ABBA
ALL THE SONGS

ABBA
ALL THE SONGS
THE STORY BEHIND EVERY TRACK

BENOÎT CLERC

CONTENTS

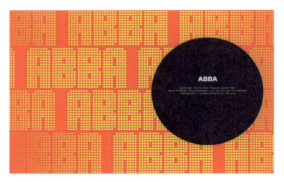

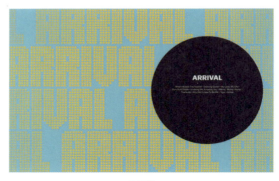

348

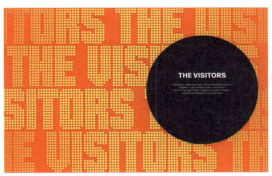

402

480

510

ABBA at the height
of their career,
April 1977.

FOREWORD

Far too often, ABBA are associated with the disco character of their many hits, such as *Dancing Queen*, *Take a Chance on Me*, *Voulez-Vous*, and *The Winner Takes It All*. Yet putting them into that musical category is a mistake that should be rectified once and for all, for their recorded work is much more complex than it seems. While the talents of the composers Benny Andersson and Björn Ulvaeus, the group's masterminds, have never been called into question, their creative genius has yet to be discovered by the uninitiated.

At the peak of a career that would last just ten years, ABBA had become the biggest group in the world. Having gone into standby mode in 1982, they disappeared from view for a time, before making a triumphant comeback in 1992, enjoying from then on the high esteem of pop fans all over the planet. Since that magical year, the importance of their music in popular culture has only increased, to the point that it has become unavoidable, obvious, and necessary. For the team

behind the *All the Songs* series, the idea of a plunge into the heart of ABBA's recorded work was thus indispensable in and of itself. While the group's songs had gone from being hits to being popular anthems, it made sense to study their varied, copious repertoire and rediscover its history, marked by the meeting, marriage, and finally divorce of Agnetha Fältskog and Björn Ulvaeus, and of Anni-Frid Lyngstad and Benny Andersson. Beyond their timeless songs, adored the world over, the group appealed through their simple lifestyle, the unforgettable performances of their charismatic female singers, and their hit songs inspired by 1950s British rock, The Beach Boys' Californian pop, and the folk songs of Fleetwood Mac. Although imbued with sadness, their compositions are luminous, and even today heal wounds like nothing else. The proof is that these 528 pages devoted to ABBA will certainly seem to you the best remedy for the worries of daily life.

Photo session for the
Ring Ring album cover
with Bengt H Malmqvist
behind the camera.

ABBA,
THE BEGINNINGS

On 13 September 1963, a young band from Västervik, a medium-sized Swedish town 160 miles (275km) south of Stockholm, entered the studios of the radio station in Norrköping to take part in the initial round of the talent show *Plats På Scen* ("On Stage"). West Bay Singers were inspired by the pop music of The Beatles and The Beach Boys, and also played songs that evoked traditional folk music as performed by the American band The Kingston Trio. The Swedish group, comprising Hansi Schwarz (vocals), Björn Ulvaeus (guitar and vocals), Johan Karlberg (guitar and vocals), and Tonny Roth (bass and vocals), were not newcomers to the music business: their sheer determination and love of performing had taken them on an impromptu tour across Europe that summer. So it was with great aplomb and brimming with self-confidence that they stood in front of the jury that day at the talent contest for young musicians. Their efforts paid off for the four twenty-somethings, as their performance took them through to the next round, scheduled for 30 September. But despite their hunger for success and their strong motivation, they had no idea that their future would be sealed in the two weeks leading up to that next round of *Plats På Scen*.

Ensnared by Polar Music

Sveriges Radio, Sweden's national radio station and the contest organizer, keen to promote its search for new talent, had placed an ad in the national daily *Expressen* about the event and the artists who had got through the first round. A photograph of West Bay Singers, featuring the four aspiring musicians looking as proud as Liverpool's Fab Four, caught the eye of Bengt Bernhag, one of the two founders of the Stockholm-based record label Polar Music. Bernhag, a renowned producer in the Swedish music industry, had created the label in 1963 with his friend Stig Anderson, a lyricist known for the hundreds of songs he had written over the years for various Swedish artists. Anderson was on the lookout for new talent to join his stable, and he contacted West Bay Singers to request a demo of their songs. The two producers were impressed with the hastily recorded cassette and they tried to lure the band to join their label before the first round of the *Plats På Scen* contest. Stig Anderson was the one who met with the musicians, presenting himself as a successful impresario and reeling off a full list of his hit songs. After meeting with the artistic directors of the prestigious RCA record company, the members of West Bay Singers decided to place their trust in Anderson and Bernhag, won over by their ambition and the fact that their label was small enough to offer a personalized service.

Polar Music's first move was to persuade the band to change its name, dropping the pop feel in favor of a smoother, more traditional image. They became Hootenanny Singers, in reference to a music trend that was very popular in the USA at the time. Represented by artists such as Pete

Noel "Paul" Stookey, Mary Travers, and Peter Yarrow formed the folk trio Peter, Paul and Mary in 1961.

Seeger and the veteran Woody Guthrie, hootenanny would go on to inspire singers on the emerging New York folk scene, led by Bob Dylan, Dave Van Ronk, and Karen Dalton, who were transforming the genre with more politically committed and often far more melancholic music than was common in American folk standards. "We wanted them to change their style, however," Stig Anderson explained in 1980. "Hootenanny was big in the States at the time and we wanted a group that sang in Swedish. Even twenty years ago all the groups sang in English."[1]

Birth of Hootenanny Singers

So it was as Hootenanny Singers that the group appeared on *Plats På Scen* on 30 September 1963, singing an American folk classic, *500 Miles Away from Home*, popularized the previous year by Peter, Paul and Mary. Not yet resolved on

singing in their mother tongue, they performed the song in English. The jury was unanimous: Hootenanny Singers qualified for the semifinals, which would be broadcast on TV several weeks later. No time to lose for Anderson and Bernhag, who saw this event as an opportunity to grow Polar Music: they sent their protégés to Metronome studios in Stockholm to record their first songs. Under the guidance of in-house sound engineer Rune Persson, four tracks were laid down during the session on 20 October 1963: *Ann-Margret, Ingen Enda Höst, Ave Maria No Morro* and *Jag Väntar vid min Mila*, a hit song by the Swedish singer and lute player Gunnar Turesson, who had released it as a 78rpm entitled *Jag Väntar* in the early 1940s.

Despite their reluctance to be seen as the heirs to Swedish traditional artists, Hootenanny Singers soon moved away from British pop and American folk when their single *Jag*

The Hep Stars, a successful Swedish band formed by Benny Andersson, Janne Frisk, Svenne Hedlund, Lennart Hegland, and Christer Pettersson.

Väntar vid min Mila ("I'm Waiting for my Love") entered the Swedish charts the following January, proving a national hit for the foursome.

Although there was no single winner of *Plats På Scen*—Sveriges Radio having decided that all the semifinalists would be winners—Hootenanny Singers would be far and away the band that benefited the most from it, because Polar Music was now committed to start production of their first album in February 1964.

The Hep Stars, "Sweden's answer to The Beatles"

While Hootenanny Singers were growing in popularity in Sweden with songs that were somewhat formulaic, other bands were more willing to embrace their British influences, riding the wave of Beatlemania that was sweeping the country after The Beatles' appearance on the Swedish TV show *Drop In* on 30 October 1963. Leading the charge was a band called The Hep Stars, whose members Sven "Svenne" Hedlund (vocals), Jan "Janne" Frisk (guitar), Lennart "Lelle" Hegland (bass), Christer "Crille" Pettersson (drums), and Benny Andersson (piano and organ) had copied John, Paul, George, and Ringo's haircuts, and were quickly dubbed "Sweden's answer to The Beatles."

By the autumn of 1965, however, the band had relinquished the title and started going their own way, with more energetic rock and an electric stage act, which appealed to a new generation of music fans looking for a rock'n'roll style with a slightly more subversive feel. Their first single, *Cadillac*, which was basically a cover of *Brand New Cadillac* by the rebellious Vince Taylor, took the band to the top of the Swedish charts in 1965. The Hep Stars soon ditched cover versions in favor of original compositions written by keyboardist Benny Andersson. The single *Sunny Girl*, released in March 1966, quickly rose up the charts, underlining Andersson's talent as a songwriter and composer. He further established himself the following May with the 45rpm *Wedding*, co-written with Hedlund, ensuring further success for his band. Andersson commented of this period: "We couldn't show our faces in

Sunday 5 June 1966 is a key date in the history of pop music, because it is the day Björn Ulvaeus and Benny Andersson met. To commemorate the 50th anniversary of that day, the two friends threw a party on 5 June 2016 at Berns Salonger in Stockholm. The over 350 guests included Agnetha Fältskog and Anni-Frid Lyngstad, who performed a touching version of *The Way Old Friends Do*. An event that many fans would have loved to attend!

any restaurant anymore, we were harassed everywhere."[2] Meanwhile, Björn Ulvaeus, Hootenanny Singers' guitarist, sensitive to the winds of change and feeling constrained by his role as a well-behaved artist, began suggesting his own compositions to the other band members, hoping to ride the coattails of The Hep Stars' growing success.

A meeting that changed the face of pop music

On 5 June 1966, a pop music festival took place on the side of the Ålleberg mountain, 240 miles (390km) from Stockholm. Topping the bill that day were two of Swedish youth's favorite bands: The Hep Stars and Hootenanny Singers. The musicians from both groups got along well, and the party continued near the hotel where both bands were staying, with two of the men ending up under an elm tree in a nearby park, playing guitar and singing songs by The Beatles and The Kingston Trio. Björn Ulvaeus and Benny Andersson instantly hit it off to the extent that they met up again in late June to discuss composing songs together. "We figured it would be a good idea to try and write a song together," Benny Andersson recalled. "I remember thinking it would be great to make a record like *Pet Sounds* by The Beach Boys, but also wondering if I did, who on earth was going to listen to it."[3]

The first song the duo wrote was *Isn't It Easy to Say*, a triplet ballad vaguely reminiscent of The Beatles' 1965 release *You've Got to Hide Your Love Away*. It would be recorded by The Hep Stars on their eponymous album several months later, along with another song Björn had previously written for his own band, called *No Time*. Ulvaeus was taking on a more prominent role in Hootenanny Singers and even sang on *En Sång en Gång för Längesen*, a Swedish-language cover

of the Porter Wagoner hit *Green, Green Grass of Home*, released in 1965 and also performed by Tom Jones in 1966. Although the Ulvaeus/Andersson partnership didn't get going immediately, the huge success of *En Sång en Gång för Längesen*, released as a single in 1967, strengthened Björn's resolve to pursue his own career outside the band. The following year, his first single, *Raring*, produced by Polar Music, with lyrics by Stig Anderson, became one of Sweden's best-selling records. Ditto for Benny, who proved his worth in 1969 when he co-composed the track *Hej Clown* ("Hi Clown") with Lars Berghagen; it was performed by Jan Malmsjö and presented that year at Melodifestivalen, the competition from which a Swedish jury chooses the country's representative for the Eurovision Song Contest. Although *Hej Clown* lost out to *Judy Min Vän* ("Judy My Friend") by Tommy Körberg, its second place firmly established Benny Andersson's reputation as a successful composer. Ninth place went to a 24-year-old red-haired singer named Anni-Frid Lyngstad.

Two singers with golden voices

Anni-Frid, known as Frida, had been performing on stage since she was 13 years old. It was while appearing with jazz singer and pianist Charlie Norman in a Malmö club on 1 March 1969 that she met someone who would completely shake up her personal life as well as her professional future. Benny Andersson was working nearby at the same time; bored, he wandered over to see what was going on in the other club. "I walked in the door and stopped dead!" he remembered in 1977. "There, up on the stage, was the most beautiful girl I'd ever seen. She wasn't just pretty—she had this atmosphere about her which rang a bell somewhere deep

Hösten, vintern, våren 1970/71

FOR ABBA ADDICTS

In the photo used for the tour operator Fritidsresor's promotional catalog in 1970, only three members of the future ABBA can be seen: Benny and Anni-Frid are in the foreground, with Agnetha visible behind them. Eagle-eyed observers will notice, however, Björn Ulvaeus's left leg showing to Frida's right. In the foreground, little Ann Lise-Lotte Fredriksson, Frida's daughter, is looking directly at the photographer, whose name is unknown.

in my memory. Anyway, I knew I had to get to meet her somehow. Luckily, I knew the owner of the club and I persuaded him to let me into her dressing room while she was still on stage. After she'd finished her encore, she came back to her room—and I was there! It was love at first sight."[4] It wasn't long before Frida fell for the charming composer, and as summer approached the two artists became inseparable. Meanwhile, Björn Ulvaeus was courting a 19-year-old singer whose career was flying high, influenced by the music of Connie Francis, Petula Clark, Sandie Shaw, Sylvie Vartan, and Rita Pavone. Agnetha Fältskog, then engaged to German producer Dieter Zimmermann, had to keep her feelings in check when she first met Ulvaeus in 1968. A few months later, in May 1969, having decided to leave her fiancé to return to her native Sweden—and thus ending her professional commitments in Germany—Agnetha was asked to appear on the TV program *Jules Sylvain Kavalkad*, on which various artists were invited to perform sketches and songs. Björn Ulvaeus was also due to appear, singing *Titta in i Min Lilla Kajuta* ("Look into My Little Cabin"), a Swedish variety classic recorded by Sven-Oloff Sandberg in 1930. The sketch accompanying the song featured Björn and Agnetha fooling about for the cameras, without viewers suspecting that there was real romance in the air on set that day.

"When I was first introduced to [Agnetha], it wasn't like meeting a stranger at all," Ulvaeus confided. "It seemed so natural and so right. I felt I'd known her forever. And she felt the same way about me. We just talked and talked and talked! I couldn't believe it! And as the filming drew towards its close, we were both afraid we wouldn't see one another again for months."[4] "Then, just as we were preparing to say our goodbyes," chipped in Agnetha, "we were told by the producer that the filming of the last bit of the show was delayed— for three days! We were over the moon about it. It was like magic—as if somebody up there knew we had to be together and had arranged the whole thing just for us!"[4] By the end of those three days, they had decided they wanted to spend the rest of their lives together. Agnetha quickly moved in with Björn on Lilla Essingen, one of the islands in the Stockholm archipelago, and at the same time, the couple became close to Benny Andersson and Anni-Frid "Frida" Lyngstad.

Four artists at the beach

As 1969 drew to a close, Benny and Björn continued working to put their status as songwriters and composers on a more professional footing, creating their own publishing house, Union Songs, with Stig Anderson and Bengt Bernhag. The duo were determined to prove their worth and write quality songs, but at first they had to settle for working on less prestigious projects, such as the soundtrack to Joseph W Sarno's erotic film *Någon att Älska* ("The Seduction of Inga"), in which there is one standout track, *She's My Kind of Girl*, which Polar Music

Sailing in the Stockholm archipelago became one of the four Swedes' favorite leisure activities.

released as a single in 1970. That same year, from 5 to 16 April, the two couples spent their vacation together at the seaside resort of Varosha in Famagusta, on the island of Cyprus. Making the most of the relaxed holiday atmosphere to play guitar and sing together on their hotel balcony, they soon discovered the chemistry between the four of them, with Frida and Agnetha complementing each other well on vocals. The Swedish tour operator Fritidsresor offered to pay all their travel costs in return for two photos that would appear in their forthcoming catalog and a concert given to United Nations forces stationed on the island. So it was in the Perroquet nightclub, famous for its legendary parties and the fresco by Cypriot artist Christoforos Savva, that the foursome gave their very first, unofficial concert.

As soon as the two couples returned to Stockholm, the Swedish press, having found out that Björn and Agnetha had become engaged during the trip, seized on the news as a major headline event, suddenly turning the two sweethearts into big stars at home. Benny and Frida, who were still finding their way as a couple, were also subject to press exposure and, from then on, the four artists were frequently seen together, with the two women vocalists often more visibly in the spotlight. Between 2 June and 10 September 1970, Björn and Benny worked on recording their first album together, *Lycka* ("Happiness"). Frida and Agnetha were asked to provide backing vocals for one track, *Hej Gamle Man!* ("Hello, Old Man!"), so that song enjoys the distinction of being the first ever to be recorded by the four future members of ABBA.

Newlyweds Björn Ulvaeus and Agnetha Fältskog, deeply in love.

Alongside this, the four put together a small cabaret show called Festfolket, which took them all over Sweden, but proved neither artistically fulfilling nor financially rewarding, as audiences were often rather thin on the ground, to say the least. This was when Agnetha, Frida, Benny, and Björn, officially this time, gave their first concert together: on stage at Trädgår'n, a live-entertainment venue in Gothenburg, on 1 November 1970. "We were horrible. The audience hated us […]," Frida would recall a few years later.[5] On 13 December, the four appeared dressed as bar girls (the ladies) and cowboys (the men), with pianist Jan "Tollarparen" Eriksson, performing the song *California, Here I Come* on the TV program *Five Minutes Saloon*. The four clearly felt they'd gone a bit too far but, remotivated by the success of the single *Hej Gamle Man!*, they decided to put the brakes on Festfolket.

A wedding ceremony fraught with pitfalls

On 6 July 1971, while Frida was enjoying the critical success of her first album, also called *Frida*, produced by her partner Benny Andersson, Björn and Agnetha were taking their wedding vows in the small church in Verum, 300 miles (500km) southwest of Stockholm.

Benny Andersson and Anni-Frid "Frida" Lyngstad in their apartment in Vallentuna, in the suburbs of Stockholm, 1972

While their engagement had been marred by the loss of Björn's ring in the waters of the Eastern Mediterranean in April 1970, their wedding was interrupted by an incident which, fortunately, didn't spoil the happy day. "After we were married there was some kind of uproar when we came out of the church," recalled Agnetha. "A police officer lost control over his horse and the animal stepped on my foot. A doctor was ever called in, but luckily it wasn't all that bad. He put a bandage around my ankle and it was okay. The entourage went to a tavern called the White Horse for the wedding dinner. [...] I will keep remembering every minute of that day.

Even when I'm an old lady, I won't forget my happiness!"[6] Their happiness was short-lived, however, as, the day after the wedding, the happy couple and their friends found out that Bengt Bernhag, co-founder of Polar Music, had taken his own life that night. The 43-year-old entrepreneur suffered from severe depression brought on by an intestinal operation and had sunk into alcoholism. Ulvaeus quickly found the strength to overcome his profound sadness and accepted Stig Anderson's offer to replace Bernhag as producer, with a specific aim in mind: to carry on the work of Polar Music's co-founder and keep his legacy alive.

Stig Anderson with his Polar Music protégés: the band that would become ABBA, Ted Gärdestad, and two members of Hootenanny Singers.

Anderson/Ulvaeus/Andersson: a winning trio

Unwilling to work without Benny Andersson, Björn accepted the job at Polar Music on condition he shared it with his friend, sacrificing half his salary in the process. The two musicians therefore became producers at the label, undertaking many artistic projects, including Ted Gärdestad's debut album. Gärdestad was a young and undeniably talented Swedish singer who would become ABBA's protégé throughout the 1970s. In 1971, while Björn and Benny were writing their second album together, Frida was savoring the success of her single *Min Egen Stad* ("My Own City"), produced by her now fiancé, Benny. In 1972, Benny, Björn, and Stig Anderson were writing a song called *Säg Det med en Sång* ("Say It with a Song") for the up-and-coming Lena Andersson, which was presented at Melodifestivalen on 12 February, in the hope that the young singer would represent Sweden at the Eurovision Song Contest. Alas, the attempt once again ended in failure, with Lena having to settle for third place. The track, rerecorded in English with the help of lyricists Wayne Bickerton and Tony Waddington and renamed *Better to Have Loved*, was a huge hit not only in Sweden, but also in Japan, where Lena Andersson was invited to take part in the 1972 Tokyo Music Festival, bringing reflected glory to Polar Music and its three representatives. But Björn and Benny had global ambitions and decided to pin all their hopes on Agnetha and Frida, whose success at home continued unabated. The decision they were about to take would change the history of pop music forever. "And then we wrote *People Need Love*," Björn said later, "and thought, 'Let's do it—the four of us.'"[7]

AGNETHA FÄLTSKOG, A RESERVED SINGER

Agnetha Åse Fältskog was born on 5 April 1950 in Jönköping, a medium-sized town about 180 miles (300km) southwest of Stockholm. She was a shy, reserved little girl who grew up in a household where music played an important role. Her father, Ingvar, was a store manager who composed in his free time; her mother, Birgit, who supported her husband in his musical ventures (which rarely extended beyond the confines of the town), was full of life. Aged five, Agnetha developed a passion for music thanks to a neighbor who taught piano, and she began her first lessons and wrote her first song on a toy piano. It was a nursery rhyme called *Två Små Troll* ("Two Little Trolls"), recounting the adventures of two trolls who become friends. At seven years old, when her parents bought her a real piano, young Agnetha showed definite talent, prompting them to enroll her in regular lessons, which she attended assiduously for ten years. After forming a vocal trio with two friends and playing the organ at her local church for several years, she joined Bernt Enghardt's orchestra as lead singer in 1966. It was a lineup well-known for shows featuring many and varied cover versions that delighted audiences.

The teenaged Agnetha, supported by her parents, shone on stage with her sparkling performances and perfect vocal mastery. When she offered the group one of her compositions, *Jag Var Så Kär* ("I Was So in Love"), about the end of her relationship with her boyfriend Björn Lilja, the musicians loved the song and a demo was quickly recorded. A cassette containing the track reached producer Karl-Gerhard Lundkvist, better known as Little Gerhard, a pioneer of Swedish rock in the early 1960s; he quickly contacted the young woman, offering to rerecord it, on condition that she agreed to part with her backing musicians. The track propelled Agnetha, still only 17, to the top of the charts and launched her singing career in Sweden. She also achieved notable success in West Germany, where she traveled many times and where she met the songwriter-composer and producer Dieter Zimmermann. He would write several songs for her and even become her boyfriend until meeting Björn Ulvaeus turned her career plans on their head.

Agnetha Fältskog is reserved and profoundly shy and she brought to ABBA a raw emotion, sometimes giving the impression that, despite her huge talent, her place in the band was merely the consequence of a series of fortuitous encounters that had changed the destiny of a young woman who was far too introverted to be propelled to global stardom. "[…] I actually didn't want to become a singer," she said in 1976. "My wish was to become a psychologist or a veterinarian. But since my first single became a hit, even my parents advised me to try my luck as a singer."[8]

ANNI-FRID LYNGSTAD,
AN EMANCIPATED YOUNG WOMAN

Anni-Frid Lyngstad, better known by the stage name Frida, the flamboyant half of the duo formed with the more introverted Agnetha Fältskog, was born on 15 November 1945 in Norway, near the town of Narvik, then under German occupation. Her mother, Synni Lyngstad, aged 19 at the time, had fallen for an enemy soldier called Alfred Hasse, but he was already married and wanted nothing to do with their child after he was demobilized. Driven by despair at the constant insults that resulted from this forbidden romance, Synni and her mother, Agny, were forced to leave the country, taking Anni-Frid with them to protect her from the trauma that these taunts might engender in the child as she grew up. In 1947, the three Norwegian women settled in the small Swedish town of Malmköping, hoping for a new life far from their homeland. Sadly, Synni died of kidney failure at the age of 21, leaving little Anni-Frid alone with her grandmother who, in 1949, decided to move to Torshälla, 25 miles (40km) further north.

When she was 11, Anni-Frid started learning the piano and was noticed for her talent as a singer at competitions and other events where she was brave enough to climb up on stage and sing her heart out. Her audacity led to offers to join various bands with whom she soon began performing, until in 1961 she joined Bengt Sandlund's orchestra, where she would develop a taste for the jazz vocals of Ella Fitzgerald and Sarah Vaughan. It was while she was with this band that she met double bassist Ragnar Fredriksson, with whom she would have two children, Hans in 1963 and Ann Lise-Lotte in 1967. That same year, she recorded her first solo single, *En Ledig Dag* ("A Day Off"), which marked the start of her career. In 1969, Anni-Frid joined the revue led by successful pianist Charlie Norman; she left the family home to live alone in Stockholm, determined to make a go of her career, and leaving Ragnar to look after the children. Her feistiness and talent, as well as the choices she made, which one imagines were difficult and which led her to cross paths with Benny Andersson in March 1969, are something she recalls clearly. "Those first months in Stockholm were terrible," she says. "I was craving for my children […]. I was pondering all the time and started to regret my decision. I hated my career, that had started to grow too big for me. I simply wasn't ready for it yet. [Benny] was the turning point in my life."[9] That chance encounter would soon propel her to the top of the charts the world over.

BENNY ANDERSSON,
A BRILLIANT COMPOSER

Göran Bror Benny Andersson was born on 16 December 1946 in Stockholm. His father, Gösta, and his mother, Laura, passed on their love of music to their young son when they gave him a small accordion for his sixth birthday. Gösta, like his own father, Efraim, was an accomplished musician, and soon the three men founded Benny's Trio. They did covers of *schlager* classics, a music style similar to folk and inspired by French *chanson*, military marches, and operetta, very much in vogue in Europe in the 1960s. The trio used to perform regularly in Stockholm and the archipelago, which led to Benny becoming a household name in the area, despite his tender years. "I was even some kind of child star and—barely being able to write— had to sign autographs," he would say in 1976.[10] When Benny's parents gave him a piano for his tenth birthday, he threw him- self into learning how to play it, working on his technique for hours on end, with the unconditional support of his family, especially his mother. "She is the one that made me feel that I was good enough. She gave me the most amazing start. [...] I played on the piano at least four hours a day. Every day. I could play as much as I wanted. She never told me I disturbed her. She didn't judge. She made me feel that what I did was good."[11] In 1961, he met and fell in love with singer Christina Grönvall, with whom he would have two children: Peter in 1963, and Heléne in 1965. By that time the couple were engaged, but they separated in 1966, as Benny's rock-star life with his new band, The Hep Stars, proved incompatible with his parental responsibilities. As the 1960s drew to a close, it seemed that nothing could stop Benny Andersson in his pro- fessional trajectory.

BJÖRN ULVAEUS,
ONE HALF OF A WINNING DUO

Björn Kristian Ulvaeus was born on 25 April 1945 on the island of Hisingen, in the northern suburbs of Gothenburg. He was six years old when his parents, Aina and Gunnar, moved to Västervik, where Gunnar's brother hired him as manager of his paper mill. Björn grew up listening to songs on the family wireless, which was dominated by *schlager* music. Melodies from the standards of this popular music trend encouraged him to work on his passion for poetry, which he used at school to seduce girls. While recorder lessons as a child failed to inspire an interest in music, the guitar proved more interesting and he became fascinated by skiffle, a combination of jazz, folk, and blues, often played on rudimentary or homemade instruments to symbolize the working-class nature of this type of music. Having improved his playing technique, Björn joined his first jazz band at school, before turning his attention to folk music, whose vocal harmonies, originating in the USA, appealed to young European music lovers.

His first stage appearances were with The Partners, before the band was renamed West Bay Singers, in homage to Västervik (or West Bay in English), the town they came from. The group were heavily influenced by British and American music, and were trying to move away from Swedish variety when they met Bengt Bernhag and Stig Anderson, who were willing to help the group reach new heights, provided they embraced the folk style and agreed to change their name again, this time to Hootenanny Singers. It was only after he left this group that Ulvaeus finally had the opportunity to exercise his talents as a lyricist, composer, and also producer, alongside Benny Andersson and the boss of the Polar Music label, Stig Anderson.

STIG ANDERSON, THE FIFTH MEMBER OF ABBA

Workaholic, loyal friend, insatiable producer, and successful lyricist, Stig Anderson was inextricably associated with ABBA's success. Born Stig Erik Leopold Anderson on 25 January 1931, he discovered music at the age of five when his mother gave him his first gramophone and six 78rpm records, which introduced the child to traditional Swedish music. He quit school at the age of 13, and worked as a delivery boy for a local grocery store, where his entrepreneurial spirit was already evident as he managed to turn a small profit by selling some items bought with his own money. Stig soon saved enough to buy his first guitar and join a few local bands. He wrote his first song following a break-up, making his ex-girlfriend the subject of the lyrics. "I went home and wrote a satirical ballad about her. Then I performed it during a meeting with the local temperance society and got a great response. That's when I realized that it's fun to write songs."[12]

In 1951, his first successful single, *Tivedshambo* ("Hambo from Tived") came out, launching his career as a songwriter and composer. He married his fiancée, Gudrun, in 1955, became a father of three, and created his own publishing house, Sweden Music, in 1960. Stikkan, as he was nicknamed, was extremely productive, churning out the hits in Sweden throughout that decade, and becoming a celebrity, even a national treasure. "For fifteen years, I was the most-played lyric writer on Swedish radio," he said in 1981. "In 1970 eight out of ten songs that I had written reached the top twenty. Those are very personal successes for me and as such mean a lot."[13]

The musical adventure alongside Bengt Bernhag

In 1963, Stig Anderson and his business partner Bengt Bernhag set up their own record label, Polar Music. Their first signing, Hootenanny Singers, in which a certain Björn Ulvaeus played the six-string and occasionally sang, gave the label the success it needed, enabling Anderson and Bernhag to start producing other Swedish artists. One of these was the group ABBA, for whom Stikkan would write many lyrics, including those for *Waterloo* (1974), *Mamma Mia* (1975), *SOS* (1975), and *Dancing Queen* (1976).

In Sweden, the popularity of the man who would always be considered the fifth member of ABBA was such that his funeral, in 1997, was broadcast live on national television, a privilege usually reserved for members of the royal family. Stig Anderson left behind him the lyrics for over 2,000 songs and the doctrine on which he built his empire: "Always work very hard. Do your best. Don't forget anything. And don't take life seriously."[14]

Single

HEJ GAMLE MAN!

(Benny Andersson, Björn Ulvaeus/3'19)

Benny Andersson and Björn Ulvaeus, respectively composer and lyricist of hit songs for Polar Music.

Musicians

Björn Ulvaeus: vocals, acoustic guitar, backing vocals
Benny Andersson: piano, backing vocals
Agnetha Fältskog: backing vocals
Anni-Frid "Frida" Lyngstad: backing vocals
John Cúonz: tambourine
Gus Horn: bass

Recording

Metronome, Stockholm: 2 June to 10 September 1970

Technical team

Producers: Björn Ulvaeus, Benny Andersson, Bengt Bernhag
Sound engineer: Michael B Tretow

Single *Hej Gamle Man!*

A-side: *Lycka*/3'05
B-side: *Hej Gamle Man!*/3'19
Released in Sweden by Polar Music: Autumn 1970
(single ref.: POS 1110)
Best chart ranking in Sweden: 5

The first song with four singers

When they returned from their vacation in Cyprus, in April 1970, Björn Ulvaeus and Benny Andersson began working on the production of *Lycka*, their first album as a duo. The initial aim was to produce a quality business card to present to possible partners (at the time, the two men wanted to specialize in writing for other artists). Recording of the album took place over five days between June and September at the Metronome studios in Stockholm, and was a joyful meeting of minds for the two friends, as they laid down 11 tracks, alternating between folk and *schlager*. One of them, *Hej Gamle Man!*, is a standout thanks to the presence of Agnetha Fältskog and Anni-Frid Lyngstad on backing vocals, and makes it the first-ever song recorded by all four future members of ABBA. Sound engineer Michael B Tretow demonstrated his talent, giving the record an amazingly sharp, precise sound, with each instrument perfectly placed in the mix. Tretow, who had already worked on projects for Björn, Benny, and Agnetha, would become ABBA's preferred partner until 1982, the year the singles *The Day Before You Came* and *Under Attack* were recorded, the last songs before a hiatus of almost 40 years.

A taste for melody

Initially, *Hej Gamle Man!* was included in the Festfolket show that the foursome staged in the spring of 1970. The song's success at these performances prompted Andersson and Ulvaeus to invite Agnetha and Frida to take part in the recording over the summer. Their names do not, however, appear on the sleeve of the single, which, when released in the autumn, became a huge hit in Sweden, reaching number 5 in the best-selling singles charts. A German version of the song was also recorded under the name *Hey, Musikant*, with lyrics by composer Hans Bradtke, but it failed to achieve the same success on the other side of the Baltic Sea. Interesting fact: a young American singer by the name of John Denver had a stratospheric hit a few months later with his folk anthem *Take Me Home, Country Roads*, whose verses bear an uncanny resemblance to *Hej Gamle Man!* We're sure this was just a coincidence…

BJÖRN BENNY & AGNETHA FRIDA

RING RING

Ring Ring (Bara Du Slog En Signal) • Another Town, Another Train • Disillusion •
People Need Love • I Saw It In The Mirror • Nina, Pretty Ballerina •
Love Isn't Easy (But It Sure Is Hard Enough) • Me And Bobby And Bobby's Brother •
He Is Your Brother • Ring Ring (Engelsk Version) •
I Am Just A Girl • Rock'n Roll Band

Released in Sweden by Polar Music: 26 March 1973 (album ref.: POLS 242)
Best chart ranking in Sweden: 2

*Note: some songs, such as Merry-Go-Round and Santa Rosa, appeared on
the B-side of the group's singles but were recorded solely by Björn Ulvaeus and
Benny Andersson for their second album as a duo, and therefore
do not form part of ABBA's official discography.*

Benny Andersson, Anni-Frid
"Frida" Lyngstad, Björn Ulvaeus,
and Agnetha Fältskog in the early
days of the band, 1973.

GENESIS OF A CULT BAND

By the time 1972 rolled round, the Festfolket show was no more. The two couples were taking a few weeks out to think things over, determined to come up with a development strategy after the show's failure. They may have been struggling to get their musical projects up and running, but when it came to their romantic lives, there were no clouds on the horizon for the four friends. Newlyweds Agnetha and Björn, like Benny and Frida, now engaged, moved out of their Stockholm apartments to Vallentuna, a nearby suburb. Life there, away from the city lights, suited the artists, as Frida explained at the time: "It's wonderful to live outside of the city. We have the woods just around the corner. It's everything we dreamed it would be. We often take long walks and go skiing when there's snow. It's such a difference to the small city apartment and the air is so much cleaner. [...] We live like most families in our spare time. We watch TV, talk, read, take walks with our dog. I draw and paint and I enjoy sewing. I have always liked that. Last year I went through Tillskärarakademien [a fashion design school] to learn how sew professionally."[15]

Continuing their quest for a tranquil lifestyle, both couples also bought small chalets on Viggsö, an island in the Stockholm archipelago, where Stig Anderson already owned a property. It was in one of these love nests in the winter of 1972 that Björn and Benny fine-tuned *People Need Love*, which they recorded on 29 March at Metronome studios, with the help of sound engineer Michael B Tretow. They then promoted the track on 30 April, performing it over playback on the children's TV show *Vi i Femman* ("We in Fifth Grade"). However, at the time the four artists weren't really a band, and *People Need Love* was just an interlude in their individual careers. When they appeared in public, they were often introduced as a male duo with female backing singers.

An ABBA stand-in

Björn & Benny, Agnetha & Anni-Frid, as they were presented on the cover of the single *People Need Love*, flew to Tokyo in November for the Yamaha World Popular Song Contest. There they were pinning their hopes on *Santa Rosa*, a song that Benny and Björn had recorded some time before, without the women. Although they didn't win the contest and didn't intend their band to be a long-term fixture, the young artists decided to prioritize recording their debut album. Production had begun on 26 September, and was progressing in line with each member's professional commitments and with Agnetha's pregnancy with her first child. She was discreetly replaced by Inger Brundin, a friend of Frida's, when the group performed *People Need Love* on the TV show *Disco*, filmed in Munich and broadcast on 6 January 1973, and for some of their promotional appearances, including on *Spotlight* in Austria on 22 March.

The rocky road to Eurovision

On 10 January 1973, Benny and Björn had a specific idea in mind when they recorded *Ring Ring (Bara Du Slog en Signal)*, a song with an irresistible melody. They wanted to enter Melodifestivalen again. The contest, where Sweden's representative for 1973's Eurovision Song Contest would be chosen, was due to take place on 10 February at Stockholm's SVT studios. This time, Stig Anderson used his contacts to produce

Agnetha expecting her baby
Linda, Valletuna, 1972.

On 18 February 1972, the Swedish adaptation of *Jesus Christ Superstar*, the hit musical by Andrew Lloyd Webber and Tim Rice, premiered at the Scandinavium in Gothenburg. Agnetha Fältskog played the role of Mary Magdalene, performed by Yvonne Elliman in the original version. Sadly, she only appeared on stage for six nights, before being replaced by Titti Sjöblom, who had also been considered for the role.

Frida in front of a blackboard at Tillskärarakademin, the Swedish Couture Academy, in 1973.

lyrics in English, which were written by Neil Sedaka and Phil Cody. A second version of the track, renamed simply *Ring Ring*, was recorded just in time for the selection process. On the day, the foursome gave a great rendition, even though Agnetha was exhausted as her due date drew near. Despite a convincing track and a visibly confident band, the attempt ended in failure, and our friends had to settle for third place, with victory going to the group Malta and their *Sommaren som Aldrig Säger Nej* ("The Summer that Never Says No"— the band would be renamed The Nova and The Dolls for the final round of the contest, and their song rewritten in English as *You're Summer*). "You have to understand one thing about the Eurovision Song Contest," Björn Ulvaeus explained in

1994. "At that time, that was the one and only vehicle to reach outside Sweden. Because there was no way anyone in England or America would listen to anything coming out of this obscure country. You could send your tapes, knowing they would throw them immediately. So the only chance was to enter the Eurovision."[7] Despite the disappointment of losing once again, *Ring Ring* was a huge hit in Sweden, where both versions, released as singles in February 1973, topped the charts.

In Belgium, Austria, Norway, and Denmark, the track—in its original version—did exceptionally well, encouraging the band to continue their musical journey with their first album, also called *Ring Ring*. It was released on 26 March under the overly long and slightly confusing band name of

Above: Frida and Benny, elegance and glamor, in 1973.
Opposite: Björn and Agnetha with their daughter Linda and their dog Ada in their apartment in Valletuna in 1973.

Björn Benny & Agnetha Frida. With its folk- and *schlager*-influenced songs, it sounds more like a collection of tracks composed at different times than a carefully planned and artistically coherent album. However, both sides of the album contain some impeccably produced melodic gems, such as *I Saw It in the Mirror, Nina, Pretty Ballerina, Love Isn't Easy (But It Sure Is Hard Enough),* and *He Is Your Brother.* The choruses are worth a close listen on their own merits, and the entire work, which met with little success outside of Scandinavia, deserves a fresh assessment. Like Donna Summer's 1974 *Lady of the Night,* the first album released by the future queen of disco, this is a record on which composers, writers, performers, and producers are finding their way, stumbling, experimenting, and struggling to relinquish their American influences. They nevertheless demonstrate a raw virtuosity in their work, which could only be a sign of a promising future for our four Swedish artists.

Sound engineer Michael B Tretow kept a low profile but is regarded as a full member of ABBA.

Overleaf: Photo session for the *Ring Ring* album cover, 1973.

MICHAEL B TRETOW, THE MAN BEHIND THE ABBA SOUND

Like many producers and studio technicians, Michael B Tretow had aspired to become a musician in his youth. Born on 20 August 1944 in the small city of Norrköping, in the south-east of Sweden, he spent his adolescence getting to know all the different recording techniques available to him, a hobby that earned him the status of sound engineer among local artists. Like any musician who believed in their projects, Michael sent his songs to a number of Swedish labels in 1965, and they came to the attention of Rune Persson, the boss and sound engineer of the prestigious Metronome recording studio in Stockholm. Persson offered Michael the opportunity to rework the mix on his demo tape, an offer that Michael promptly accepted. His songs didn't achieve the hoped-for success, however, and by 1967 he had abandoned his dreams of glory. It was then that he got a call from Metronome. Persson had been sufficiently impressed with the work Tretow had done on his own songs to offer him a job as a sound engineer.

An irreplaceable partner

From 1967, Michael B Tretow worked with all the groups on the Swedish rock scene, including The Hounds, Ola & the Janglers, and Hootenanny Singers (featuring a certain Björn Ulvaeus), as well as on the second album of a young singer called Agnetha Fältskog. When Ulvaeus and Benny Andersson joined forces as producers at Polar Music in 1970, Metronome became the place where the magic happened, thanks to the technical knowledge of the in-house sound engineer and the growing chemistry between him, Björn, and Benny. From the first recording sessions for the *Ring Ring* album in 1972, the trio became inseparable, as the three men spoke the same language and were able to build a coherent body of work. Over the years, Michael B Tretow became an integral part of ABBA's success, and would remain their only sound engineer until 1981's *The Visitors*. He was soon dubbed the sixth member of ABBA, with fifth spot already occupied by Stig Anderson, the group's manager and producer. Although he was globally renowned for his work with ABBA, for a long time the "B" in his name remained a mystery. He himself explained it as follows: "It stands for 'Bo.' That's all. […] I started using just 'B' very early on because of Hank B Marvin, the Shadows' guitarist."[16]

Single

RING RING (BARA DU SLOG EN SIGNAL)

(Benny Andersson, Stig Anderson, Björn Ulvaeus/3'03)

Musicians

Agnetha Fältskog: vocals, backing vocals
Anni-Frid "Frida" Lyngstad: vocals, backing vocals
Björn Ulvaeus: electric guitar, backing vocals
Benny Andersson: piano, Mellotron, backing vocals
Janne Schaffer: electric guitar
Rutger Gunnarsson: bass
Ola Brunkert: drums, maracas, tambourine

Recording

Metronome, Stockholm: 10 January 1973
Europa Film, Stockholm: January 1973

Technical team

Producers: Björn Ulvaeus, Benny Andersson
Sound engineers: Michael B Tretow, Björn Almstedt (Europa Film)
Assistant sound engineers: Rune Persson (Metronome), Åke Eldsäter (Metronome)

Single

A-side: *Ring Ring (Bara Du Slog en Signal)*/3'12
B-side: *Åh, Vilka Tider*/2'31
Released in Sweden by Polar Music: 26 March 1973
(single ref.: POS 1172)
Best chart ranking in Sweden: 1

Genesis

As 1972 drew to a close, Benny, Björn, Agnetha, and Frida decided to retreat to the chalets they had just bought on Viggsö island in the Stockholm archipelago. Although this was intended to be a rest period, Benny and Björn were busy writing new material: they were concentrating in particular on the song they wanted to present at Melodifestivalen on 10 February, in the hope of being selected to represent Sweden at the next Eurovision Song Contest. With the working title *Klocklåt*, which roughly translates as "bell song," the track is an American-influenced pop salvo built around rousing verses and excellent choruses with a heady melody. In the minds of its composers, the song that they presented had to be overflowing with energy, quite the opposite of the syrupy ballads served up every year by prospective candidates. "We wanted to do something poppy, something that reflected the popular music tastes of today. We wanted to get rid of all the pomp and circumstances surrounding the Eurovision Song Contest: the dinner-jackets and the evening dresses,"[17] said Stig Anderson, whom Ulvaeus and Andersson called in to hastily write some lyrics.

On 10 January, the musicians were at Metronome in Stockholm to record *Ring Ring (Bara Du Slog en Signal)*, which, with a little help from destiny, would, they hoped, get them into Eurovision this time round. The Melodifestivalen jury weren't convinced, but the song was very successful with the public, encouraging the four artists to carry on their journey together and persuading Ulvaeus and Andersson to drop the idea of a second duo album in favor of a debut album with their romantic partners. Although Michael B Tretow had previously worked with all four future members of ABBA, it was on *Ring Ring (Bara Du Slog en Signal)* that the sound engineer really came into his own. Engrossed at the time in *Out of His Head: The Sound of Phil Spector*, a book by Richard Williams that explored in minute detail the working method of the infamous producer and revealed the recording technique he used to create his celebrated Wall of Sound, Tretow decided to draw inspiration from this model for the takes of *Ring Ring (Bara Du Slog en Signal)*. As well as using space as a natural reverberation tool, Spector, who produced many hits in this way—*River Deep–Mountain High* by Ike and Tina Turner, The Ronettes' *Be My Baby*, The Crystals' *Da Doo Ron Ron (When He Walked Me Home)*…—would record multiple

HEADPHONES AT THE READY 🎧

Although both writers denied it, the guitar riff on *Ring Ring (Bara Du Slog en Signal)*, along with the piano gimmick played on the eighth note, sound as if they were inspired by the ones on *Underdog*, a song by the Italian Giorgio (aka Giorgio Moroder), on his third album, *Son of My Father*, released in 1972 and distributed in Sweden by…Polar Music.

tracks of each instrument to completely fill the sound space. It was through studying Spector's production technique that Tretow came to a decision that would give *Ring Ring (Bara Du Slog en Signal)* a very special sound.

Production

Without telling Ulvaeus and Andersson, Tretow experimented with two identical takes of the song recorded on 10 January 1973. He decided to play with the cassette speed when mixing one of them, giving it a slightly more bass sound and unavoidably conferring an astonishing color on the whole, as the pitch of the notes differed slightly between the two takes. This infuriated radio stations, who rang Polar Music to report a problem with the mixing of the track, thus confirming that the sound engineer had achieved what he set out to do, namely, to get people to notice the risk he had taken. "[…] I could make the sound enormous…that's how we got the sound that is ABBA's alone. For some reason, no foreign producer has discovered it."[18]

The band were still called Björn Benny & Agnetha Frida when they performed *Ring, Ring (Bara Du Slog en Signal)* at Melodifestivalen on 10 February 1973.

ANOTHER TOWN, ANOTHER TRAIN

(Benny Andersson, Björn Ulvaeus/3'10)

Musicians

Agnetha Fältskog: vocals, backing vocals
Anni-Frid "Frida" Lyngstad: vocals, backing vocals
Björn Ulvaeus: vocals, acoustic guitar
Benny Andersson: piano, Mellotron, backing vocals
Janne Schaffer?: acoustic guitar
Rutger Gunnarsson: bass
Ola Brunkert?: drums
Roger Palm?: drums

Recording

Metronome, Stockholm: 17 October 1972 to 15 March 1973
KMH studios, Stockholm: March 1972 to March 1973
Europa Film, Stockholm: March 1972 to March 1973

Technical team

Producers: Björn Ulvaeus, Benny Andersson
Sound engineer: Michael B Tretow
Assistant sound engineers: Rune Persson (Metronome), Åke Eldsäter (Metronome), Lennart Karlsmyr (KMH studios), Björn Almstedt (Europa Film)

Single

A-side: *Another Town, Another Train*/3'04
B-side: *I Am Just a Girl*/3'00
Released in the USA by Playboy Records: March 1973
(single ref.: P 50018)
Best chart ranking in the USA: did not make the charts

Genesis

In 1972, with the intention of introducing his protégés' music to the American public, Stig Anderson forged a relationship with Playboy Records to distribute *People Need Love*, the first single of the band, in the US market. The punching power of the label, owned by Hugh Hefner's Playboy Enterprises group, did not live up to Anderson's expectations, and when success came knocking in 1974, the decision was made to find a bigger partner, and one that would be more committed to the development of ABBA. Despite the failure of *People Need Love* in the USA, Playboy Records nevertheless distributed a handful of singles between 1972 and 1973. One of these was *Another Town, Another Train*, on which Björn Ulvaeus crooned in the style of Gilbert O'Sullivan—an Irish singer who was then riding the wave of success of his single *Clair*—to tell the story of a couple separating. The song's epilog compares the split to a train leaving, a recurrent theme in American country music, of which Ulvaeus was particularly fond. The single, distributed by Playboy Records, presented the group as follows: Björn & Benny (with Anna & Frieda). *Another Town, Another Train* was also released as a single in Japan and Venezuela, and rerecorded, in a translation by Austrian author Friedrich Alex Jacobson, as *Wer im Wartesaal der Liebe Steht* ("Who Stands in the Waiting Room of Love") for the B-side of *Ring Ring* when it was released in Germany. It was subsequently covered by numerous artists, including British singer Dave Mills and a band called Schytts, who performed it in Swedish after Stig Anderson rewrote the lyrics.

Production

Popularized by The Beatles' *Lucy in the Sky with Diamonds* in 1967, then used on David Bowie's *Space Oddity* two years later, the Mellotron is the keyboard that stands out on *Another Town, Another Train*, with Benny Andersson using flute sounds to kick off the track. If the sound produced by the famous instrument (here a white-lacquered MS400 model) seems to bear an uncanny resemblance to a recorder, this is because it operates on tapes with real recordings, triggered by the keys in the order chosen by the user. Despite the revolutionary nature of this instrument, Andersson would stop using it after the *Ring Ring* and *Waterloo* albums.

Björn Ulvaeus and Benny Andersson on the streets of Stockholm, 1972.

DISILLUSION

(Agnetha Fältskog, Björn Ulvaeus/3'05)

Musicians
Agnetha Fältskog: vocals, backing vocals
Anni-Frid "Frida" Lyngstad: backing vocals
Björn Ulvaeus: acoustic guitar
Janne Schaffer: electric guitar
Mike Watson: bass
Ola Brunkert: drums
Benny Andersson: piano

Recording
Metronome, Stockholm: 14 March 1973

Technical team
Producers: Björn Ulvaeus, Benny Andersson
Sound engineer: Michael B Tretow
Assistant sound engineers: Rune Persson, Åke Eldsäter

Genesis

Misogyny is far from being a recent phenomenon. In ABBA's early days, Agnetha and Frida were frequently presented as mere backing singers, then as singers, talented ones it was true, but they weren't spared all kinds of sickening stereotypes. Throughout the 1970s, for example, the media were more than happy to dub Agnetha "the nicest bottom in show business," and Frida was criticized for abandoning her children to pursue her career, whereas Benny Andersson was never accused of any such thing. Let's not forget that when *Ring Ring* was released, Frida and Agnetha already had solid careers behind them as performers and had also worked as composers in the 1960s. However, *Disillusion* is the only track in ABBA's entire studio discography that bears the signature of Agnetha Fältskog, who wrote both the chord sequences and the melody. In the song, she portrays a young girl dumped by a lover, and she delivers a performance that is the only one of its kind in the group's repertoire, showcasing her powerful and subtle voice. There are traces of Joni Mitchell and Elton John in this melancholic ballad, which betrays Fältskog's sensitivity while revealing to listeners her full vocal range. Unfortunately, from then on, Fältskog preferred to leave the composing to Ulvaeus and Andersson in the belief that her songs weren't as good as theirs. In 1975, she recorded *Mina Ögon* ("My Eyes"), the Swedish version of *Disillusion,* for her album *Elva Kvinnor i ett Hus* ("Eleven Women in a House").

Production

Until 1978, the year ABBA started recording their albums at Polar Music studios, Benny Andersson used only one acoustic piano, the Bolin grand at Metronome studios, made in the 1960s by luthier Georg Bolin for the jazz pianist and composer Bill Evans. Metronome acquired the legendary instrument in 1967. Benny Andersson was delighted with it and used it to record many ABBA songs, including *Waterloo, Mamma Mia, SOS, Dancing Queen*, and *Knowing Me, Knowing You.* The piano was put up for auction at Sotheby's in 2015, but failed to find a buyer. At the time of writing, it is still part of the equipment at Metronome studios, renamed Atlantis Grammafon in 1983, then Atlantis Studios a few years later.

Despite her undeniable talent, Agnetha soon decided to stop composing for the band, leaving that to Benny and Björn.

Single

PEOPLE NEED LOVE

(Benny Andersson, Björn Ulvaeus/2'43)

Musicians
Agnetha Fältskog: vocals, yodel, backing vocals
Anni-Frid "Frida" Lyngstad: vocals, yodel, backing vocals
Björn Ulvaeus: vocals, acoustic guitar
Benny Andersson: piano, backing vocals
Janne Schaffer: electric guitar
Mike Watson: bass
Ola Brunkert: drums

Recording
Metronome, Stockholm: 29 March, 5 April 1972

Technical team
Producers: Björn Ulvaeus, Benny Andersson
Sound engineer: Michael B Tretow
Assistant sound engineers: Rune Persson, Åke Eldsäter

Single
Swedish version
A-side: *People Need Love*/2'44
B-side: *Merry-Go-Round (En Karusell)*/3'24
US version **(Björn & Benny [with Svenska Flicka])**
A-side: *People Need Love*/2'35
B-side: *Merry-Go-Round*/3'16
Released in Sweden by Polar Music: May 1972
(single ref.: POS 1156)
Released in the USA by Playboy Records: September 1972
(single ref.: P 50014)
Best chart ranking in Sweden: 17
Best chart ranking in the USA: 114

Genesis
In September 1972, when *People Need Love*, the first single by the future ABBA, was released, it wasn't attributed to a group, but to a male duo accompanied by two pretty young women. With typical delicacy, the US distributor Playboy Records gave the name on the sleeve as "Björn & Benny (with Svenska Flicka)," which translates as "Björn & Benny (with Swedish Girls)." Times change, but back then no one made a fuss about how the two female singers, who in fact carry the entire song, were eclipsed by Ulvaeus and Andersson. The song was recorded in spring 1972 and wasn't originally intended to launch a quartet—it was simply the result of the four of them having fun in the studio. The success of *People Need Love* in Sweden persuaded Benny and Björn to continue their venture, and in the course of the next few months they began producing the *Ring Ring* album.

Production
Produced in a *schlager* style that the two men were still finding hard to relinquish, *People Need Love* is about harmony between couples, and indeed between human beings in general. It is typical of the pacifist songs that had been hits in the late 1960s/early 1970s, such as Jackie DeShannon's *What the World Needs Now Is Love* (1965) and Brotherhood of Man's *United We Stand* (1970). Such songs already felt outdated when *People Need Love* was released in 1972, by which time youngsters were only interested in the glam-rock revolution spearheaded by David Bowie in Great Britain. By choosing to take inspiration from the vocal harmonies of Roger Cook and Madeline Bell of the British group Blue Mink, whose single *Melting Pot* was an international hit in 1970, rather than from the sexy rock of T. Rex, the Swedes appeared somewhat out of touch with their era. Adding the yodel at the end of the track didn't much help either, firmly placing it in a musical past. But it was exactly this uniqueness that led to ABBA's success several months later, with the band members choosing to follow their instincts by placing melody at the heart of their compositions, regardless of the dictates of fashion. That's the mark of great artists.

I SAW IT IN THE MIRROR

(Benny Andersson, Björn Ulvaeus/2'33)

Musicians
Björn Ulvaeus: vocals, acoustic guitar
Agnetha Fältskog: vocals, backing vocals
Anni-Frid "Frida" Lyngstad: vocals, backing vocals
Benny Andersson: vocals, Fender Rhodes
Janne Schaffer: acoustic guitar
Mike Watson: bass
Ola Brunkert: drums

Recording
Metronome, Stockholm: 15 to 16 March 1973

Technical team
Producers: Björn Ulvaeus, Benny Andersson
Sound engineer: Michael B Tretow
Assistant sound engineers: Rune Persson, Åke Eldsäter

Genesis

Benny Andersson and Björn Ulvaeus wrote *I Saw It in the Mirror* in 1970 for singer Billy Gezon, aka Billy G-son, previously of The Violents. The two composers loved the singer's deep voice, which they compared to the American Joe Cocker, and they wrote a single for him called *There's a Little Man*, on which Agnetha Fältskog sang backing vocals. On 27 February 1970, just after that song was recorded, Billy also laid down *I Saw It in the Mirror* on tape. It featured on the B-side of *There's a Little Man*, but would not propel the singer to stardom: he remained unknown until returning to the limelight in 1988 at Melodifestivalen with a song called *Måndag i mitt Liv* ("Monday in my Life"). Once again, the artist failed to break through and, despite releasing the song as a single, he will not be remembered by posterity.

Production

When Björn Ulvaeus and Benny Andersson completed production of *Ring Ring* in 1973, the album appeared to be one track short. So they decided to rerecord *I Saw It in the Mirror*, changing the arrangements to give it more of a soul sound, which suited it perfectly. Performed with great grace, with the melody foregrounded, Björn and Benny singing in unison and Agnetha and Frida's backing vocals executed to perfection, the song was given a second lease of life. Its sheer simplicity and efficiency shine through. *I Saw It in the Mirror* alone makes it worth listening to this first album by the future ABBA, as it underlines the skill of the two pop-writing virtuosos and their minimalist production style.

NINA, PRETTY BALLERINA

(Benny Andersson, Björn Ulvaeus/2'52)

Musicians

Anni-Frid "Frida" Lyngstad: vocals, backing vocals
Agnetha Fältskog: vocals, backing vocals
Björn Ulvaeus: vocals, electric guitar, backing vocals
Benny Andersson: piano, backing vocals
Janne Schaffer: electric guitar
Rutger Gunnarsson: bass
Ola Brunkert: drums

Recording

KMH studios, Stockholm: 2 November 1972

Technical team

Producers: Björn Ulvaeus, Benny Andersson
Sound engineer: Michael B Tretow
Assistant sound engineer: Lennart Karlsmyr

Genesis

Had it been released in the London of the Swinging Sixties, *Nina, Pretty Ballerina* would have been a hit. Many a young Londoner would have danced the watusi, the jerk, or the swim to this catchy song with its staccato rhythm and typical pop theme: a bored office girl whose life is only meaningful when she goes dancing every Friday night and gets the opportunity to show off her moves. An initial version of the instrumental part of the track was recorded on 17 October 1972 at Europa Film studios in Stockholm, and *He Is Your Brother* was recorded at the same time with various session musicians who never again worked with Benny and Björn. Neither man was satisfied with the takes and only the ones from *He Is Your Brother* were retained for the album, while *Nina, Pretty Ballerina* was rerecorded on 2 November in the studios of Kungliga Musikhögskolan—KMH, Stockholm's Royal College of Music—with musicians who had already played brilliantly during other *Ring Ring* sessions. The song was released as a single in Austria, France, Kenya, and the Philippines.

Production

Benny Andersson and Michael B Tretow used a technique that we now call Vari-Speed, well known to today's sound engineers but pioneering at the time, to record the piano part for the choruses of *Nina, Pretty Ballerina*. As Andersson was having difficulty playing his sixteenth-note chords, Tretow reduced the tape speed before recording him. This enabled the pianist to lay down his score on tape easily before the song returned to its original tempo, this time with an additional piano line that appears to have been executed with astonishing dexterity.

Funny guy and virtuoso sound engineer, Michael B Tretow was very much part of the ABBA adventure.

LOVE ISN'T EASY (BUT IT SURE IS HARD ENOUGH)

(Benny Andersson, Björn Ulvaeus/2'52)

Musicians

Björn Ulvaeus: vocals, acoustic guitar, backing vocals
Agnetha Fältskog: vocals, backing vocals
Anni-Frid "Frida" Lyngstad: vocals, backing vocals
Benny Andersson: piano, backing vocals
Janne Schaffer: electric guitar
Mike Watson: bass
Ola Brunkert: drums

Recording

Metronome, Stockholm: 14 March 1973

Technical team

Producers: Björn Ulvaeus, Benny Andersson
Sound engineer: Michael B Tretow
Assistant sound engineers: Rune Persson, Åke Eldsäter

Genesis

Never has the influence of The Beatles on Ulvaeus and Andersson's creations been so obvious as in this pop anthem, which, like many of the album's other tracks, should have made *Ring Ring* a cult record. The two composers had never made a secret of their love of the Fab Four's music, and when the Swedish press tried to compare ABBA to them, Benny and Björn agreed, while making the extent of their admiration abundantly clear. "To start with we dislike any comparison with The Beatles because they are the strongest influence that we've had," Björn said. "They are more like 'God' to us."[19] Over and above their esteem for the British stars, it was Lennon and McCartney's concept of writing music that influenced the Swedes. Until then, bands had simply been content to cover the standards, adapting them to produce hits that felt hackneyed. "It was the idea that two people in a group could write their own songs and we thought, if they can do it, why can't we? That changed everything for us. Before The Beatles, songwriters were very anonymous people and nobody paid any attention to them," said Benny.[20]

Production

But The Beatles' influence didn't end there, as their open-to-anything spirit also inspired the Swedes to develop a varied repertoire. As early as 1973, this was already a mix of rock, pop, *schlager*, and folk, to which would soon be added reggae, disco, and new wave. "The Beatles [...] showed that you explore different paths," concluded Ulvaeus. "You didn't have to be a rock group only, you could do different things on the same album, [...] which is necessary for us to do because we play around with different styles and that is what we have fun doing."[19] *Love Isn't Easy (But It Sure Is Hard Enough)* was recorded on the same day as *Disillusion*, but unfortunately wasn't released as a single in Sweden, only in Denmark, with *I Am Just a Girl* as the B-side. To make up for this, Polar Music reissued the single across Europe on 19 May 2023.

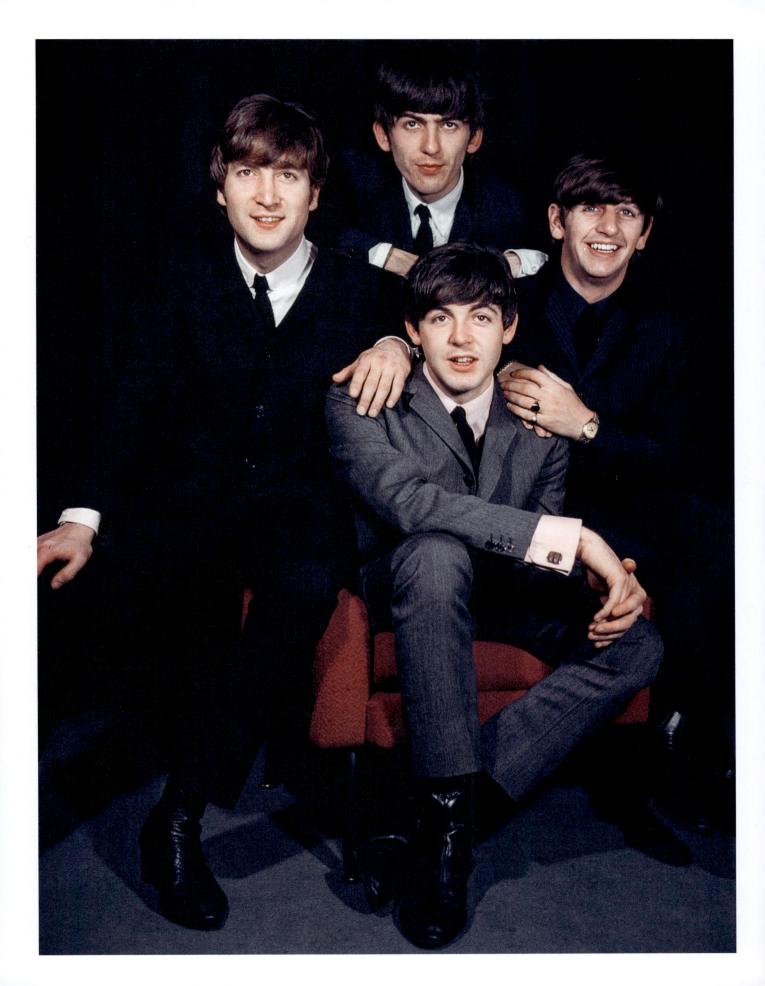

ME AND BOBBY AND BOBBY'S BROTHER

(Benny Andersson, Björn Ulvaeus/2'49)

Musicians
Anni-Frid "Frida" Lyngstad: vocals, backing vocals
Agnetha Fältskog: backing vocals
Björn Ulvaeus: vocals, acoustic guitar, backing vocals
Benny Andersson: piano, backing vocals
Rutger Gunnarsson: bass
Roger Palm: drums
?: flute

Recording
KMH studios, Stockholm: 25 January 1973

Technical team
Producers: Björn Ulvaeus, Benny Andersson
Sound engineer: Michael B Tretow
Assistant sound engineer: Lennart Karlsmyr

Genesis

In this song, Frida tells us a story dreamed up by Benny Andersson and Björn Ulvaeus (who wrote the lyrics for the track together), about a fictitious childhood when she used to play with a friend called Bobby and his brother. In real life, things were quite different, as Anni-Frid's childhood was much less rosy than the song suggests. She was born in Norway but forced to flee at a young age. She lost her mother two years later and was raised by her loving grandmother, as her father, a German officer, had vanished without a trace from young Anni-Frid's life. "I'm definitely carrying a lot of problems from my younger years with me," she confided in 1976. "I believed everything would become easier to take with the passing of time. But in reality it's the contrary. I don't know what would have become of me, if I didn't have Benny in my life."[9] Right from the start, ABBA's songs need to be listened to carefully to hear the subtext, as the discography is full of joy while also taking into account the personal traumas of each of its members.

Production

Once again, the shadow of The Beatles hovers over the track's production. This time, it's hard not to think of the Fab Four's *Magical Mystery Tour* when Benny Andersson on piano launches into a rhythmic section based on a quarter-note chord, exactly as The Beatles did when they recorded *Your Mother Should Know* at London's Chappell Recording Studios in August 1967. This cabaret atmosphere perfectly suited the Liverpool boys' burlesque world and works well with the somewhat old-fashioned feel of *Ring Ring*. Admittedly, Björn, Benny, Agnetha, and Frida seemed to have missed the boat somewhat by recording a song like this in 1973, but no matter: their sense of fun shines through and introduces audiences to the sheer joy of the group's music at the time.

Single

HE IS YOUR BROTHER

(Benny Andersson, Björn Ulvaeus/3'17)

Musicians

Björn Ulvaeus: vocals, electric guitar
Anni-Frid "Frida" Lyngstad: vocals, backing vocals
Agnetha Fältskog: vocals, backing vocals
Benny Andersson: piano, backing vocals
Janne Schaffer: electric guitar
Stefan Brolund: bass
Jan Bandel: drums
Håkan Jansson: saxophone

Recording

Metronome, Stockholm: 29 October 1972

Technical team

Producers: Björn Ulvaeus, Benny Andersson
Sound engineer: Michael B Tretow
Assistant sound engineers: Rune Persson, Åke Eldsäter

Single

Swedish version
A-side: *He Is Your Brother*/3'18
B-side: *Santa Rosa*/3'02
US version
A-side: *He Is Your Brother* (Stereo)/3'18
B-side: *I Saw It in the Mirror*/2'34
Released in Sweden by Polar Music: November 1972
(single ref.: POS 1168)
Released in the USA by Playboy Records: 1973
(single ref.: P 50037)
Best chart ranking in Sweden: did not make the charts
Best chart ranking in the USA: did not make the charts

Genesis

Following on from the success in Sweden of the single *People Need Love*, Björn Ulvaeus, Benny Andersson, and their manager Stig Anderson decided to carry on with the Björn & Benny, Agnetha & Anni-Frid combo and give the public a new single from the band. Andersson and Ulvaeus composed *He Is Your Brother* in the same pacifist, humanist spirit, releasing it as a single in November of the same year, 1973. Alas, it didn't make it into the Swedish charts, let alone *Billboard* in the USA. This was despite its being distributed by Playboy Records, who this time round, rather than printing "Björn & Benny (with Svenska Flicka)"—"Björn and Benny (with Swedish Girls)"—on the labels, wrote "Björn & Benny with Anna and Frieda." While we appreciate the effort, they still managed to misspell "Frida," and the band decided to rename Agnetha "Anna" in the hope of boosting international sales by erasing the group's slightly foreign feel. "According to my passport, my name is Anna Agnetha Fältskog—therefore both names are right," she would say in 1976. "When I started my career as a solo singer in Sweden eight years ago, I called myself Agnetha. With ABBA, I changed it into Anna, because it was the start of a completely new career for me. My husband Björn calls me Anna as well."[8] While the world now knows her as Agnetha, the name Anna appeared quite frequently in articles about ABBA in the early 1970s.

Production

The first bar of the song features a glissando on piano, which reappeared in the intro to *Dancing Queen* in 1976, and the song as a whole is built around a pop rhythm and verses sung alternately by Björn and Frida/Agnetha. Swedish saxophonist Håkan Jansson, who had revealed his talent in 1969 on the debut album from musician and producer Lars Samuelson's band Dynamite Brass, accompanies the choruses with a discreet woodwind note. As well as specializing in accompanying some of the biggest names in Swedish music, Dynamite Brass were known for appearing on numerous TV shows. Their bassist, Mike Watson, also appeared on *Ring Ring*, playing the four-string on *People Need Love*. He featured on many other ABBA tracks, too, including *SOS*, *The Winner Takes It All*, and *Super Trouper*. Håkan Jansson, on the other hand, wasn't seen again in the group's discography.

Always dressed smartly, the four Swedes took as much care of their appearance as they did of their music.

RING RING (ENGELSK VERSION)

(Benny Andersson, Stig Anderson, Björn Ulvaeus, Neil Sedaka, Phil Cody/3'03)

Musicians

Agnetha Fältskog: vocals, backing vocals
Anni-Frid "Frida" Lyngstad: vocals, backing vocals
Björn Ulvaeus: electric guitar, backing vocals
Benny Andersson: piano, Mellotron, backing vocals
Janne Schaffer: electric guitar
Rutger Gunnarsson: bass
Ola Brunkert: drums

Recording

Metronome, Stockholm: 10, 17 January 1973
Europa Film, Stockholm: January 1973

Technical team

Producers: Björn Ulvaeus, Benny Andersson
Sound engineers: Michael B Tretow, Björn Almstedt (Europa Film)
Assistant sound engineers: Rune Persson (Metronome), Åke Eldsäter (Metronome)

Single

Swedish version
A-side: *Ring Ring* (English version)/3'06
B-side: *She's My Kind of Girl*/2'46
UK version
A-side: *Ring Ring*/3'00
B-side: *Rock'n Roll Band*/3'08
Released in Sweden by Polar Music: 14 February 1973
(single ref.: POS 1171, single ref. 2: POS 1172)
Released in the UK by CBS/Epic: 14 February 1973
(single ref.: S EPC 1793)
Best chart ranking in Sweden: 2
Best chart ranking in the UK: 32

Genesis

While his protégés, Björn & Benny and Agnetha & Frida, were getting ready to compete in 1973's Melodifestivalen, hoping that their song *Ring Ring (Bara Du Slog en Signal)* would be their entry ticket to the Eurovision Song Contest, their manager Stig Anderson was looking to the future. He felt the song would benefit from international exposure, especially if it were to be selected for Eurovision, so he asked the legendary Neil Sedaka to work on an English version of the lyrics. Sedaka was an iconic figure associated with the Brill Building (a breeding ground for songwriters and composers in 1960s New York) and was one of the first Americans to sing his own songs rather than cover versions. He had become a global star with the hit songs he penned and mostly performed, since his debut in 1957. *Oh! Carol*, the best-known globally, along with another, *The Dreamer* (1963), were even given to the young Agnetha Fältskog as a Christmas gift in 1964. Sedaka enlisted the services of his partner Phil Cody to write the English version of the track, based on the same theme as the original, namely, a young woman spurned by her boyfriend and waiting by the telephone for the call that never comes.

Production

The original version of *Ring Ring (Bara Du Slog en Signal)* was recorded in January 1973 at both Stockholm's Metronome studios (with Michael B Tretow as sound engineer) and Europa Film studios, where another technician, Björn Almstedt (in-house sound engineer for Europa), would do the vocal takes for the English version. Sedaka, who had agreed to work on the song on the condition that it really appealed to him, had high hopes for it, believing it to be a potential hit. This turned out to be the case in Sweden, where both versions entered the charts simultaneously. Although it was as good as all the other ABBA hits, *Ring Ring* was not included on the famous *ABBA Gold* compilation of 1992, which relaunched the band's popularity worldwide. Inevitably, it remains a song for true fans, despite its melody and production making it one of the most delightful of ABBA numbers.

Stig Anderson and his
daughter Marie at the Polar
Music offices in 1974.

I AM JUST A GIRL

(Benny Andersson, Stig Anderson, Björn Ulvaeus/3'02)

Musicians

Agnetha Fältskog: vocals, backing vocals
Anni-Frid "Frida" Lyngstad: vocals, backing vocals
Benny Andersson: piano, backing vocals
Björn Ulvaeus: vocals, acoustic guitar
Hasse Rosén: acoustic guitar
Bo Dahlman: acoustic guitar
Rutger Gunnarsson: bass, backing vocals
Derek Skinner: drums
Kjell Öhman: piano, celesta, harpsichord
Arnold Johansson: trumpet
Gösta Nilsson: trumpet
Jörgen Johansson: trombone
Christer Torgé: trombone
Åke Jelving: violin
Anders Dahl: violin
Gert Lundberg: violin
Gunnar Michols: violin
Harry Teike: violin
Herbert Konvicka: violin
Inge Lindstedt: violin
Kryztof Zdrzalka: violin
Per Sandklef: violin
Sixten Strömvall: violin
Lars Arvinder: viola
Niels Heie: viola
Kjell Bjurling: cello
Gunnar Östling: cello
Kerstin Bagge: backing vocals
Kerstin Dahl-Boquist: backing vocals
Annica Risberg: backing vocals

Recording

Europa Film, Stockholm: 11 to 12 September 1972
Metronome, Stockholm: March 1973

Technical team

Producers: Björn Ulvaeus, Benny Andersson
Sound engineer: Michael B Tretow
Assistant sound engineers: Rune Persson (Metronome),
Åke Eldsäter (Metronome), Björn Almstedt (Europa Film)
String arrangements: Sven-Olof Walldoff

Genesis

After composing the music for the erotic film *Någon Att Älska* ("The Seduction of Inga") in 1970, Benny Andersson and Björn Ulvaeus were offered work with film director Per Berglund, who was in the middle of producing the film *Ture Sventon—Privatdetektiv* ("Ture Sventon, Private Detective"), based on a successful Swedish children's book. Berglund asked the two men to compose a song that would be performed by the lead actor, Jarl Kulle. With lyrics by Stig Anderson, the song *Jag Är Blott en Man* ("I Am Just a Man") was submitted but rejected by the film's producer, who preferred another track called *Ture Sventon*, after the film's main character. Both songs subsequently appeared on a single released by Polar Music in 1972, but would be completely forgotten. When Benny and Björn launched production of the *Ring Ring* album in 1972, they took this sweet ballad out of their bag of tricks, kept the backing tracks, and rerecorded the vocals in March 1973 for inclusion under the title *I Am Just a Girl*.

Production

Although the song is highly enjoyable, its production does not quite match that of the album's other tracks. With string arrangements by Sven-Olof Walldoff, who had worked with Hootenanny Singers on several occasions and would soon become part of ABBA's inner circle, the track sounds as if it had been recorded a decade earlier, and it didn't help people to see Björn & Benny, Agnetha & Frida as a band of its time. But regardless of the critics, who pointed to the lack of artistic coherence in *Ring Ring*, often seen as a compilation of songs rather than a carefully designed album, *I Am Just a Girl* testifies to a period when Benny and Björn were beginning a working relationship that would prove amazingly effective. It heralded, in many ways, the emergence of the greatest pop-writing duo of the late 20th century.

The two couples in
1972, shortly before
ABBA was formed.

From *Ring Ring (Bara Du Slog en Signal)* to *Under Attack*, guitarist Janne Schaffer was a constituent part of the ABBA sound.

Overleaf: The Polar Music stable in its glory days, 1973.

Single

ROCK'N ROLL BAND

(Benny Andersson, Björn Ulvaeus/3'07)

Musicians

Björn Ulvaeus: vocals, acoustic guitar, backing vocals
Agnetha Fältskog: backing vocals
Anni-Frid "Frida" Lyngstad: backing vocals
Benny Andersson: piano, backing vocals
Janne Schaffer: electric guitar
Rutger Gunnarsson: bass
Roger Palm: drums

Recording

Europa Film, Stockholm: 30 August 1972
Metronome, Stockholm: 26 September 1972

Technical team

Producers: Björn Ulvaeus, Benny Andersson
Sound engineer: Michael B Tretow
Assistant sound engineers: Björn Almstedt (Europa Film), Rune Persson (Metronome), Åke Eldsäter (Metronome)

Single

A-side: *Rock'n Roll Band*/3'02
B-side: *Another Town, Another Train*/3'04
Released in the USA by Playboy Records: July 1973
(single ref.: P 50025)
Best chart ranking in the USA: did not make the charts

Genesis

Autumn 1972. As the Scandinavian winter set in, the days were getting shorter in Sweden and the four future members of ABBA were active on all fronts, especially when it came to developing their own personal careers. Agnetha Fältskog was enjoying acclaim with the single *Tio Mil Kvar till Korpilombolo* ("Ten Miles Left till Korpilombolo"), released by Cupol, which quickly became a hit. The same applied to Anni-Frid Lyndstad, whose single *Man Vill ju Leva Lite Dessemellan* ("You Want to Live a Little in Between") met with similar success. Benny Andersson and Björn Ulvaeus were hard at work producing the song *Love Has its Ways*, composed by Japanese composer Koichi Morita for Epic, the label that distributed ABBA's songs in the UK and was trying to break into the Japanese market. The B-side of *Love Has its Ways* was a track called *Rock'n Roll Band*, which felt heavily inspired by one of Ulvaeus' favorite groups, The Beach Boys.

Production

Following the release of the single *Love Has its Ways*, the two men decided to reuse the song on the Björn & Benny and Agnetha & Frida album they were currently working on. The Swedes had officially launched production on 26 September, when they had begun reworking *Rock'n Roll Band*, adding a guitar track played by Janne Schaffer, who would later become one of ABBA's main partners, leaving his mark on dozens of their songs. Although Benny and Björn have admitted they were not overly keen on the song, it is nevertheless a quality track. And although it makes *Ring Ring*'s lack of coherence obvious, as the album consists of songs recorded over a long period of time, the group's next albums would more than compensate for this minor bump in the road.

ABBA (BJÖRN, BENNY, AGNETHA & FRIDA)

WATERLOO

Waterloo • Sitting In The Palmtree • King Kong Song • Hasta Mañana •
My Mama Said • Dance (While The Music Still Goes On) • Honey, Honey •
Watch Out • What About Livingstone • Gonna Sing You My Lovesong •
Suzy-Hang-Around • Waterloo (English Version)

Released in Sweden by Polar Music: 4 March 1974 (album ref.: POLS 252)
Released in the UK by CBS/Epic: 4 March 1974 (album ref.: S EPC 80179)
Released in the USA by Atlantic: 4 March 1974 (album ref.: SD 18101)
Best chart ranking in Sweden: 1
Best chart ranking in the UK: 28
Best chart ranking in the USA: 145

OUT TO CONQUER EUROPE

The failure of The Nova and The Dolls at the Eurovision Song Contest on 7 April 1973—due to the victory of the French singer Anne-Marie David, who was competing for Luxembourg—aroused a strong feeling of injustice in Sweden, especially among fans of Björn & Benny, Agnetha & Frida, whose song *Ring Ring (Bara Du Slog en Signal)* had been a triumphant success across the country. Complaints persuaded the organizers of the next edition of the Melodifestivalen to modify the selection process for the jury. Until then, this had been made up of so-called experts, who had clearly failed in their duty. It was therefore decided henceforward to take into account votes by the audience, who would appoint some of the jurors for the following year.

The multitude of projects Ulvaeus, Andersson, Fältskog, and Lyngstad worked on during 1973 confirmed their place on the Swedish music scene, and this hard-won credibility drove them to pursue their venture as a foursome. During the winter, a decision was taken that would make this plan a reality. "I couldn't be bothered to keep on saying all four names of the group as on the disc label," reported Stig Anderson, the group's manager and head of their label, Polar Music, "so I mixed up their initials and came up with ABBA. That didn't much please the two boys, because ABBA is very similar to the name of a noted brand of pickled herring in Sweden, but in the end they agreed it was a neat, commercial, easy-to-remember tag for a pop group."[21] However, before giving the group that name, Anderson took the trouble of asking the permission of the company in question, which gave its agreement—a wise decision for its popularity among Swedes. "[…] The factory said, 'OK, as long as you don't make us feel ashamed for what you're doing,'" Agnetha recalled with amusement twenty years later. "I think we did a good job."[7]

The ABBA four on Viggsö island

It was with unparalleled combativeness that the members of ABBA attacked the year 1973. Nothing seemed to stop the two composers, who shut themselves away in their chalets on the island of Viggsö where, armed with an old upright piano and an acoustic guitar, they launched into writing the successor to *Ring Ring (Bara Du Slog en Signal)*. At the same time, Stig Anderson completed his promotion of the group all over Europe, having them record Spanish and German versions of *Ring Ring*. As summer drew to a close, and the four went into the studio to record their new compositions, another goal was occupying the minds of the Polar Music trio. With the intention of correcting an obvious auditioning error made the previous year, the Melodifestivalen selection committee granted ABBA the right to take part once more in the national competition, which was to be held on 9 February 1974.

Immediately, the priority for the musicians and their manager was to choose which song to perform. They were torn between two of their new compositions, *Hasta Mañana* and *Waterloo*, both by Björn and Benny, with lyrics by Stig Anderson. However, the latter quickly chose for his protégés the second song, which had the advantage of pop choruses and would make an impression in a competition where traditional songs—whether from France, Italy, or Sweden—still reigned supreme.

"I'm sure I'm right," Anderson told them, with characteristic clarity and intuition, "but if it is a disaster, then you can cut my throat afterwards."[21]

Contestants in outfits of light

When ABBA performed the Swedish version of *Waterloo* at Melodifestivalen in Stockholm, on 9 February 1974, they caused a surprise not only because of their very rock-like and melodious song. Their clothes also unsettled the audience, so starkly did they contrast with the sensible image the group had presented the previous year. It was in the shop Gröna Moln och Blått Gräs ("Green Clouds and Blue Grass"), opened in Stockholm in 1972 by the stylist Inger Svenneke, that the four artists had found their stage outfits. These drew inspiration from the British glam rock movement and its most famous ambassadors—David Bowie's group The Spiders from Mars. Frida, who had fallen in love with a silver jacket covered with chains and various metal trinkets displayed in the shop window, had urged the others to come and source their costumes there.

It was in this futuristic garb that the members of ABBA would win with flying colours, despite a performance occasionally marred by imprecise voice control. From now on, the group and their manager had an open door through which to conquer, if not the world, then at least the European continent. From the following day, Stig Anderson began negotiations, determined to get the group known before they took part in the Eurovision Song Contest, to be held on 6 April at the Brighton Dome in England.

Stikkan active on all fronts

Anderson, whom his associates had nicknamed Stikkan, had only two months to carry out his plan of attack. He decided that the group's new album, *Waterloo*, due for release on 4 March and this time bearing the name ABBA (for Agnetha, Björn, Benny, and Anni-Frid), would be his most effective weapon. Ready for action as ever, he immediately set about moving heaven and earth to make sure his group was known across all Europe in no time. "The morning after we won here, I had all my master tapes available, a Swedish version and English version, and I had photos, films, etc. I took the plane and swept over Europe to every record company who represented us already and said, 'Press it, and have it ready tomorrow.' Thanks to that, they started playing it on stations all over Europe. When we came to Brighton, people in Germany, Switzerland, and Italy already had heard it on the radio."[22]

It was thus with unprecedented self-confidence and preparation that ABBA went on stage at the Brighton Dome on 6 April 1974, still wearing their coloured outfits and with Björn Ulvaeus sporting a star-shaped guitar designed for the occasion by the Swedish luthier Göran Malmberg. That day, *Waterloo* was performed perfectly by Agnetha and Frida, Björn and Benny in playback, alongside their musicians Ola Brunkert (drums) and Rutger Gunnarsson (bass guitar). Guitarist Janne Schaffer was unable to join them because the rules limited the number of artists on stage to six. As for the orchestra, Sven-Olof Walldoff, who had written the string arrangements for *I Am Just a Girl* in 1972, took the place of conductor, dressed up as Napoleon Bonaparte—because the song *Waterloo* draws a parallel between the emperor's defeat at the famous Battle of Waterloo in Belgium in 1815 and a romantic disappointment suffered by the female narrators of ABBA's song. The performance—before 500 million television viewers—was thus a success, but when the group returned to their dressing room, tension was at breaking point. "While

ABBA's success at the Eurovision Song Contest meant that 6 April 1974 became a key date in music history, and made Sweden famous the world over.

waiting for the votes to come in, our nerves were boiling up again," Agnetha explained. "The excitement was so intense that it almost hurt. My head was buzzing and my heart was pounding peculiarly. Then, the votes of the international jury started to come in. You could hear a pin drop in the waiting room. At one moment one contestant was ahead, at another moment the other. In a fascinated manner we all gazed at the screens on which the results were projected. At one moment I got the impression that we didn't make it after all [...] then Finland gave us five points which gave us the lead position again. And then it was all over. *Waterloo* had acquired 24 points [...]"[23]

From the Brighton Dome to *Top of the Pops*

ABBA's victory that evening had all the look of a good omen for the group and their manager, Stig Anderson. The latter, fixated on his goal, distributed singles of *Waterloo* to all the clubs in Brighton that very night, so that the song would be played, while over the following days the group made many public appearances, held press conferences, and attended official receptions. After four days in Brighton, they went to London where, notably, they appeared on the television program *Top of the Pops*, the holy grail for any band wanting to see their career take off. "To be whisked up to London in a Rolls-Royce directly to *Top of the Pops*, that was a dream come true, appearing in the same place that The Beatles had," Björn said.[24]

Back in Sweden, they rested briefly before thinking of future events, including a national tour planned for the summer—along the way cancelling Benny and Frida's wedding, originally scheduled for July 1974. "The date was set," Andersson explained, "the invitations had been sent—but at the last moment something came in between: our Eurovision victory in Brighton with *Waterloo*. After that, we received so many offers that we had to postpone our wedding [...]. Maybe

On 2 November 1974, ABBA appeared on stage in East Berlin in the television program *Ein Kessel Buntes*. On that side of the Berlin Wall, the group encountered a problem. "I remember we were paid in whatever currency they had —East German marks or whatever—which you couldn't change when you got to the west," Björn said. "Nobody would take it. I had one day to get rid of it, so I bought everyone in the bar a drink!"[28]

we'll have time for it next year, in January we will finally have two weeks off…"[25] For Agnetha and Björn, too, the return to Vallentuna was complicated by a turbulent reunion with their young daughter, Linda, who did not seem to recognize her parents on their return from the UK. Profoundly hurt by this situation, Björn and Agnetha gave their assurance that they would never again absent them-selves in that way and, by agreement with Frida and Benny, cancelled the Swedish tour planned for the summer of 1974. Although the reason for it was admirable, the decision infuriated certain professionals, who accused the group of preferring to concentrate on their career abroad rather than to play before Swedish audiences. This is why Sweden's national television network invited ABBA to appear only a very few times in the following two years, despite the success of *Waterloo*. "When we are asked why we never appear on Swedish television, I always reply that we are never asked," Björn explained in 1977. "In 1975, we only performed once. And do you know why? Because the other group, that had been invited first, was unable to attend due to health problems!"[26]

A tour meets with muted success

The summer of 1974 was thus devoted to family life and various musical projects. Frida and Agnetha put the finishing touches to their respective solo albums, *Frida Ensam* ("Frida Alone") and *Elva Kvinnor i Ett Hus* ("Eleven Women in One House"). The writing of ABBA's third album proceeded apace, despite an increasingly crowded timetable for Björn and Benny, who were decidedly busy on all fronts. In September the group flew to New York, where three days of promotion awaited them. With *Waterloo* having soared to number 6 on *Billboard* in July, the team from Polar Music, led by the formidable Görel Hanser, Stig Anderson's secretary and in charge of the label's press relations, was determined to establish a lasting presence for the group in the USA. Once back in Scandinavia, the musicians prepared their first tour, which was needed to promote them, despite the reservations of Frida and Agnetha, who were already showing their aversion to this kind of obligation. "I'm a little scared of giant tours like this," Frida said. "You are on the road constantly, you have to get up on stage every night and [you are] completely exhausted afterwards. There's not much time for love in these circumstances…"[25]

Despite this reluctance, the tour began on 17 November at the Falkoner Centret in Copenhagen, Denmark. It continued until the beginning of 1975, ending on 22 January at the Universum in Umeå, Sweden, having taken in Germany, Austria, Switzerland, and Norway. Other countries, including France, the Netherlands, and the UK, had initially been considered, but the absence of a solid fan base outweighed the wishes of manager Stig Anderson and tour organizer Thomas Johansson, who decided to reconsider and concentrate mostly on Scandinavia. Although the tour was formative for ABBA, it was symptomatic of a problem they encountered at the time. The period following *Waterloo* seems to have been difficult as they struggled to create new singles for their fans and confirm their potential in the eyes of professionals in the industry. *Honey, Honey*, released as a single in the USA, did not follow up on the success of its predecessor, and the group quickly began producing their third album, with the aim of

1974

finding a hit that could permanently cement their reputation in North America. In November, *So Long*, which had been recorded over the summer, was hardly convincing, and flopped disastrously in the UK. ABBA were losing momentum, and now needed to think of their future. "It was a very difficult period," Björn Ulvaeus admitted. "[…] Everyone had decided we were a one-hit wonder because we came from Eurovision. And, with very few exceptions, they are one-hit wonders. [...] We didn't have anything really good on that first

album to release. [...] We went back to write and be better, not thinking 'hits.' It was the same attitude we always had: be as good as possible, treating every song as though it could be a single, never knowingly recording 'B' tracks."[27] It was a wise decision by the two composers who, in the intimate setting of their chalet on the island of Viggsö, would create two songs that were to firmly establish ABBA on the international pop scene.

Janne Schaffer in 1976, shortly before the release of his album *Katharsis*.

Overleaf: Benny and Björn at Marcus Music studios in Solna, 1974.

JANNE SCHAFFER, ABBA'S ROCK TOUCH

Born 24 September 1945, Jan Erik Tage Schaffer grew up in a family of musicians, and studied at Sweden's Royal College of Music. His father played the violin and his mother taught piano; it was a household where music took pride of place. "I heard a lot of pupils coming and going, maybe four or five a day. I was surrounded by music, though it was mainly classical and I wasn't hugely into that."[29] Having become proficient on acoustic guitar, the young Jan discovered the possibilities offered by the electric guitar. "[...] Hearing Elvis was really quite special. *Heartbreak Hotel* was on the radio and that was it for me. I went to another style of music and never looked back!"[29]

A Swedish success

During the 1960s Schaffer played guitar with several groups, including Ted and the Caracas and The Sleepstones. He made his way on the Swedish music scene, and met Benny Andersson, who asked him to work on Ted Gärdestad's first album, produced by Polar Music in 1972. During the same period Schaffer took part in the recording of *People Need Love* for Björn & Benny, Agnetha & Anni-Frid, and joined the team for *Waterloo*, on which his incisive playing and saturated guitar sound are instantly recognizable. At the same time, he began making his first solo album, where jazz, funk, pop, and blues were blended, and from then on described himself as a fusion guitarist. This diversity endowed him with a major role on ABBA's records, as a musician who could adapt to all styles. That first album, entitled simply *Janne Schaffer*, met with huge success in Sweden and launched his career. "I was Number One in the Swedish charts for six weeks, and even before ABBA at that time! The only time in history I was before ABBA. When [...] they asked me to go [on tour with them], I was playing with an American singer called Shawn Phillips. I played that for two months and my son was one year old. [...] I said I can go on recording with you but I can't do any tours, and then they called Lasse Wellander who is a fantastic, excellent guitar player."[30] While he shared ABBA recording sessions with Wellander throughout the 1970s, Schaffer became a well-known session guitarist, and left his mark on most of the group's hits, including *Waterloo, Voulez-Vous, I Have a Dream*, and *Super Trouper*. "Altogether there were 98 songs and I played on around 50. Looking back, we sold over 380 million records and I'm on over half, which is pretty cool!"[29]

Single

WATERLOO

(Benny Andersson, Stig Anderson, Björn Ulvaeus/2'45)

Musicians
Agnetha Fältskog: vocals, backing vocals
Anni-Frid "Frida" Lyngstad: vocals, backing vocals
Benny Andersson: piano, Minimoog, backing vocals
Björn Ulvaeus: acoustic guitar, backing vocals
Janne Schaffer: electric guitar
Rutger Gunnarsson: bass guitar
Ola Brunkert: drums
Christer Eklund: saxophone

Recording
Metronome, Stockholm: 17 December 1973, January to February 1974

Technical team
Producers: Björn Ulvaeus, Benny Andersson
Sound engineer: Michael B Tretow

Single
Swedish version (in Swedish)
Side 1: *Waterloo* (Swedish version)/2'46
Side 2: *Honey, Honey* (Swedish version)/2'55
Swedish version (in English)
Side 1: *Waterloo* (English version)/2'46
Side 2: *Watch Out*/3'46
UK and USA versions
A-side: *Waterloo*/2'46
B-side: *Watch Out*/3'46
Released in Sweden by Polar Music: 4 March 1974
(single in Swedish ref.: POS 1186, in English ref.: POS 1187)
Released in the UK by CBS/Epic: April 1974 (single ref.: S EPC 2240)
Released in the USA by Atlantic: May 1974 (single ref.: 45-3035)
Best chart ranking in Sweden (Swedish version): 2
Best chart ranking in Sweden (English version): 3
Best chart ranking in the UK: 1
Best chart ranking in the USA: 6

Genesis
It was in Björn and Agnetha's chalet on Viggsö that *Waterloo* saw the light of day. In the autumn of 1973, aiming to enter a pop song in the Melodifestivalen due to be held on 9 February the following year, Benny and Björn composed two songs with great potential: a ballad with old-fashioned charm, entitled *Who's Gonna Love You?,* and then *Hasta Mañana*, also a ballad, in a more pop vein. They recorded a preliminary version of the latter with piano and guitar, accompanied by a hummed melody, and sent it to their lyricist, manager, and producer, Stig Anderson. When Stikkan started writing, in December 1973, he wanted to give the song an irresistible catchiness, and opted for a chorus with a word or expression with just three syllables. The first thing that came into his head was "honey pie"—possibly inspired by *I Can't Help Myself (Sugar Pie Honey Bunch)*, a Motown standard sung by the Four Tops in 1965. The idea was quickly dropped in favour of the name of a Belgian town, Waterloo, scene of a bloody battle between the troops of Napoleon Bonaparte and an Allied army under the command of the Duke of Wellington and Field Marshal Blücher. Before even writing the song's lyrics, which were to draw a parallel between the defeat of Napoleon on 18 June 1815 and that of a woman rejected by her lover, Anderson concentrated on the title itself. "The title is the most important thing," he explained a few years later. "It has to be short and quickly visible on the TV screen. It must be understandable in Poland and Yugoslavia as well."[31]

Production
Once Stig Anderson had written the Swedish lyrics of *Waterloo*, an English version, heavily reworked by Björn Ulvaeus, was also produced. The voices of Frida and Agnetha, in unison, were added to the backing tracks recorded the previous December. The song's production was fairly similar to that of *Ring Ring (Bara Du Slog en Signal)* as, once again, the sound engineer Michael B Tretow recreated Phil Spector's famous "wall of sound," with the aim of giving the song a 1960s rock feel. References to that genre are obvious, starting with the intro, borrowed from that of *Da Doo Ron Ron* by The Crystals, produced in 1963 by…Phil Spector. Although the rhythmic base provided by bass guitarist Rutger Gunnarsson and drummer Ola Brunkert makes a nod to The Beach Boys, the overall production recalls that of Tony Visconti on the T. Rex

1974

Frida and Agnetha preparing to record the German version of *Waterloo*.

Overleaf: ABBA posing at Waterloo Station in London, 10 April 1974.

albums *Electric Warrior* (1971) and *The Slider* (1972). The onomatopoeic sounds sung by Agnetha and Frida at the end of the choruses (especially at 00'54) are a clear reference to *Runaway* by Del Shannon, produced by Harry Balk in 1961. And the whole song pays homage to the pop music beloved of Ulvaeus and Andersson. "So the true pop songs, the really good pop songs, that's where we were coming from," Björn explained. "And that's what we wanted to express with *Waterloo*."[32] Frida and Agnetha recorded two other versions of the song in 1974: first a German one, at Mackans studios in Stockholm on 15 March, then a French one in the Vogue recording studios in Villetaneuse, a suburb of Paris. Vogue had become ABBA's distributor in France.

The Briton Robert Gunnell, head of Radio Brighton, was a bad loser. He decided to boycott *Waterloo* after ABBA's success at the Eurovision Song Contest. "That song can be number one one hundred thousand times but that doesn't mean that I have to like the record or that I have to play it," he declared at the time. "I believe that our listeners don't like the record, that's why I don't play it."[33]

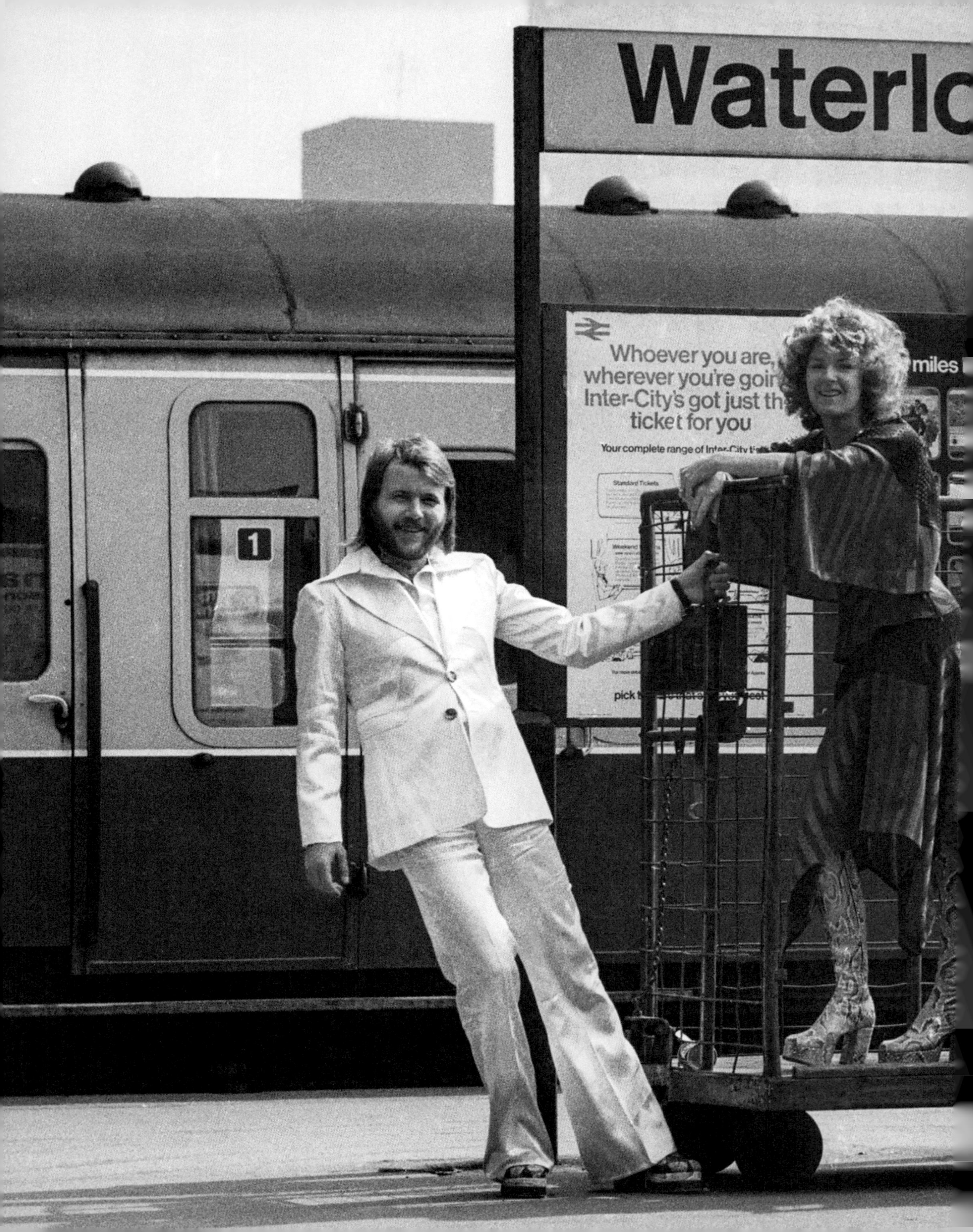
Waterlo
Whoever you are,
ticket for you
1

SITTING IN THE PALMTREE

(Benny Andersson, Björn Ulvaeus/3'39)

Musicians
Björn Ulvaeus: lead vocals, backing vocals
Agnetha Fältskog: backing vocals
Anni-Frid "Frida" Lyngstad: backing vocals
Benny Andersson: Minimoog
Janne Schaffer: electric guitar
Rutger Gunnarsson: bass guitar
Ola Brunkert: drums
Malando Gassama: congas, güiro

Recording
Metronome, Stockholm: 18 to 19 December 1973

Technical team
Producers: Björn Ulvaeus, Benny Andersson
Sound engineer: Michael B Tretow

Genesis

Mother and Child Reunion, which Paul Simon sang in 1972, is considered the first time a pop singer ventured into the reggae style. It opened the door for numerous groups from the English-speaking world to pile in without discrimination, at the risk of distorting this highly spiritual musical genre, and turning it into a style fashionable in the nightclubs of Western capitals. Led Zeppelin tried their hand at Jamaican slang with *D'Yer Mak'er* in 1973, Eric Clapton massacred The Wailers' *I Shot the Sheriff* in 1974, Graham Parker sang *Don't Ask Me Questions* in 1976, and 10cc had a global hit with their dreadful *Dreadlock Holiday* in 1978. The entire international rock scene had a crack at the reggae style, even if it meant sometimes coming off the worse for it. ABBA were no exception, leaping into the fray with *Sitting in the Palmtree*, which gives off a pleasant whiff of ocean spray and sun cream, but contains writing of unconvincing quality. Even though it displays considerable innocence, in the seaside song genre Elton John's *Jamaica Jerk-Off*, released in 1973 on *Goodbye Yellow Brick Road*, proved more popular. Nevertheless, a few years later Björn Ulvaeus defended his having been inspired by this musical trend, even though he emphasized its qualities, and proclaimed the open-mindedness of those who had got involved with it. "[…] I don't see anything new happening in the States. Here reggae is very strong and it seems to develop in its own directions now. […] I think you have to live here and have to feel that constant pulse to really part of it. We don't feel the reggae influence."[19]

Production

Janne Schaffer, who played the electric guitar riffs on *Waterloo*, shines here for his mastery of reggae-style muted plucking, even though more broadly the whole team around ABBA displays rock-solid technique and shows impressive adaptability, going from pop to reggae with noticeable ease. It must be said that Schaffer had the right experience, having worked with Bob Marley in 1971 when the latter, at the request of the American singer-songwriter Johnny Nash, had come to Stockholm to work on the soundtrack of Gunnar Höglund's movie *Vill Så Gärna Tro* ("Really Want to Believe"). During that stay Marley recorded his legendary *Acoustic Medley*, which was made available from 1992 on the box set *Songs of Freedom*. On percussion, the Gambian musician Malando Gassama made

Although his scores were hidden in the mix, percussionist Malando Gassama worked on many ABBA recordings, including *When I Kissed the Teacher*, *Dancing Queen*, and *The Name of the Game*.

his debut on congas and güiro. He had previously worked with Janne Schaffer, who introduced him to Björn Ulvaeus and Benny Andersson. Gassama's subtle playing, with its discreet but formidable groove, would become one of ABBA's secret weapons; they would make use of his services until 1979, when he went down in history as having supplied an unforgettable conga part for the disco number *Voulez-Vous*.

Malando Gassama grew up in Banjul, the capital of Gambia. He then lived for almost 25 years in Sweden, where his talents as a session musician led him to work with international artists such as Al Jarreau, Quincy Jones, and Eric Bibb.

KING KONG SONG

(Benny Andersson, Björn Ulvaeus/3'14)

Musicians
Björn Ulvaeus: lead vocals, backing vocals
Agnetha Fältskog: vocals
Anni-Frid "Frida" Lyngstad: backing vocals
Benny Andersson: piano, Minimoog
Janne Schaffer: electric guitar
Rutger Gunnarsson: bass guitar
Ola Brunkert: drums

Recording
Metronome, Stockholm: 14 November 1973

Technical team
Producers: Björn Ulvaeus, Benny Andersson
Sound engineer: Michael B Tretow

Genesis

Did the international success of *Jungle Boogie*, a funk hit by Kool & The Gang that made the whole planet dance in November 1973, lead Björn Ulvaeus to think of a jungle theme? Whether it did or not, there is certainly a primate here, even if it is a fictional character—King Kong, the giant gorilla created by the imagination of film-makers Merian C Cooper and Ernest B Schoedsack in 1933. Judging by the song's lyrics, seeing the movie caused the narrator to be inspired by this theme, even though Ulvaeus insisted that the title alone made him want to write about this subject, perfect for giving the song an effective chorus. Unfortunately, the song's humorous side highlights the album's lack of coherence, and it later became one of the tracks the musicians themselves detested most, as Agnetha Fältskog testified in 2013: "There are some [ABBA songs I hate] but not so many. The worst was the *King Kong Song*. 'You do the King Kong Song, gotta sing along.' Oh dear, maybe we should have that left out."[34]

Production

With its glam rock quality, which Benny and Björn seem to enjoy and which is emphasized here by the guitar riff written and played by Janne Schaffer, the song would have been effective if it had not had such flimsy lyrics. Having been used to leaving their manager to write the words to their songs, Andersson and Ulvaeus were not yet comfortable with this task, though Ulvaeus took over this role completely from 1979. "As far as I was concerned, I hated writing lyrics," Andersson said in 2006. "[…] It's tricky, writing lyrics—it's not just putting words together. Björn is a true lyricist, although [he] didn't know it then, and he didn't enjoy it any more than I did."[35] "Stig was much the more accomplished lyricist between the two of us," Ulvaeus added. "I hadn't written that many lyrics at that point, and was really only starting out, but I did work on the English version of *Waterloo*, and changed it around a bit. I learned from Stig during that first couple of years."[35]

HASTA MAÑANA

(Benny Andersson, Stig Anderson, Björn Ulvaeus/3'05)

Musicians
Agnetha Fältskog: lead vocals, backing vocals
Anni-Frid "Frida" Lyngstad: backing vocals
Benny Andersson: Mellotron
Björn Ulvaeus: acoustic guitar, backing vocals
Janne Schaffer: electric guitar
Rutger Gunnarsson: bass guitar
Ola Brunkert: drums

Recording
Metronome, Stockholm: 18 to 19 December 1973

Technical team
Producers: Björn Ulvaeus, Benny Andersson
Sound engineer: Michael B Tretow

FOR ABBA ADDICTS
Agnetha Fältskog paid further homage to Connie Francis in 2004, when she included *I Can't Reach Your Heart* (sung by Francis in 1963) as a track on her album of covers, *My Colouring Book*.

Genesis

It was during the very last sessions for the album *Waterloo* that the two songs in the running for the Melodifestivalen to be held on 9 February 1974 were written and recorded. In December, Benny and Björn, who had already sent Stig Anderson a preliminary version of what would become *Honey Pie* and subsequently *Waterloo*, then recorded and sent on a mid-tempo ballad. Anderson, who was on holiday in the Canary Islands, was inspired by a phrase he heard every evening on television, when the presenter said goodbye to viewers: *"Hasta mañana,"* meaning "until tomorrow." Having discarded the song's provisional title, *Who's Gonna Love You?*, and replaced it with this Spanish expression, in the course of the lyrics Anderson developed the theme of the end of a holiday romance, giving the song an undeniable coherence. He dictated the words to Andersson and Ulvaeus over the telephone, and the latter then asked Agnetha and Frida to come and record the song at the Metronome studios.

All that remained was to choose which of the two was more likely to win—the final straight to the Eurovision Song Contest. "[*Hasta Mañana* was] a good song," Benny Andersson explained, "but we said, 'No, we should have something that would represent what we want to do.' Not necessarily what they might like at the Eurovision, which is more of European traditional *schlager*."[36] On Stig Anderson's return to Stockholm, it was decided to drop *Hasta Mañana* in favour of *Waterloo*.

Production

The fact that Agnetha sang the song as a solo was another reason for dropping it, as the group preferred a song sung by both their female vocalists. The two women tried to record the song during the session, but the results did not convince Ulvaeus and Andersson. Agnetha therefore decided to draw inspiration from one of the idols of her youth, Connie Francis, in performing the song. "Connie Francis is my nostalgic singer," Agnetha said in 2013. "I was very affected by her voice. It's something very hurting in her voice. She also did harmonies in the songs, and there I could really hear what you could do with a song, and she's still a big big favorite."[37] *Hasta Mañana* was released as a single in South Africa, Italy, Japan, Madagascar, and Portugal, where it was a clear success. Soon, ABBA would continue down this route, recording several of their songs in Spanish.

1974

Janne Schaffer in the studio
with his famous 1959 Gibson
Les Paul Standard "Burst."

MY MAMA SAID

(Benny Andersson, Björn Ulvaeus/3'14)

Musicians

Agnetha Fältskog: vocals, backing vocals
Anni-Frid "Frida" Lyngstad: vocals, backing vocals
Benny Andersson: Fender Rhodes, Minimoog, xylophone, backing vocals
Björn Ulvaeus: electric guitar, backing vocals
Janne Schaffer: electric guitar
Rutger Gunnarsson: bass guitar
Ola Brunkert: drums, tambourine

Recording

Metronome, Stockholm: 24 September 1973 to 20 February 1974

Technical team

Producers: Björn Ulvaeus, Benny Andersson
Sound engineer: Michael B Tretow

Genesis

Here is a sound that isn't heard in ABBA's early records. Funk music, to our great surprise, seems to have found its way into the group's work. It is a safe bet that the influence of guitarist Janne Schaffer, who at the time was recording his first solo album in the Europa film studios, played a big part in the production of *My Mama Said*. Indeed, at the time he was blending into his work all the kinds of music that had inspired him, including funk, which, in the mid-1970s, was about to develop into the all-powerful disco. In September 1974, a few days before ABBA recorded *My Mama Said* with Schaffer, Vertigo, the guitarist's record label in the UK, had issued a promotional version of the unreleased *Dr. Abraham*. This was an instrumental number with a groove to strike fear into the hearts of the Americans of Kool & The Gang, with the goal of alerting the press to the arrival of Schaffer's first album. It is impossible, therefore, not to appreciate the influence the song had on Benny Andersson and Björn Ulvaeus, who immediately decided to record their own funk anthem.

Production

With its single-note motif hidden in the right-hand side of the stereo recording, and its unison voices, there can be no doubt about the influence the song had on disco groups with female vocalists after the release of ABBA's album. First and foremost were the German group Silver Convention and their multitude of languorous songs such as *No, No Joe, Thank You Mr. D.J.*, and especially *The Boy with the Ooh-La-La* (1976), which also copied the use of the marimba, played by Benny Andersson on *Mama Mia* in 1975. This was a totally successful foray into the funk style, carried by the voices of Björn, Agnetha, and Frida, who at the time testified to the enjoyment she had experienced during the sessions at Metronome: "I like it best when I sing together with the others. Then I get a feeling of security from them. We have a security among us. I don't have to feel alone, little, scared and nervous. And it's wonderful to work together with Benny."[15]

1974

DANCE (WHILE THE MUSIC STILL GOES ON)

(Benny Andersson, Björn Ulvaeus/3'05)

Musicians
Agnetha Fältskog: vocals, backing vocals
Björn Ulvaeus: vocals, acoustic guitar
Anni-Frid "Frida" Lyngstad: backing vocals
Benny Andersson: piano?, Minimoog, Mellotron, backing vocals
Janne Schaffer: electric guitar
John "Rabbit" Bundrick: piano?
Per Sahlberg: bass guitar, percussion
Ola Brunkert: drums

Recording
Metronome, Stockholm: September 1973

Technical team
Producers: Björn Ulvaeus, Benny Andersson
Sound engineer: Michael B Tretow

Genesis

Even more than on *Ring Ring* or *Waterloo*, the influence of Phil Spector productions is palpable on hearing this song, totally inspired by 1960s ballads and above all by The Ronettes' 1963 hit *Be My Baby*, produced by Spector and composed by him, Jeff Barry, and Ellie Greenwich. It is difficult therefore to see ABBA as an innovative, even revolutionary group, so little do the influences of Björn Ulvaeus and Benny Andersson appear to have been assimilated at the time. Michael B Tretow, despite his undeniable ability, does nothing to improve matters, tirelessly imitating the recording methods of his American idol. But this homage through imitation does not spoil the listener's enjoyment, for the composition is nevertheless perfect, with choruses that belong to another era but have effective melodies. The choice of title seemed clear to Ulvaeus, who did not call it simply *Dance* but decided to add words from the lyrics to produce the eventual name, *Dance (While the Music Still Goes On)*.

Production

Unusually for an ABBA record, Benny Andersson did not play the piano part. At least, that is according to the session musician John "Rabbit" Bundrick, who insists he himself played it during a session while he was staying in Stockholm in September 1973. "I did a lot of work with Janne Schaffer, a famed guitarist in Sweden, in the past Nash days," Bundrick wrote in his journal in 1973, referring to a period when he had worked with the American singer-songwriter Johnny Nash, "so I always called him up when I went to Sweden, as I did this time, and he invited me to work with him in the studio. One of these sessions was with the unknown singers, who were later to become ABBA. At the time they were just a group of backing singers for other artists in Sweden, and were trying their luck at doing their own record, so Janne invited me on the session to play piano. Little did we all know that they would become ABBA."[38] Although Bundrick confirmed he was the pianist in *Dance (While the Music Still Goes On)*, he is not credited on the record, and Andersson never admitted to making way for this guest during the September 1973 session.

Single

HONEY, HONEY

(Benny Andersson, Stig Anderson, Björn Ulvaeus/2'55)

Musicians

Agnetha Fältskog: vocals, backing vocals
Anni-Frid "Frida" Lyngstad: vocals, backing vocals
Björn Ulvaeus: vocals, acoustic guitar, backing vocals
Benny Andersson: piano, Minimoog, autoharp
Janne Schaffer: acoustic guitar
Rutger Gunnarsson: bass guitar
Ola Brunkert: drums
Alfred Pisuke: violin
Anders Dahl: violin
Claes Nilsson: violin
Gunnar Michols: violin
Harry Teike: violin
Inge Lindstedt: violin
Kryztof Zdrzalka: violin
Martin Bylund: violin
Sixten Strömvall: violin
Åke Jelving: violin

Recording

Metronome, Stockholm: October to November 1973

Technical team

Producers: Björn Ulvaeus, Benny Andersson
Sound engineer: Michael B Tretow
String arrangements: Sven-Olof Walldoff

Single

A-side: *Honey, Honey*/2'55
B-side: *Dance (While the Music Still Goes On)*/3'05
Released in the USA by Atlantic: August 1974 (single ref.: 45-3209)
Best chart ranking in the USA: 27

Genesis

It was the summer of 1974. As ABBA struggled to maintain their momentum in the UK following their April victory in the Eurovision Song Contest, their British label CBS/Epic decided to edit the single *Ring Ring*, in order to release it again in their territory. After a few saxophone and guitar overdubs, and an atrocious slowing down of the tape to give it a more rock feel, the song was released again—and was a monumental flop. The situation, which seems to have been beyond Ulvaeus and Andersson's control, sent them into a rage, all the more since the label then turned down another song, *Honey, Honey*, which the group had favoured as the new single from the *Waterloo* album. To add to ABBA's disappointment, a British duo, Sweet Dreams, recorded *Honey, Honey* at the same time and reached number 10 in the British charts on 20 July! "It taught us a lesson about taking advice from other people who thought they knew what we should do," Benny Andersson said. "We always wanted to do exactly what we wanted to do."[35] The song was, however, released as a single in many countries, including the USA, where only the name ABBA appeared on the sleeve, thus inaugurating the new name of the group, who had first appeared as ABBA (Björn, Benny, Anna & Frida) on the sleeve of *Waterloo* a few months earlier.

Production

The lyrics of *Honey, Honey*, which portray a couple in which the woman cannot resist her partner's sex appeal, are the very cliché of a 1970s disco song, even though the instrumental part yet again references the writers' love of 1960s pop. "I have to confess that the lyrics for *Honey, Honey* are a little stupid!" said Ulvaeus. "They do make me cringe a bit. Stig and I wrote the words—it was about half and half between us—so I'm afraid I do have to take my share of the responsibility […] I think we paid much more attention to creating a hook, to find a title that would stand out and be very, very catchy, perhaps more so at the time than a British or American songwriter, because they didn't need to think along those lines."[35]

ABBA in 1974, sporting their extravagant glam-rock-influenced costumes.

WATCH OUT

(Benny Andersson, Björn Ulvaeus/3'46)

Musicians
Björn Ulvaeus: lead vocals, electric guitar
Agnetha Fältskog: backing vocals
Anni-Frid "Frida" Lyngstad: backing vocals
Benny Andersson: Minimoog
Janne Schaffer: electric guitar
Rutger Gunnarsson: bass guitar
Ola Brunkert: drums
Recording
Metronome, Stockholm: 17 December 1973
Technical team
Producers: Björn Ulvaeus, Benny Andersson
Sound engineer: Michael B Tretow

Genesis

Although it possesses undeniable qualities, including an addictive guitar riff played (and probably composed) by the virtuoso Janne Schaffer, *Watch Out* proves that in 1973 Ulvaeus and Andersson seemed incapable of giving their group a coherent artistic direction. Their influences, whether from the UK or the USA, were interfering with what they were trying to achieve with ABBA. Here, it was with a clear nod to British glam rock—which, however, was nearing the end of its life following the death of Ziggy Stardust, David Bowie's avatar, on stage at the Hammersmith Odeon, London, the previous 3 June—that ABBA came up with a very rock number. It was recorded on the same day as *Waterloo*— yet another demonstration of the two composers' eclectic character at the time, for the songs are artistic opposites. "If it hadn't been for Janne Schaffer's guitar riff, it would have been a completely worthless track," Benny Andersson says in Carl Magnus Palm's book *ABBA: The Complete Recording Sessions*, which is essential reading. "We had this feeling in the beginning that we should try to do a bit more rock'n'roll, which, of course, was a bloody stupid idea. I don't know why we tried to do that—it never turned out any good."[39]

Production

Besides glam rock, another musical trend from the UK influenced ABBA and their musicians during the recording of *Waterloo*, and especially in the making of *Watch Out*: heavy metal. Championed notably by Deep Purple and Led Zeppelin, this style appealed to Janne Schaffer, who drew inspiration from it in writing the song's riff, played on a Gibson Les Paul plugged into an Ampeg amplifier. "On *Watch Out*, I was using a guitar synthesizer for the intro…" Schaffer explained [probably an EMS Synthi Hi-Fli, which went on sale in 1972 and was very fashionable at the time]. "You can hear the octave effect on that little phrase I repeat at the beginning. We had a lot of fun in the studio, trying different things out. Early on Björn [Ulvaeus] and Benny [Andersson] weren't exactly sure which direction ABBA should move to. From the third album onwards, I think Benny had more of an understanding of how he wanted the band to sound…"[40]

1974

Björn and Benny hard at work at Glen Studio in Stocksund, 1974.

WHAT ABOUT LIVINGSTONE

(Benny Andersson, Björn Ulvaeus/2'54)

Musicians
Agnetha Fältskog: vocals, backing vocals
Anni-Frid "Frida" Lyngstad: vocals, backing vocals
Benny Andersson: piano, Minimoog
Björn Ulvaeus: backing vocals
Janne Schaffer: electric guitar
Rutger Gunnarsson: bass guitar
Ola Brunkert: drums

Recording
Metronome, Stockholm: 17 October 1973

Technical team
Producers: Björn Ulvaeus, Benny Andersson
Sound engineer: Michael B Tretow

Genesis

Just four years after the American Neil Armstrong's first steps on the moon, Björn Ulvaeus wrote lyrics celebrating the exploits and adventures of another famous explorer: the Scottish physician David Livingstone, who travelled through Africa during the 19th century and searched, notably, for the source of the Nile. Livingstone, who died of malaria and dysentery on one of his expeditions, inspired Ulvaeus to write an ode to the glory of those who lost their lives on journeys of discovery. Over a very 1960s pop instrumental accompaniment reminiscent of some songs on the album *Ring Ring*, Agnetha and Frida sing, in unison, the praises of Livingstone, offering the listener a return to the group's first musical loves. This is to the great pleasure of Ulvaeus, who in various interviews reiterated the enjoyment he derived from writing light songs, such as those that marked the year before the group's first album.

Production

Just as it figures in many songs on *Waterloo*, the Minimoog synthesizer is omnipresent in *What About Livingstone*, doubling Rutger Gunnarsson's bass line; it is so prominent in the mixing that it is impossible to say whether or not Gunnarsson was retained in the song's final version. "[The Minimoog is] the best synthesiser, because it's got its very own sound, soft and musical,"[41] Benny Andersson explained in 1979, before revealing a secret about his relationship with this revolutionary instrument. "I actually don't know so much about the technical side of it. In the beginning I would simply sit and turn the knobs until I got a sound I liked. [...] But during the first years I think Michael and Björn suffered quite a lot while I was fooling around with the knobs."[41]

1974

GONNA SING YOU MY LOVESONG

(Benny Andersson, Björn Ulvaeus/3'35)

Musicians
Agnetha Fältskog: backing vocals
Anni-Frid "Frida" Lyngstad: vocals, backing vocals
Benny Andersson: piano, Minimoog, Mellotron
Björn Ulvaeus: backing vocals
Janne Schaffer: electric guitar
Rutger Gunnarsson: bass guitar
Ola Brunkert: drums

Recording
Metronome, Stockholm: 13 December 1973

Technical team
Producers: Björn Ulvaeus, Benny Andersson
Sound engineer: Michael B Tretow

Genesis

After the very touching *Disillusion*, sung on *Ring Ring* by Agnetha Fältskog (who had also co-written it), it was Frida Lyngstad's turn to take lead vocals in ABBA's second real ballad, with Agnetha and Björn Ulvaeus enhancing it with backing vocals. *Gonna Sing You My Lovesong* seems to have been written for Frida by her fiancé, Benny Andersson, who with this produced his last lyrics for an ABBA song, before definitively leaving the task to Björn and Stig Anderson, and to Björn alone a few years later.

Production

As with many ABBA songs, a pervading melancholy is hidden behind sound engineer Michael B Tretow's flashy production. Tretow knew better than anyone how to bring to life the group's compositions, which were subsequently highlighted by the vocal feats of Frida and Agnetha. "This kind of happy-sad, this jubilant melancholia, is something that is perhaps very Nordic," Björn Ulvaeus explained. "I don't hear that in Germany or America or the UK or France. But in Swedish folk music, definitely. And then there's the ladies' voices together. The way it sounds is jubilant. Whatever they sing, however sad the song is, they manage to sound uplifting."[24] To heighten the emotion created by the vocal parts in *Gonna Sing You My Lovesong*, Benny Andersson added several string parts played on a Mellotron keyboard. It was the last time he used this instrument, made popular by the introduction to the 1967 Beatles song *Strawberry Fields Forever*; he later declared that it could produce only "horrible" sounds.

1974

ABBA on Viggsö island,
where their greatest songs
were composed.

Overleaf: ABBA and Lorne
Michaels, creator and
producer of *Saturday Night
Live*, November 1975.

SUZY-HANG-AROUND

(Benny Andersson, Björn Ulvaeus/3'11)

Musicians

Benny Andersson: lead vocals, Minimoog, backing vocals
Agnetha Fältskog: backing vocals
Anni-Frid "Frida" Lyngstad: backing vocals
Björn Ulvaeus: acoustic guitar, backing vocals
Janne Schaffer: electric guitar
Rutger Gunnarsson: bass guitar
Ola Brunkert: drums

Recording

Metronome, Stockholm: 16 October 1973

Technical team

Producers: Björn Ulvaeus, Benny Andersson
Sound engineer: Michael B Tretow

Genesis

Doubtless because he had written its lyrics, Benny Andersson decided to sing *Suzy-Hang-Around* himself. It is a pop song that tells the story of a nine-year-old girl rejected by a group of boys a year older than her, who exhort her to come back to them when she is older. At the time Benny was engaged to Anni-Frid Lyngstad, and perhaps he drew inspiration from his sweetheart's unhappy childhood memories: the offspring of a relationship between her Norwegian mother and a German soldier during World War Two, she had to flee their home country to escape the unpleasantness that the family had to endure. It is a plausible theory, especially since Frida herself made no secret of the special importance the role of mother had for her because of her past, even though her children, born of her first marriage, then lived with their father. "Being together with my children is also very important to me," she said in an interview around this time. "If I didn't have the children, my life would seem empty! […] Sometimes they can be with me for weeks. It's good for their father to get some rest every now and then, since he has them most of the time. Naturally, I have missed them terribly sometimes, but we do have each other. We talk to each other over the phone several times a week. […] I like it when they turn to me, I enjoy giving them advice and help."[15]

Production

Even though his voice is perfectly matched to the song's pop style, Benny Andersson never again sang lead vocals on an ABBA song. He swore he would never do it again, being of the opinion that his friend Björn's voice was better suited to the group's songs, especially thanks to its highly original timbre. In 1976, when fans and observers asked Benny if he would do more singing, he replied unequivocally that he thought he sounded terrible and would never be caught singing solo again. As time went by, Björn too gradually stepped aside, making way for Agnetha and Frida, who represented ABBA's unique vocal identity for the wider public. True fans are probably sorry that this was Benny's only foray into solo singing, which is an interesting exception in the group's recorded work.

1974

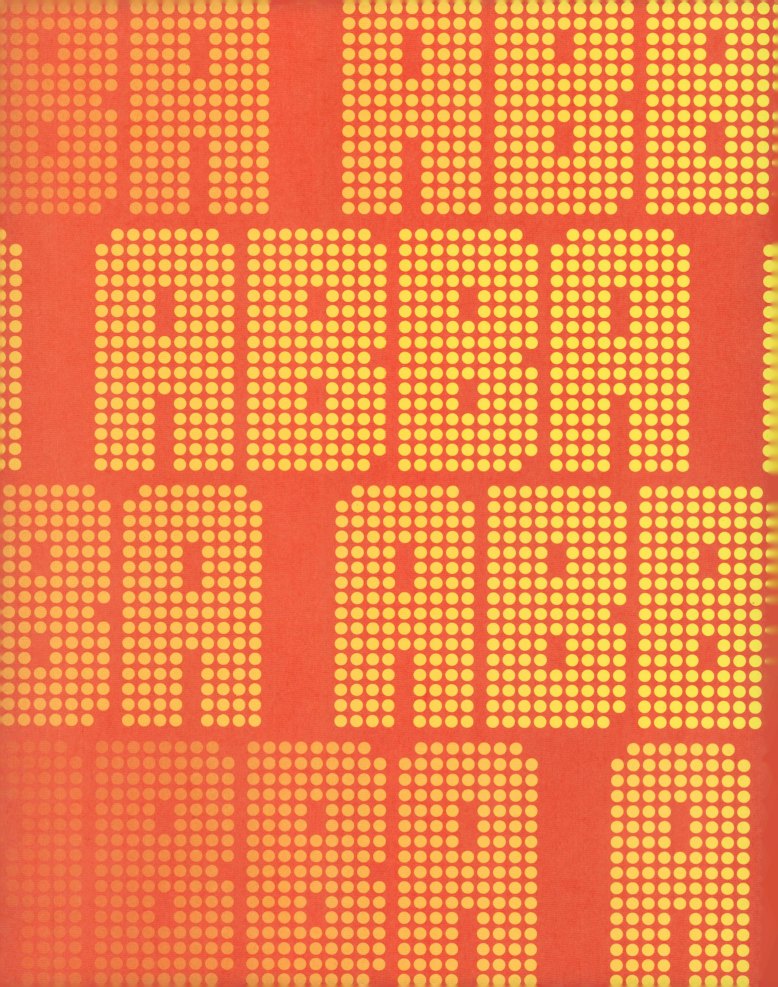

ABBA

Mamma Mia • Hey, Hey Helen • Tropical Loveland • SOS •
Man In The Middle • Bang-A-Boomerang • I Do, I Do, I Do, I Do, I Do • Rock Me •
Intermezzo No. 1 • I've Been Waiting For You • So Long

Released in Sweden by Polar Music: 21 April 1975 (album ref.: POLS 262)
Released in the UK by CBS/Epic: 21 April 1975 (album ref.: S EPC 80835)
Released in the USA by Atlantic: 21 April 1975 (album ref.: SD 18146)
Best chart ranking in Sweden: 1
Best chart ranking in the UK: 13
Best chart ranking in the USA: 174

INTERNATIONAL RECOGNITION

The first sessions for ABBA's new album, which began during the summer of 1974, allowed Benny and Björn to concentrate on their group's musical aesthetic, which until then had been undefined because the two composers liked to blend their many influences in their compositions. Shut away in Björn and Agnetha's chalet, and seemingly paying no attention to fashion, the two friends created a handful of new songs, hoping to release the group's third album before the end of the year. In November, the failure of the single *So Long* in the UK sent a clear message: trying to make a new *Waterloo* was pointless; the world needed something new. It must be said that since 1973 the record industry had been exceptionally prolific, and in the space of less than two years had seen a stunning list of major albums come on to the market, most of them revolutionary. Despite their victory at Eurovision, ABBA needed to compete with the international success of Pink Floyd's *The Dark Side of the Moon*, David Bowie's *Diamond Dogs*, and Queen's *Sheer Heart Attack*. As audiences turned to these new trends, ABBA realized they needed to reinvent themselves in order to break their image as a "one-hit group," and find the formula that would restore their glory in the UK where, they were sure, an audience awaited them.

Back into the studio

The first songs the group recorded (such as *Man in the Middle, I've Been Waiting for You,* and *SOS*) bear witness to Ulvaeus and Andersson's inexhaustible inspiration. Others quickly joined the list, and soon the aesthetic of the forthcoming album began to take shape. Although the two composers still struggled to shake off their *schlager* influences, the almost automatic use of the Minimoog synthesizer gave their productions a more modern feel, which fitted in with the music being written at the time. The change needed was also a personal one, for at this time the two couples left their homes in Vallentuna. While Björn and Agnetha moved into a big house in the upmarket suburb of Lidingö, Benny and Frida returned to the capital, opting for an apartment in the Gamla Stan district.

In another marked change, as ABBA were having increasing difficulty booking the recording slots needed to make their songs at Metronome, they decided to transfer the recording of their new album to the district of Långängen, in Stocksund, where Bruno Glenmark's studios were located. Glenmark was a musician and producer who had also competed in the 1974 Melodifestivalen with Glenmarks, a group formed with his wife, Ann-Louise Hanson, his niece Karin, and his nephew Anders. Although their song *I Annorlunda Land* ("In a Different Land") had not measured up to the standard of *Waterloo*, Glenmark did not hold that against the members of ABBA, and even suggested they come and work in his studio, where most of their new album would be recorded. The success of *Waterloo* having given them a degree of financial security, they were able to work there in a relaxed manner, with the assistance of their faithful sound engineer. "Before we won the Eurovision Song Contest with *Waterloo*, Benny Andersson and I had been in a rat race," said Björn Ulvaeus. "We were running around producing other people's records, writing songs for other people, even going on tours in different constellations just to pay the rent. But from *Waterloo*, when the royalties came pouring in, from that time

In front of the big wheel at Gröna Lund amusement park in Stockholm in 1975, where ABBA performed that summer.

Overleaf: ABBA in New York, on the set of the *Saturday Night Live* program broadcast on 15 November 1975..

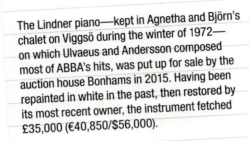

The Lindner piano—kept in Agnetha and Björn's chalet on Viggsö during the winter of 1972—on which Ulvaeus and Andersson composed most of ABBA's hits, was put up for sale by the auction house Bonhams in 2015. Having been repainted in white in the past, then restored by its most recent owner, the instrument fetched £35,000 (€40,850/$56,000).

we could afford to say no to everything else and just concentrate on the writing."[42]

Return to the Folkparks

While production was forging ahead at Glen Studio, Agnetha and Frida worked on their own account with the choreographer Graham Tainton, who had already given Frida lessons in 1969, and would collaborate with the group for several years. The aim was to prepare for the Folkparks Tour scheduled for the summer of 1975. It was essential for Swedish artists who wished to meet their audience to tour the country's amusement parks, where concerts were organized. But ABBA had not done this since winning Eurovision, preferring instead to concentrate on family life. This failure had provoked rage in the national press, but ABBA were now driven by a desire to go back to their roots, for the four friends had once played in various amusement parks, individually or with other groups.

When their new album, *ABBA*, was released on 21 April 1975, it was rapturously received in Sweden, which boded well for the forthcoming summer tour. Although the release of the single *I Do, I Do, I Do, I Do, I Do* in April did not herald the hoped-for artistic revival, that of *SOS* in June acted like a spark. Driven by its Minimoog musical line and Agnetha's voice, the song was the coup Ulvaeus and Andersson needed in order to convince the world that their group had real potential. At the same time, the four hired the film-maker Lasse Hallström to make four promotional clips for them, promoting the songs *I Do, I Do, I Do, I Do, I Do, Mamma Mia, SOS*, and *Bang-A-Boomerang*. Shot over two days in April, the videos were sent to media the world over. They bore witness to the group's strong visual identity, thanks above all to the ingenuity of Hallström, who filmed Agnetha and Frida in close-up—one facing the camera and the other in profile—which became one of ABBA's hallmarks over the years.

SOS lights the fuse

The impact of these videos was immediate, and contributed to the success of *SOS* in several countries. In the UK, the song reached number 6 in the charts, and finally convinced the press of ABBA's potential: they no longer looked like a one-hit wonder. In the autumn of 1975 the group flew to the USA for a short promotional tour, taking in San Diego, Las Vegas, Los Angeles, and New York. They appeared on *The Mike Douglas Show, Dinah!*, and *American Bandstand*, where they were interviewed by Dick Clark after performing *SOS* in playback—a performance that became legendary both for the quality of the song and for the outfits of Agnetha and Frida, designed by Owe Sandström and Lars Wigenius, and inspired by Kissen, Sandström's Burmese cat. Although the USA also seemed delighted with the song and rewarded it with number 15 on *Billboard*, it was the Australian public who most rapturously welcomed the resurgent ABBA, riding the wave of their new single, *Mamma Mia*, in November 1975 (it was not until the following May that the song was released as a

Above: Stylists Lars Wigenius and Owe Sandström created ABBA's wardrobe.
Opposite: Frida and Agnetha signing the band's second album.

single in the USA). Very quickly, the Australian star television presenter Ian "Molly" Meldrum suggested to the group a meeting in Stockholm as part of his program *Countdown*. Broadcast the following March, this lit a fuse under a public that was now seduced by ABBA's music. Seeing their songs taking Australia by storm, the group planned a tour there in order to meet their fans. But in the summer of 1975, well before that project was finalized, Benny and Björn resumed work, and wrote a piece with an enigmatic title, *Boogaloo*, strongly influenced by the burgeoning disco style. Quickly renamed *Dancing Queen*, it soon propelled the group to the top of the world's charts.

Although ABBA were idolized by the Swedish public, in 1975 the press turned against them, accusing them of over-commercialism in their artistic development. Sarcastic remarks were rife, as were parodies of the group. Nevertheless, one of these amused the musicians: a parody of the sleeve of *ABBA*, which appeared on the cover of the album *Hög Standard* by the group Peps Blodsband.

LASSE WELLANDER– A BLUESMAN WITH ABBA

Lasse Wellander was born on 18 June 1952 in Skrekarhyttan, 145 miles (230km) west of Stockholm. In 1959 his parents, who owned a small grocer's shop in the village, moved to Nora, a quiet town on the shores of the lake of the same name, a short distance to the north. During this time the young Lasse learned the recorder and the accordion. When The Beatles appeared on the Swedish television program *Drop In* on 30 October 1963, it made him want to switch to the guitar. "A lot of other young guys were doing much the same thing at the time," Wellander said. "I guess we all heard The Beatles and … decided [we] wanted to be like them."[43] Wellander played the guitar and even the bass guitar with various local groups during the 1960s, and in 1968 joined Peps & Blues Quality. With his parents' agreement, he took a year's sabbatical to spend time with the band, even though he was still only at high school. Other musical projects followed, such as Wellander & Ronander and Low Budget Blues Band, which enabled him to find his place on the Swedish musical scene and subsequently join the backing band of a young singer who had been signed by Polar Music: Ted Gärdestad. One evening, when Gärdestad was performing a concert with his group Nature at the Alexandra club in Stockholm, two members of ABBA were in the audience. "Björn and Benny were very involved in Ted's career […] They liked what and how we played," Wellander remembered. "[…] Then they came to a rehearsal sometime in '74 and asked me if I wanted to do an ABBA session."[44] During that first session, Wellander played guitar on *Intermezzo No. 1* and *Crazy World*.

From *ABBA* to *Voyage*

Like his friend Janne Schaffer, with whom he shared sessions with ABBA during the following years, Lasse Wellander mastered many musical styles. But blues seemed to be his favorite—witness his first solo album, *Electrocuted*, released in 1976, where the influence of his heroes John Mayall, Eric Clapton, and Peter Green is dominant. He worked with many other musicians during the 1980s and 1990s, featuring on more than 6,331 songs (spread over 1,600 albums!), and played a large part in the ABBA legend, accompanying the group on stage during their tours and recording guitar lines in many of their songs, such as *Knowing Me, Knowing You*, *Take a Chance on Me*, and *The Winner Takes It All*. He was also involved in the making of the soundtracks of the movies *Mamma Mia!* (2008) and *Mamma Mia! Here We Go Again* (2018), and was invited to join ABBA from 2017 for the recording of the album *Voyage*. Lasse Wellander died on 7 April 2023. His was an exceptional career, and he will always be remembered as a pre-eminent part of the ABBA adventure.

Single

MAMMA MIA

(Benny Andersson, Stig Anderson, Björn Ulvaeus/3'32)

Musicians

Agnetha Fältskog: vocals, backing vocals
Anni-Frid "Frida" Lyngstad: vocals, backing vocals
Benny Andersson: piano, marimba, Minimoog, Fender Rhodes, backing vocals
Björn Ulvaeus: backing vocals
Janne Schaffer: electric guitar
Finn Sjöberg: electric guitar
Mike Watson: bass guitar
Roger Palm: drums
Anders Dahl: violin
Inge Lindstedt: violin
Gunnar Michols: violin
Sixten Strömvall: violin
Harry Teike: violin
Kryztof Zdrzalka: violin
Niels Heie: viola
Håkan Roos: viola
Kjell Bjurling: cello
Olle Gustafsson: cello
Lars-Erik Rönn: oboe

Recording

Metronome, Stockholm: 10 to 12 March 1975

Technical team

Producers: Björn Ulvaeus, Benny Andersson
Sound engineer: Michael B Tretow
String arrangements: Sven-Olof Walldoff

1975

Single

UK and USA version
A-side: *Mamma Mia*/3'32
B-side: *Tropical Loveland*/3'05
Released in the UK by CBS/Epic: December 1975
(single ref.: S EPC 3790)
Released in the USA by Atlantic: 22 May 1976
(single ref.: 45-3315)
Best chart ranking in the UK: 1
Best chart ranking in the USA: 32

Genesis

At the start of spring 1975, as production of ABBA's new album was nearing completion, Benny Andersson and Björn Ulvaeus considered that they needed two more songs to complete the record's track listing. As Sweden's vinyl-pressing facilities were at that point packaging the group's new single, *I Do, I Do, I Do, I Do, I Do,* the musicians realized they needed to perfect ABBA's musical aesthetic and finally break free of their influences to create something truly original—the only way to survive in the merciless music world. In the intimate setting of the Metronome studios, where the team had set up again after having recorded most of the album at Bruno Glenmark's home, something magical happened on this day in March 1975. The musicians Finn Sjöberg, Mike Watson, and Roger Palm, alongside Benny and Björn, created a new song which earned ABBA the international recognition they had sought from the beginning. "[…] This was the period when we started to try something that was us, rather than trying to interpret or impersonate somebody else's work […]," Benny explained. "And that came from the confidence you get when things are going well, when people are buying your singles and albums and you know they like them. This gives you a lot of extra buoyancy."[35]

Although it was not intended as a single, *Mamma Mia* was one of the four songs that Lasse Hallström filmed the following April. Even though ABBA were betting everything on *I Do, I Do, I Do, I Do, I Do,* the Australian public, who discovered these four clips in August, fell for *Mamma Mia*'s incomparable choruses, and demanded it be released as a single. Negotiations proceeded apace between the group's various labels across the world (CBS/Epic in the UK, RCA in Australia, Atlantic in the USA, and Polar Music in Sweden) and, following the song's triumph in Australia, each record company agreed to release *Mamma Mia* as a single in its own country, where it met with considerable success. Only Polar Music, already busy planning what would follow ABBA's rise to fame, failed to release the song as a single in 1975.

1975

Production

The final song recorded for ABBA's third album, *Mamma Mia* initially featured a chorus with bass guitar, drums, and guitars. "It was not convincing," Björn Ulvaeus said. "So one of us said, 'Why not do [it] the other way around, take everything away on the chorus to see what happens?', and of course that was wonderful."[35] However, although the song's production was complete, Benny Andersson decided to add his personal touch to it, using the Metronome studios' marimba, which had been put away in a corner. Striking the instrument's small wooden blades, Andersson punctuates the song with these little notes that give it all its charm. "I just wanted to see what it sounded like," he said. "… And it changed the course of the song … it made for a really catchy start."[45] Leaving nothing to chance, when they came to write the lyrics Björn Ulvaeus and Stig Anderson opted for a simple story (a woman determined to stand up for herself against an unfaithful lover), but chose a title that could be understood and sung in all languages. Since the Italian expression *Mamma mia* (literally "mother of mine," but in fact meaning something like "my goodness!") was much used in Sweden at the time, it seemed suitable to appeal to the wider public. Be that as it may, the song was built on this formula, and the lyrics were written around this irresistible vocal motif. It was a wise decision, which made *Mamma Mia* one of the biggest hits of the group's career.

HEY, HEY HELEN

(Benny Andersson, Björn Ulvaeus/3'16)

Musicians
Agnetha Fältskog: vocals, backing vocals
Anni-Frid "Frida" Lyngstad: vocals, backing vocals
Benny Andersson: piano, Hohner Clavinet D6, backing vocals
Björn Ulvaeus: backing vocals
Janne Schaffer: electric guitar
Rutger Gunnarsson: bass guitar
Roger Palm: drums, tambourine

Recording
Glen Studio, Stocksund: 14 September 1974

Technical team
Producers: Björn Ulvaeus, Benny Andersson
Sound engineer: Michael B Tretow

Genesis

Although the American singer Tammy Wynette became a legend in 1968 by singing the progressive lyrics of *D-I-V-O-R-C-E,* describing the sadness but also the self-confidence of a woman who is leaving her husband, her compatriot Loretta Lynn had also asserted her status as a strong-willed woman with *Fist City,* a country hit in which she warns a young woman that she will make her see stars if she dares to go near her partner.

In 1973 the British television series *Helen: A Woman of Today*—featuring a young mother of two children, played by Alison Fiske, who decides to leave her unfaithful husband of ten years—doubtless inspired Björn Ulvaeus to write *Hey, Hey Helen,* which deals with a woman who has fought for her freedom and now faces the harsh reality of divorce. Songs about women who initiate separation from badly behaved husbands have become a symbol of hard-won women's emancipation and, in the age of #MeToo, have taken their rightful place in the repertoire of American female singers. A prime example is the magnificent *Julianna Calm Down* by The Chicks, an ode to courage released on their album *Gaslighter* in 2020.

Production

Despite a glam rock quality that the group seemed to have trouble shedding in making their third album—the influence of David Bowie's *The Rise and Fall of Ziggy Stardust and the Spiders from Mars* is undeniable here—the record demonstrates ABBA's willingness to take artistic risks. Although the marimba in *Mamma Mia* is often cited as a quirk in the recording studio that contributed to the song's success, Benny Andersson's use of a Hohner Clavinet D6 in *Hey, Hey Helen* is worth a mention. Designed in 1964 by the engineer Ernst Zacharias and popularized in 1972 by Stevie Wonder with his hit *Superstition,* the German-made keyboard makes a noteworthy appearance at 2'08 in *Hey, Hey Helen,* Andersson hammering its keys with a groove he had never shown before. It is a foray into the 1970s funk style that had begun the previous year with *My Mama Said,* and to which ABBA's two composers would soon prefer the dance-like sounds of disco music.

Alison Fiske, star of the series *Helen: A Woman of Today*, inspired Björn's lyrics for *Hey, Hey Helen*.

TROPICAL LOVELAND

(Benny Andersson, Stig Anderson, Björn Ulvaeus/3'05)

Musicians
Anni-Frid "Frida" Lyngstad: lead vocals, backing vocals
Agnetha Fältskog: backing vocals
Benny Andersson: accordion, marimba, synthesizers
Björn Ulvaeus: backing vocals
Lasse Wellander: electric guitar
Mike Watson: bass guitar
Roger Palm: drums
Recording
Metronome, Stockholm: 21 February 1975
Technical team
Producers: Björn Ulvaeus, Benny Andersson
Sound engineer: Michael B Tretow

Genesis

A return to the reggae style for ABBA, who had already tried their hand at it in 1974 with *Sitting in the Palmtree*. At a time when the music industry revered as royalty Bob Marley and his group The Wailers, who had just released their most authentic trilogy (the term "roots" best describes it)—*Catch a Fire* and *Burnin'* in 1973, followed by *Natty Dread* in 1974—*Tropical Loveland* must have earned ABBA much mockery from reggae lovers. In the UK, talented artists such as Aswad, Steel Pulse, and The Cimarons managed to make a success of the style in Europe. Since ABBA were not specialists in the genre, however, their attempt seems shallow, even though it remains entertaining. This was a time of euphoria for reggae, which young Europeans enjoyed during evening dances or on beach holidays, without knowing its philosophy or history. Benny confessed to never really having wanted to tackle this musical style, but the song's provisional title—*Reggae*—would seem to contradict this.

Production

Although the presence of Benny's accordion is enough to have reggae fans tearing their dreadlocks out, that of the red-headed lead vocalist is perfectly in keeping with the song's cheerful tone. Here, Frida is given her sole moment of glory as a soloist on the record, Agnetha having excelled in *SOS* and also in *I've Been Waiting for You*. Frida's vocal timbre is less melancholy than Agnetha's, and the allocation of roles in the studio seemed often to depend on the musical tone of the piece to be recorded. In 1975 Frida drew an interesting analogy regarding the two women in the pages of the magazine *Bravo*: "It's revealing in which position one sleeps. I always sleep on my back, completely stretched out. This means that I'm not afraid of the world and I feel secure. Anna on the other hand sleeps on her belly, snuggled into her pillow. She is in need of affection, she needs a lot of love and always wants to be protected…"[46] In other words, Frida seems perfect for bright songs, and Agnetha for the sadder ones. ABBA's history would prove that Anni-Frid Lyngstad was perhaps right on this point.

1975

ABBA performed four times on the German TV show *Disco* in 1975, including on 6 December, when they sang *SOS*.

Overleaf: Braving the sub-zero temperatures of their native Scandinavia, the four members of ABBA didn't hesitate to strip off for fans.

Single

SOS

(Benny Andersson, Stig Anderson, Björn Ulvaeus/3'22)

Musicians
Agnetha Fältskog: lead vocals, backing vocals
Anni-Frid "Frida" Lyngstad: backing vocals
Benny Andersson: piano, Minimoog
Björn Ulvaeus: acoustic guitar
Janne Schaffer: electric guitar
Mike Watson: bass guitar
Ola Brunkert: drums

Recording
Glen Studio, Stocksund: 22 to 23 August 1974

Technical team
Producers: Björn Ulvaeus, Benny Andersson
Sound engineer: Michael B Tretow

Single
A-side: *SOS*/3'22
B-side: *Man in the Middle*/3'00
Released in the UK by CBS/Epic: 8 September 1975
(single ref.: S EPC 3576)
Released in the USA by Atlantic: 20 September 1975
(single ref.: 45-3265)
Best chart ranking in the UK: 6
Best chart ranking in the USA: 15

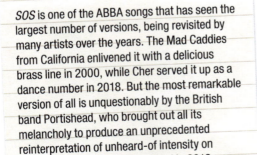

SOS is one of the ABBA songs that has seen the largest number of versions, being revisited by many artists over the years. The Mad Caddies from California enlivened it with a delicious brass line in 2000, while Cher served it up as a dance number in 2018. But the most remarkable version of all is unquestionably by the British band Portishead, who brought out all its melancholy to produce an unprecedented reinterpretation of unheard-of intensity on the musical platform SoundCloud in 2016.

Genesis

When Benny Andersson and Björn Ulvaeus went into the studio in August 1974, it was a time of introspection. Although *Waterloo*, which had seen ABBA win the Eurovision Song Contest the previous April, was a huge success worldwide, the group needed to face up to various obstacles in developing their career. Certainly, the Swedish public had opened their hearts to the four, ignoring the critics in the conformist press who accused them of making music designed exclusively to appeal to the widest possible audience. "Commercialism is a controversial concept," Björn said with annoyance in 1976. "No one knows exactly where it begins and where it ends. If it sells, then it's commercial."[47] On 22 August, Ulvaeus and Andersson began the production of three new songs that would become *Man in the Middle*, *So Long*, and *SOS*. Although *So Long* was chosen as the group's new single on 18 November, it struggled to find an appreciative audience outside Sweden, as *I Do, I Do, I Do, I Do, I Do* did a few months later. Yielding to the demands of CBS/Epic, their British distributor, which had a cast-iron belief in the piece's potential, the group agreed to release *SOS* as a single in September 1975, and Agnetha also recorded a version in Swedish for her solo album *Elva Kvinnor i ett Hus* ("Eleven Women in a House"), scheduled for release in December 1975. The song's quality earned the group an unhoped-for success in Britain, which was confirmed by the international triumph of *Mamma Mia* a few months later. It is well known that Pete Townshend, The Who's legendary guitarist, personally approached Björn Ulvaeus in a restaurant to congratulate him, describing *SOS* as "the best pop song ever written." As for Glen Matlock, the Sex Pistols' first bass guitarist, the song had such an influence on his playing that he confessed to having borrowed its bass line to use in *Pretty Vacant*, a punk anthem that features on the group's only studio album, *Never Mind the Bollocks, Here's the Sex Pistols*, released in 1977.

Production

Apart from its cheerful pop choruses, it is undoubtedly Agnetha Fältskog's breathtaking performance of verses filled with sadness that makes *SOS* so profound. Some insist that she recorded her line with sobs in her voice, but that is not the case, for with each successive recording for ABBA Agnetha seems to have found a specific way of singing, producing

1975

performances where emotion is palpable in every bar. In his speech at ABBA's induction into the Rock & Roll Hall of Fame in 2010, Benny Andersson tried to explain the role of melancholy in ABBA's music. "[…] Above […] the 59 degrees latitude, from eastern Russia, through Finland into Scandinavia, there's this 'melancholy belt' […]. And if you live in a country like Sweden with five, six months of snow, and the sun disappears totally for like two months, that would be reflected in the work of artists […] It's definitely in the Swedish folk music, you can hear it in the Russian folk songs, you can hear it in the music from Jean Sibelius, or Edvard Grieg from Norway, you could see it in the eyes of Greta Garbo, and you can hear it in the voice of Jussi Björling. And actually, you can hear it in the sound of Frida and Agnetha on some of our songs too […]."[48] Endowed with a title that could be pronounced in all languages (the hallmark of lyricist Stig Anderson), *SOS* alternates between somber verses and joyous choruses, a structure that gradually became the group's signature, and can be heard in numerous ABBA songs, such as *Fernando* and *I Have a Dream*.

MAN IN THE MIDDLE

(Benny Andersson, Björn Ulvaeus/3'00)

Musicians
Björn Ulvaeus: lead vocals
Agnetha Fältskog: backing vocals
Anni-Frid "Frida" Lyngstad: backing vocals
Benny Andersson: Hohner Clavinet
Janne Schaffer: electric guitar
Mike Watson: bass guitar
Ola Brunkert: drums
Ulf Andersson: alto saxophone

Recording
Glen Studio, Stocksund: 22 to 23 August, 23 October 1974

Technical team
Producers: Björn Ulvaeus, Benny Andersson
Sound engineer: Michael B Tretow
Brass arrangements: Björn J:son Lindh

HEADPHONES AT THE READY
At 2'29 in the song, the robotic voice of Björn Ulvaeus comes in, singing "in the middle." In order to give Ulvaeus's voice this timbre, Michael B Tretow had plugged his microphone into one of Janne Schaffer's guitar-effect pedals. Curiously, the French version of *ABBA* released by Vogue in 1975 contains a different mixing of *Man in the Middle*, which lacks this vocal effect. The same goes for the Japanese version of the CD, released by Polydor in 1986.

Genesis
Man in the Middle is proof of ABBA's diversity, showing that they were capable of giving their fans songs as funky as Stax Records' Southern soul productions. The song had the working title *Dance with the Devil*, and was recorded from 22 August 1974, as the group were working on new ideas for their next album. Björn features as lead vocalist, taking over that role from Agnetha and Frida, who are relegated to being backing vocalists. Not since *My Mama Said* in 1974 had the group tackled music so firmly rooted in American popular culture. Since Benny and Björn aimed to conquer the US market, this musical approach seems, with hindsight, entirely appropriate to reveal the group's skill and that of their talented musicians Janne Schaffer on guitar, Mike Watson on bass guitar, and Ola Brunkert on drums. These three masterfully executed what the two composers demanded, rewarding us with three minutes of pure funk. "We still want to achieve a definitive breakthrough in England and America," Benny Andersson declared in 1975. "Then, we will have achieved everything that's within our possibilities. Our records always made the American top 100, but we still haven't been really accepted."[49]

Production
Although the line Benny Andersson plays on the Clavinet is reminiscent of that of the keyboard player Ray Jackson on Bill Withers' *Use Me*, released in 1972 on the album *Still Bill*, the similarity with the American singer ends there. ABBA here demonstrate their mastery of the funk style, thanks especially to the support of saxophonist Ulf Andersson, who supplies a few discreet lines before ending the song with a solo. It would have been good to hear that last a little longer, rather than dying away into a premature fade—a sign that Benny and Björn had no desire to enrich their songs with long sequences of solo instruments, as pop music from the English-speaking world loved to do at the time. They should not be blamed for that, for ABBA's specialty was above all to compose pop songs with timeless melodies. Let us leave instrumental displays to the Americans, and instead enjoy Swedish expertise in songwriting!

BANG-A-BOOMERANG

(Benny Andersson, Stig Anderson, Björn Ulvaeus/2'50)

Musicians

Agnetha Fältskog: vocals, backing vocals
Anni-Frid "Frida" Lyngstad: vocals, backing vocals
Benny Andersson: piano, synthesizers, backing vocals
Björn Ulvaeus: acoustic guitar, backing vocals
Janne Schaffer: electric guitar
Rutger Gunnarsson: bass guitar
Roger Palm: drums
Bruno Glenmark: trumpet

Recording

Glen Studio, Stocksund: 16, 25 September 1974

Technical team

Producers: Björn Ulvaeus, Benny Andersson
Sound engineer: Michael B Tretow

Genesis

On 15 February 1975 the traditional Melodifestivalen competition was held, to select the group or artist who would have the privilege of representing Sweden at the next Eurovision Song Contest. Among the ten contestants were the duo Svenne & Lotta, whose song, *Bang-A-Boomerang*, had been written by ABBA's winning trio—Benny Andersson, Björn Ulvaeus, and Stig Anderson. The song, recorded in September 1974 to feature on ABBA's next album, was finally re-recorded in January 1975 and offered to Svenne & Lotta, its composers considering that it had the potential to secure a win for Sweden a second year running. Moreover, Ulvaeus and Andersson knew Sven "Svenne" Hedlund, for he had been the vocalist of the group The Hep Stars, for whom Benny was the keyboard player. When Svenne & Lotta came third—the winner being Lasse Berghagen with his *Jennie, Jennie*—Björn and Benny decided to recover the tapes of the first version of *Bang-A-Boomerang* and include it on ABBA's third album. The song benefited from a clip shot by Lasse Hallström when it was released as a single in France, Madagascar, and South Africa in 1975. The same year, it appeared under the title *Som en Boomerang* on the B-side of the single *Til et Solgyldent Land* ("To a Sun-Golden Land") by the Danish singer Ulla Pia.

Production

Besides its catchy choruses, the most noteworthy sequence of *Bang-A-Boomerang* is of course its introduction, which has a powerful synthesizer line. Much though ABBA connoisseurs may argue about it, sometimes quite virulently, it is impossible to establish what keyboard instrument Benny Andersson used in this passage. The ARP Solina String Ensemble, which went on sale in 1974 and which David Bowie used extensively from 1977, is a serious candidate—it is a string-machine type of keyboard, which produces synthetic strings sounds. But there remains a complete mystery over this instrument, used in several ABBA songs at the time, for Andersson only very rarely said anything precise about the different synthesizers he was using then.

Single

I DO, I DO, I DO, I DO, I DO

(Benny Andersson, Stig Anderson, Björn Ulvaeus/3'15)

Musicians
Agnetha Fältskog: vocals, backing vocals
Anni-Frid "Frida" Lyngstad: vocals, backing vocals
Benny Andersson: piano, backing vocals
Björn Ulvaeus: backing vocals
Lasse Wellander: electric guitar
Mike Watson: bass guitar
Roger Palm: drums
Ulf Andersson: alto saxophone

Recording
Metronome, Stockholm: 21, 23 February 1975

Technical team
Producers: Björn Ulvaeus, Benny Andersson
Sound engineer: Michael B Tretow

Single
UK version
A-side: *I Do, I Do, I Do, I Do, I Do*/3'15
B-side: *Rock Me*/3'03
US version
A-side: *I Do, I Do, I Do, I Do, I Do*/3'15
B-side: *Bang-A-Boomerang*/3'01
Released in the UK by CBS/EPIC: July 1975
(single ref.: S EPC 3229)
Released in the USA by Atlantic: March 1976
(single ref.: 45-310)
Best chart ranking in the UK: 38
Best chart ranking in the USA: 15

1975

Genesis
On 24 May 1975, ABBA went to Hamburg, West Germany, where they appeared on the TV show *Disco*, presented by Ilja Richter. Before filming began, the program's head of production, Hans Stürzer, categorically refused permission for Agnetha and Frida to wear their "cat" dresses, recently created by Owe Sandström and Lars Wigenius. "They are showing too much leg," he said "and when they dance you can even see their knickers [underwear]. We can't show that…"[50] Instead, the two singers wore the long version of their stage outfit and, thus attired, performed *I Do, I Do, I Do, I Do, I Do* without upsetting the program's audience. Although it was pleasing and featured a very effective chorus, the song was symptomatic of the problem ABBA faced in 1975: they were incapable of making a clean break from their past influences and creating a coherent piece of work that was, above all, rooted in its time. Although it was only with the release of *Arrival* in 1976 that ABBA really became ABBA, the first three albums—*Ring Ring*, *Waterloo*, and *ABBA*—are, thanks to vital songs such as *I Do, I Do, I Do, I Do, I Do*, dear to fans' hearts. A touch of *schlager* music in the arrangements, a rhythm influenced by Motown soul, production inspired by the techniques of Phil Spector, and lyrics that sing of eternal love: that was the recipe for *I Do, I Do, I Do, I Do, I Do*.

Production
On 21 February 1975, Benny Andersson and Björn Ulvaeus entered the studio at Metronome to record two new songs, which became *Tropical Loveland* and *I Do, I Do, I Do, I Do, I Do*. That day, they were accompanied by guitarist Lasse Wellander, drummer Roger Palm, and bass player Mike Watson. As usual, the group ran through the song Andersson and Ulvaeus had provided, and each musician proposed a part for his instrument. Quickly, Watson suggested a bass guitar line, which was turned down by his bosses. Faced with a general lack of inspiration, the group went to lunch, then tried again, in vain, to find the arrangements that would have allowed them to record *I Do, I Do, I Do, I Do, I Do*. As the day drew to a close, with no one having managed to convince Benny and Björn, Mike Watson tried again. "I started to play the same bass that I did at eleven o'clock, and [Benny] said, 'Oh, that's how we wanna do it!'"[51]

For the piece's general tone, the musicians wanted to pay homage to one of the idols of their youth, the American singer Billy Vaughn. Celebrated for having led his orchestra to fame with such albums as *Blue Hawaii* (1959), *Theme from a Summer Place* (1960), *Theme from the Sundowners* (1960), and *Berlin Melody* (1961), this arranger and musician had succeeded in creating a sound of his own, doubling his saxophone lines—his favorite instrument—to locate them on both sides of stereo recordings. To achieve their goal, Benny and Björn called on Ulf Andersson, who chose an alto saxophone for the song. This professional musician, who had already taken part in the recording sessions for *Man in the Middle* in October 1974, was now familiar with Benny Andersson's way of working: despite being a composer of genius, Benny could not read music. "Whenever I went to record with ABBA they would say to me, 'Don't forget to bring music paper,'" Ulf recalled. "When I played *I Do*, Benny sat down by the piano and showed me exactly what I should do and I put it down on the paper and in three or four hours the whole thing was done and recorded [...]. The way Benny composes, he put it down on the tape, recorded whatever he came up with, then someone had to sit down and copy what he was playing."[52]

Glam-rock outfits, pop culture, and rock songs: ABBA sometimes created a real mish-mash of genres!

Overleaf: Sound checks for the concert at Stockholm's Konserthuset on 11 January 1975.

ROCK ME

(Benny Andersson, Björn Ulvaeus/3'03)

1975

Musicians
Björn Ulvaeus: lead vocals
Agnetha Fältskog: backing vocals
Anni-Frid "Frida" Lyngstad: backing vocals
Benny Andersson: piano, Hohner Clavinet, backing vocals
Finn Sjöberg: electric guitar
Lasse Wellander: electric guitar
Rutger Gunnarsson: bass guitar
Roger Palm: drums

Recording
Glen Studio, Stocksund: 18, 21 October 1974

Technical team
Producers: Björn Ulvaeus, Benny Andersson
Sound engineer: Michael B Tretow

Genesis

Although Benny Andersson would later disown the very rock-like *Watch Out*, which features on *Waterloo*, *Rock Me*, which was cut from the same cloth, found favor with him, and he completely committed to recording such a song. With its introduction inspired by that of Gary Glitter's *Rock And Roll Part 1*, released in 1972, the piece features prominently a chorus melody that recalls the music of The Supremes (especially *Baby Love)*. It then rolls out the red carpet for Björn, who is the main performer, and in the verses mimics the glam rock singers who were in vogue at the time, such as Slade's Noddy Holder, who had sung his lungs out on *Mama Weer All Crazee Now* in 1972. A song impregnated with influences, then, but one that provides the album with a variety of styles, as was already the case with *Waterloo*. "That [was] something we learned from The Beatles," Benny explained. "They were always in their style in a way, much more so than we were, but what they did was, you heard a song with them, then the next single was nothing close to the previous one, or the third, or the fourth, or the fifth. [...] And another great thing, I have to say, that goes for many [groups that have] more that one singer; it helps you. You have John and Paul or you have Fleetwood Mac, you have The Eagles: it's great to have two singers, because they make a difference between the tracks as well."[53]

Production

Initially recorded to be sung by Agnetha Fältskog, *Rock Me* (whose working title was *Baby*) was finally sung by Björn himself, accompanied by ABBA's musicians, whose line-up varied between sessions, because all were already regularly engaged in working with other artists. Whether guitar was played by Finn Sjöberg, Lasse Wellander, or Janne Schaffer, bass guitar by Mike Watson or Rutger Gunnarsson, and drums by Ola Brunkert or Roger Palm, the magic created at Glen Studio or Metronome was the same, with the artists capable of an unprecedented degree of collaboration. "They don't play the same way as American studio musicians, but they are just as good," said sound engineer Michael B Tretow. "They play in an entirely different way. That must be the reason that Abba's records sound exotic."[18]

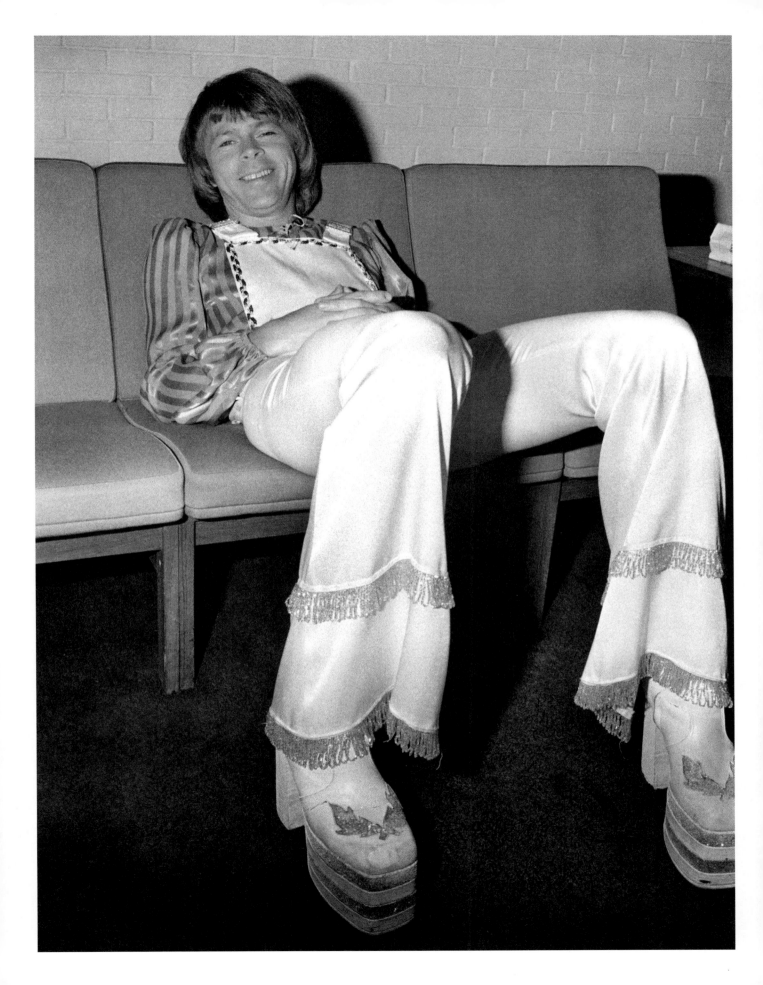

INTERMEZZO NO. 1
(FEATURING BENNY ANDERSSON)

(Benny Andersson, Björn Ulvaeus/3'48)

Musicians

Benny Andersson: piano, Minimoog
Finn Sjöberg: electric guitar
Lasse Wellander: electric guitar
Rutger Gunnarsson: bass guitar
Roger Palm: drums, timpani
Gunnar Michols: violin
Claes Nilsson: violin
Bertil Orsin: violin
Harry Teike: violin
Snorri Thorvaldsson: violin
Lars Arvinder: viola
Niels Heie: viola
Hans-Göran Eketorp: cello
Erik Dybeck: cello
Gunnar Gunrup: trumpet
Gösta Nilsson: trumpet

Recording

Glen Studio Stocksund: 16, 23 October 1974
Metronome, Stockholm: 11 December 1974

Technical team

Producers: Björn Ulvaeus, Benny Andersson
Sound engineer: Michael B Tretow
String arrangements: Sven-Olof Walldoff
Brass arrangements: Björn J:son Lindh

Genesis

Like many musicians at the time, Benny Andersson showed a real interest in the albums of the composer Wendy Carlos. She introduced the world to Moog synthesizers through her hit album *Switched-on Bach* (1968), in which she revisited the music of J S Bach using the revolutionary keyboard. Carlos achieved recognition in 1971 when the film director Stanley Kubrick entrusted her with making the soundtrack to his *A Clockwork Orange*, notably featuring reinterpretations of works by Gioacchino Rossini and Ludwig van Beethoven executed on the Moog synthesizer. The influence of classical composers on Benny Andersson's repertoire is undeniable, but in 1974 it was still more or less imperceptible, apart from the organ introduction he had played on *Wedding* by The Hep Stars in 1966. Deciding to give credit where it is due, in the autumn of 1974 Benny launched into the recording of the instrumental *Intermezzo No. 1*. In the beginning it had the working title *Bach-låten*, which means "melody by Bach."

Production

In the early 1970s the boundary between pop and classical music was fairly tenuous. The Brazilian pianist Eumir Deodato revisited the works of Claude Debussy in 1973, Roger Daltrey sang over music by Franz Liszt and Richard Wagner in Ken Russell's movie *Lisztomania* in 1975, and Walter Murphy made the entire world dance to his funk version of Beethoven's fifth symphony in 1976. The whole world seemed to appreciate these strange combinations—and the appearance of Queen's *Bohemian Rhapsody* in October 1975 was undoubtedly the culmination of these unorthodox musical mixtures.

ABBA therefore raised few eyebrows in offering an instrumental track lasting almost four minutes that shows its composer's classical influences. Supported by guitar parts played in unison by Schaffer and Wellander, and brass arrangements by Björn J:son Lindh, a flautist and keyboard player who regularly accompanied his friend Janne Schaffer on stage, the track sparkles. ABBA frequently performed it live, and it was the soundtrack for a whole scene in *ABBA: The Movie* in 1977.

In 1974, Wendy Carlo, a pioneer of electronic music, was enjoying the success of the soundtrack to Stanley Kubrick's *A Clockwork Orange* she had written three years earlier.

Agnetha wearing her famous "*Tyck om dej!*" ("Take care of yourself") T-shirt for the cover of *Hennes* magazine, May 1974.

Overleaf: Famous ABBA photo session in which Ola Lager concealed the artists' bodies and focused on their faces.

I'VE BEEN WAITING FOR YOU

(Benny Andersson, Stig Anderson, Björn Ulvaeus/3'39)

Musicians
Agnetha Fältskog: lead vocals, backing vocals
Anni-Frid "Frida" Lyngstad: backing vocals
Benny Andersson: Minimoog
Björn Ulvaeus: acoustic guitar
Janne Schaffer: electric guitar
Finn Sjöberg: electric guitar
Rutger Gunnarsson: bass guitar
Roger Palm: drums

Recording
Glen Studio, Stocksund: 15 September 1974

Technical team
Producers: Björn Ulvaeus, Benny Andersson
Sound engineer: Michael B Tretow

Genesis

Agnetha Fältskog sings of eternal love in this ballad, which has a timeless quality. Folk guitar, a discreet guitar solo, a modest tempo set by the drums, and "na-na-nas" galore support the singer's delicate voice. Her tessitura, as well as her reputation as a fragile young woman in love, find a perfect home here. ABBA fans, and journalists the world over, ceaselessly questioned Agnetha about her relationships with men during the 1970s and 1980s, men who were seduced by her charm, sensitivity, and kindness. "I have my own perceptions of a relationship with a man," she said in 1981. "In my opinion, honesty is the most important thing in a relationship. And reliability—that you can depend on someone. This creates an atmosphere wherein one can feel secure."[54] "I don't think I'm beautiful or sexy," she added, speaking to the magazine *Privé* that same year. "I don't have any confidence in that. But I do have confidence in what's inside my head. I do think that I'm intelligent. Men really seem to be impressed by me and by the fact that I'm rather smart. They also seem to be scared off by the knowledge that I have built a big career. I don't know why, they should be proud of my career, but they are not."[5]

Production

To bring to life this slow ballad, which was released as a single in Australia in 1975 and in New Zealand in 1977, Agnetha endowed her performance with the same emotion as that which is apparent in *Disillusion*, which she had written and sung on the group's first album in 1973. To achieve this, she had a certain way of doing things in studio sessions, always sitting down while she recorded her sung lines. "[…] I discovered it could affect how I sang. I decided to sit close to the mic to maintain my posture. That way, I could bring my voice down when the lyrics called for that. It reinforced my feeling that I wasn't just singing but also relating the lyrics."[39]

1975

Single

SO LONG

(Benny Andersson, Björn Ulvaeus/3'06)

Musicians
Agnetha Fältskog: vocals, backing vocals
Anni-Frid "Frida" Lyngstad: vocals, backing vocals
Benny Andersson: piano, Minimoog, backing vocals
Björn Ulvaeus: electric guitar, backing vocals
Janne Schaffer: electric guitar
Mike Watson: bass guitar
Ola Brunkert: drums
Bruno Glenmark: trumpet
Recording
Glen Studio, Stocksund: 22 to 23 August, 25 September 1974
Technical team
Producers: Björn Ulvaeus, Benny Andersson
Sound engineer: Michael B Tretow

Single
A-side: *So Long*/3'04
B-side: *I've Been Waiting for You*/3'38
Released in Sweden by Polar Music: 18 November 1974
(single ref.: POS 1195)
Released in the UK by CBS/Epic: 18 November 1974
(single ref.: S EPC 2848)
Best chart ranking in Sweden: 7
Best chart ranking in the UK: did not make the charts

1975

HEADPHONES AT THE READY
At 2'47 in *So Long*, Bruno Glenmark adds a touch of trumpet to the song. As a nod to the heavy metal influences on Ulvaeus and Andersson, he echoes the vocal theme in the introduction to *Immigrant Song*, sung by Robert Plant on *Led Zeppelin III* (1970).

Genesis

Following ABBA's win at the Eurovision Song Contest with *Waterloo*, Benny and Björn found themselves at an impasse. Their second album did not contain any other potential hit and, outside Sweden, they struggled to bounce back after this success, which was as ephemeral as it was sudden. The summer of 1974 was thus a time for reflection. Focused on writing new songs, the two men felt they needed to produce a new single to win back the hearts of the British public and press, who spurned them and considered them a one-hit wonder. "The obvious song to release was *Honey Honey*, which had been covered [by Sweet Dreams in the UK]," Björn explained. "But we thought we should release something that was more rock'n'roll. That was a mistake."[27] During the summer, with the music of bands such as Sweet or Mud in mind, ABBA recorded *So Long*, hoping to establish themselves as a fixture on the international rock scene. "We had been trying to be a rock band more than a pop band," Björn said in another interview. "Then we found out that it was not us."[35]

Production

Recorded during the very first sessions at Bruno and Ann-Louise Glenmark's home in the summer of 1974, *So Long* benefited from a unique acoustic treatment. The house had an indoor swimming pool, and sound engineer Michael B Tretow decided to take advantage of its natural reverberation, immediately installing the speaker of Janne Schaffer's guitar amplifier there. The noise of recording takes shattered the quiet of the place, and the peace of the Glenmarks' children and their grandmother, whose rooms were immediately above it. "The group worked incredibly hard," Bruno Glenmark recalled. "They could rehearse a song over and over."[55] As this was clearly a time to experiment, Tretow also decided to let Schaffer use his different effects pedals as he wished, especially on *So Long*, in which his 1959 Gibson Les Paul Standard "Burst" came out with some strange sounds. "[…] For that I used a Morley [in all likelihood Evo-1] echo pedal that I could push down for extra swirly sounds," Schaffer recalled. "You can hear it at the beginning."[40]

The musician Björn J:son Lindh had the honor of providing the unforgettable string arrangements for *Crazy World*.

CRAZY WORLD

(Benny Andersson, Björn Ulvaeus/3'45)

Musicians

Björn Ulvaeus: lead vocals, acoustic guitar
Agnetha Fältskog: backing vocals
Anni-Frid "Frida" Lyngstad: backing vocals
Benny Andersson: piano, synthesizers, backing vocals
Finn Sjöberg: electric guitar
Lasse Wellander: electric guitar
Rutger Gunnarsson: bass guitar
Roger Palm: drums
Gunnar Michols: violin
Claes Nilsson: violin
Bertil Orsin: violin
Harry Teike: violin
Snorri Thorvaldsson: violin
Lars Arvinder: viola
Niels Heie: viola
Hans-Göran Eketorp: cello
Erik Dybeck: cello

Recording

Glen Studio, Stocksund: 16, 23 October 1974

Technical team

Producers: Björn Ulvaeus, Benny Andersson
Sound engineer: Michael B Tretow
String arrangements: Björn J:son Lindh

Single *Money, Money, Money*

A-side: *Money, Money, Money*/3'05
B-side: *Crazy World*/3'47
Released in the UK by CBS/Epic: 1 November 1976
(single ref.: S EPC 4713)
Released in the USA by Atlantic: 1 November 1976
(single ref.: 3434)
Best chart ranking in the UK: 3
Best chart ranking in the USA: 56

Genesis

Some songs are doomed to an unhappy fate. *Crazy World* is one of them. Recorded the same day as *Intermezzo No. 1*, it is the sort of ballad that rock and heavy metal artists knew how to write during the 1970s, and is sung with unprecedented emotion by Björn Ulvaeus. Sadly, the song did not satisfy its writers enough to be included on the group's third album. It was dropped, and joined the list of rare ABBA outtakes (such as *Terra Del Fuego* and *Rikky Rock'n'Roller*, two more of their unloved songs), before being dusted off during the sessions for *Arrival* a few months later. Having been reworked, the song failed miserably on the B-side of the single *Money, Money, Money* in November 1976. If ABBA had preferred it to *I Do, I Do, I Do, I Do, I Do*, there is no doubt that it would have been a single with great potential, in the tradition of high-quality slow numbers of the 1970s, alongside *Your Song* by Elton John (1970), *Spaceman* by Journey (1977), and *Wuthering Heights* by Kate Bush (1978). Many young lovers must have missed out on their first kiss after this delicate song was sidelined.

Production

The song's theme is universal: a man goes to his beloved's house and sees another man coming out. At the end of the song, the narrator's pain dissipates when his sweetheart informs him it was her brother, so their love has remained intact. The real-life Björn, though, seems not to have been worried about losing his beloved and loving Agnetha in 1975, and was open with journalists who asked him about the men prowling around his wife: "I really don't care one tiny bit. They can do what they like. Agnetha is around me most of the time, so why should I worry?"[49] The string arrangements written by Björn J:son Lindh, a keyboard player and flautist who was invited to take part in some of the group's sessions during the autumn of 1974, endow the piece with a well-balanced element of melancholy starting from the second verse, and never lapse into caricature. With its moving verses and effective choruses, the song reappeared, to fans' great delight, in 1994 on the box set *Thank You for the Music*, which combines hits with some of the group's rarely heard songs.

PICK A BALE OF COTTON – ON TOP OF OLD SMOKEY – MIDNIGHT SPECIAL

(traditional/4'24)

The picture says it all: ABBA are off to conquer the world!

Overleaf: The dresses worn by Agnetha and Frida were designed by Lars Wigenius and Owe Sandström, and inspired by Kissen, the former's cat.

Musicians

Agnetha Fältskog: vocals, backing vocals
Anni-Frid "Frida" Lyngstad: vocals, backing vocals
Benny Andersson: piano, Minimoog, backing vocals
Björn Ulvaeus: vocals, acoustic guitar, backing vocals
Finn Sjöberg: electric guitar
Rutger Gunnarsson: bass guitar
Roger Palm: drums

Recording

Glen Studio: 6 May 1975
Metronome, Stockholm: 14 May 1975

Technical team

Producers: Björn Ulvaeus, Benny Andersson
Sound engineers: Michael B Tretow (Glen Studio), Janne Hansson (Metronome)

Compilation *Stars Im Zeichen Eines Guten Sterns*

Released in Germany by Polydor: 1975 (single ref.: 2437 321)
Released in Austria by Polydor: 1975 (single ref.: 2437 350)

Genesis

In 1975, ABBA agreed to take part in the making of a charity compilation called *Stars Im Zeichen Eines Guten Sterns* ("Stars in the Sign of a Good Star") released by Polydor Germany, in aid of Deutsche Krebshilfe, an association that combated cancer in the country. Having been given the choice of what to cover for the recording, the group decided to pay homage to the blues favorites of Benny Andersson and Björn Ulvaeus, delving into the repertoire of American blues and folk. On 6 May, Benny, Björn, and their musicians recorded a medley of three traditional tunes, giving Agnetha and Frida a welcome break (they would never again be heard covering other artists with ABBA, except in *Tivedshambo* by their friend Stig Anderson, which they reinterpreted and recorded for the latter's birthday in 1981). *Pick a Bale of Cotton* is a traditional song about cotton picking by African-American slaves, and has been sung over the years by various blues musicians, including the famous Leadbelly. *On Top of Old Smokey* was a big hit for The Weavers when they covered it in 1951, with the title *Smoky*. The third song, *Midnight Special*, is well known to fans of Creedence Clearwater Revival, because the group, who were lovers of traditional American tunes, covered it on their album *Willy and the Poor Boys* in 1969.

Production

The song was reworked in the Metronome studio on 14 May 1975, when it was taken in hand by a sound engineer other than Michael B Tretow—something very rare in ABBA's career. Tretow had left Metronome for Bruno Glenmark's studios, and was not available that day, so Janne Hansson took charge of the session. Since *Stars Im Zeichen Eines Guten Sterns* had not been sold outside West Germany, the members of ABBA decided to dig the medley out again and put it on the B-side of the single *Summer Night City* in September 1978. Renamed *Medley: Pick a Bale of Cotton—On Top of Old Smokey—Midnight Special* and subsequently nicknamed simply *Folk Medley* by fans, the song became one of the group's legendary rarities, and was remembered with pleasure by its members, because they had recorded it without pressure or constraints. "It was fun to do it," Björn confirmed. "We felt free because it wasn't our own material, and I think it turned out quite well."[56]

MADE IN SWEDEN
FOR EXPORT

ARRIVAL

When I Kissed The Teacher • Dancing Queen • My Love, My Life •
Dum Dum Diddle • Knowing Me, Knowing You • Money, Money, Money •
That's Me • Why Did It Have To Be Me • Tiger • Arrival

Released in Sweden by Polar Music: 11 October 1976 (album ref.: POLS 272)
Released in the UK by CBS/Epic: 5 November 1976 (album ref.: EPC 86018)
Released in the USA by Atlantic: 5 November 1976 (album ref.: SD 18207)
Best chart ranking in Sweden: 1
Best chart ranking in the UK: 1
Best chart ranking in the USA: 20

ABBA in the costumes created
for their appearance on the TV
show *Sylvester Tanz Party* on
31 December 1975.

FOR ABBA ADDICTS

It was at Barkarby airfield, 12 miles (20km) northwest of Stockholm, that Ola Lager took the photo of ABBA on board a Bell 47G helicopter that was used on the cover of *Arrival*. To pay tribute to its national stars, the helicopter (minus its tail) was displayed in Terminal 5 of Stockholm's Arlanda airport in April 2015, giving fans the opportunity to take a photo in front of the legendary aircraft.

ABBA SUPERSTARS

1976

Following the international success of the singles *SOS* and *Mamma Mia*, ABBA found themselves in an exciting but precarious position. After such a huge triumph, which had seen the band achieve one of its major ambitions—topping the UK charts—where were they going to go from there? As Benny and Björn worked on writing and producing Frida's solo album *Frida Ensam* and Agnetha's *Elva Kvinnor I Ett Hus*, they took some time out in the studio to plan a new single to keep ABBA fans happy while they waited for the group's new album. Once again, Glen Studio was where the magic happened, enabling the band to win the public's hearts once and for all.

Birth of disco

The 1970s need to be viewed as a musical kaleidoscope. While the 1960s had been about pop in all its forms, the 1970s saw a series of trends, sometimes in complete opposition to one another. A variety of different musical styles—heavy metal, rock, glam rock, funk, punk, country, *krautrock*, and folk—came and went during this decade. It was a key period in the record industry and the boundaries of music seemed to dissolve. In 1975, when ABBA had just completed their trilogy of what could best be described as *schlager* pop—the albums *Ring Ring*, *Waterloo*, and *ABBA*—they wanted their music to reflect the times while retaining their identity. That year, a music genre, tailor-made for the nightclubs that were springing up everywhere, hit the airwaves and the dancefloors. Its name was disco. Built on four-beat bars with a tempo of around 120 beats per minute, it got people hooked; everyone had been dancing to the music for months. By 1975, the ambassadors of disco, whether former masters of funk

who had changed tack or the rising stars of the genre, were releasing a multitude of albums to get people on to the dancefloor. The discotheques were full. People were going crazy for Donna Summer's *Love to Love You Baby*, Gloria Gaynor's *Never Can Say Goodbye*, *Main Course* by the Bee Gees, Van McCoy's *Disco Kid*, and the second, eponymous album by KC and The Sunshine Band. A forerunner of this trend, which would ultimately prove as fleeting as it was revolutionary, was the American George McCrae with *Rock Your Baby*. Released in April 1974, it was one of the biggest hits of the disco era.

McCrae's single, a copy of which was lying around at Glen Studio, captivated Benny and Björn, and in the summer of 1975 they decided to write a song based on these new sounds the whole world was raving about. In August, while the two men were recording *Fernando* for Frida's album, they began work on *Boogaloo*, which they sensed had commercial potential. It would soon be renamed *Dancing Queen*. They also felt the arrangements of *Fernando* worked well and decided to record an English version.

A host of compilations

Surprisingly, ABBA's biggest success as 1975 drew to a close was not their third album, *ABBA*, released in April, but a collection of their best-known songs. In agreement with the group's various labels around the world, Polar Music released a series of compilations, which seems a little odd for a band still on its way up. It's impossible to give an exhaustive list, but these compilations included different versions of *The Best of ABBA*, released in Japan, Australia, New Zealand, and the

1976: the love story between ABBA and Australia begins.

Overleaf: Legendary shot of the group on a bench in Djurgärden, Stockholm, used on the cover of the *Greatest Hits* compilation.

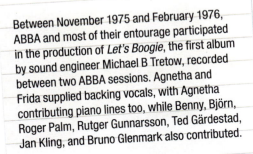

Between November 1975 and February 1976, ABBA and most of their entourage participated in the production of *Let's Boogie*, the first album by sound engineer Michael B Tretow, recorded between two ABBA sessions. Agnetha and Frida supplied backing vocals, with Agnetha contributing piano lines too, while Benny, Björn, Roger Palm, Rutger Gunnarsson, Ted Gärdestad, Jan Kling, and Bruno Glenmark also contributed.

1976

Netherlands; a *Golden Double Album* in France; *16 ABBA Hits* and *The Very Best of ABBA* in West Germany; a *Greatest Hits* in Europe and the UK; and even just plain simple *ABBA* in Portugal, reusing the cover image from the 1975 album and with a varied tracklist of songs. The worldwide release of these albums gave ABBA increased visibility and they now had to choose between the two songs they had recorded that summer. *Dancing Queen* got the most votes in the band, mainly thanks to its up-to-the-minute production and irresistible melody, but the song that ended up being chosen was *Fernando*, closer to the *schlager* style so beloved of its two composers. Released as a single in March 1976, it was a huge international hit, topping the charts in Sweden, reaching number two in the UK, and even number 13 on the American *Billboard* charts. ABBA, it seemed, were unstoppable and in early March they flew to Australia, where their growing fanbase was clamoring for more of their sparkling pop.

The Australian adventure

ABBA's arrival on the tarmac at Sydney airport was testimony to their massive success in Australia. Thousands of fans jostled to catch a glimpse of their favorite band in scenes of unprecedented frenzy. Some even chased the foursome as they were driven to their hotel, occasionally forcing their vehicle to stop. "When we came to Australia," recalled Benny Andersson, "they had so much ABBA all around. ABBA on pillows, ABBA on soaps, ABBA on everything."[57]

The band appeared on various TV programs almost non-stop for two weeks, culminating in a special edition of Bandstand on 9 March to promote the single *Fernando* and the compilation *The Best of ABBA*, which helped generate sales of over a million albums. ABBA's colossal success in Australia was comparable (and compared) to The Beatles' conquest of America in 1964. While Benny and Björn savored this long-awaited glory, Frida and Agnetha seemed to struggle to keep pace with the promotional commitments and to grasp the sheer magnitude of their success. Multiple press conferences, police escorts wherever they went, hotels besieged by fans, and the collective hysteria were all tough for the young women to contend with.

Being so far from her daughter Linda soon became a big problem for Agnetha, and tensions began to mount in the group. The peace and quiet of their little island of Viggsö seemed a long way away. But ABBA's success down under was nothing compared to what awaited them in the months to come.

ABBA about to hit the tarmac at Warsaw Airport, Poland, 7 October 1976.

Dancing Queen conquers the world

As soon as the *Dancing Queen* single was released on 16 August 1976, it became a smash hit worldwide. It reached number one in 12 countries—South Africa, Germany, Australia, Belgium, Denmark, Ireland, Mexico, New Zealand, the Netherlands, the UK, the USSR, and the USA—enabling ABBA to achieve their most cherished dream: conquering America. The band's success was now sealed and its name became a logo designed by graphic artist Rune Söderqvist, the man behind the legendary, albeit strange, cover for the *Greatest Hits* album in Sweden. "That came up during a photo session [in Wolfgang "Bubi" Heilemann's studio in Hamburg in February 1976] for *Bravo* magazine," said Agnetha Fältskog. "We had to hold our initial letter in life-size. Benny turned around his B and we only noticed this when the pictures were ready. We liked it so much that we decided to copyright that logo."[58] While *Dancing Queen* was turning the members of ABBA into global superstars, Ulvaeus and Andersson were already busy recording tracks for the band's next album. *Arrival* was released on 11 October 1976, packed with potential hits ready to take the world by storm. *Money, Money,*

Money, When I Kissed the Teacher, Knowing Me, Knowing You, and, of course, *Dancing Queen* made the album a benchmark in the world of pop music, despite it being an artful mix of musical styles, with disco—hugely trendy at the time—never lording it over Benny and Björn's first loves, *schlager* and rock. The album was heavily promoted and the band pulled out all the stops to publicize it around the world.

ABBA and the critics

The triumph of *Arrival* also attracted growing criticism from detractors. In the UK, where the media loves to hate popular artists (remember the outpouring of hate directed at Queen in the mid-1970s), ABBA were criticized because their music was too "light," too "joyful," and their success antagonized certain journalists. In Sweden, where lyrics were, and still are, often political, certain critics somehow managed to overlook ABBA's millions of fans and never missed an opportunity to criticize the perceived lack of depth in the words to their songs. In the TV special *ABBA from the Beginning*, aired in Australia on 27 October 1976, and then in Sweden as *ABBA-Dabba-Dooo!!* on 5 November, the musicians were practically

Agnetha Fältskog on the set of the Polish TV show *ABBA w Studio 2* on 7 October 1976.

subjected to an interrogation about their music, with the presenter pressurizing them to respond to the worst of the criticism. Expressionless but clearly irritated, the band put on a brave face and answered without flinching: "We are making records for an audience as huge as possible. And not for a couple of critics who slate our records in the paper and then secretly take one of our albums home with them."[33] When asked why they didn't relocate to Holland for a bit of peace and quiet, Benny replied, "That would be a cowardly act. It would say: critics, we are running away from you. We would never do that. We will stay here and keep resisting unfair criticism."[33]

The revenue generated by ABBA's successive hits was also a major reason behind some of the vitriol directed at the band, even though they never showed any desire to leave Sweden, despite the 85 percent income-tax rate at the time. "I really don't get why people have to moan about this," said Agnetha. "Everyone is doing well in Sweden and we are doing a little better, but we've worked very, very hard for it. People tend to forget that."[33]

Around the world

While *Arrival* was bulldozing its way up the charts around the world, ABBA were preparing a European and Australian tour. It was an ambitious project, and testament to their fame in Europe and the Antipodes. The European leg kicked off on 28 January 1977 at Ekebergshallen in Oslo, Norway, and ended on 14 February in London's Royal Albert Hall. On 3 March, ABBA landed in Sydney for concerts at the Sydney Showground and then in Melbourne, Adelaide, and Perth, where the tour ended on 12 March. With 28 concerts in six weeks across Europe and Australia, the band had to cope with life on the road, which was both exhilarating and grueling, as Agnetha would reveal in her autobiography *As I Am. ABBA Before & Beyond*, in 1997: "Yes, the Australian tour was the most incredible of all the things that I experienced with ABBA. There was fever, there was hysteria, there were ovations, there were sweaty, obsessed crowds. Some-times it was awful. I felt as if they would get hold of me and I'd never get away again [...]. On occasions they would grab hold of us in the most unpleasant ways and there were times when we cried once we were inside the car."[59]

Benny Andersson and Agnetha Fältskog on stage at the Congress Center-CCH in Hamburg, Germany, on 8 February 1977.

Inevitably, Agnetha's relationship with the stage, and more broadly with public exposure in all its forms, gradually became more complicated, as she felt that her place was with her daughter Linda rather than out on the road. ABBA finally had success at their fingertips and internal tensions were starting to emerge, but they didn't show it and made the most of their position as the kings and queens of pop.

Although people generally prefer the original to the copy, fans would probably like Nashville Train's *Abba in Our Way*, a 1976 album released by Polar Music on which five Swedish musicians (including Rutger Gunnarsson and Roger Palm, respectively bass player and drummer of ABBA) perform country-style versions of ABBA's songs. A special shout-out to their rendition of *Waterloo*, which has you itching to gallop across the prairies of Midwest America.

Rutger Gunnarsson was behind one of ABBA's most famous bass lines, as well as some of their best string arrangements.

RUTGER GUNNARSSON, THE MASTER OF GROOVE

Rutger Gunnarsson was born on 12 February 1946 in Linköping, 125 miles (200km) southwest of Stockholm. At the age of 12, he discovered classical guitar, which he practiced assiduously. He studied music theory and arrangements and was influenced by guitar virtuosos such as Australia's John Williams and Britain's Julian Bream. Gunnarsson soon became a bass player in a number of bands. "After I played classical guitar for ten years I finally decided to change to bass because it felt lonely playing on my own all the time. I wanted to be in a group playing with other musicians and classical guitar did not fit into group-style playing."[60] After enrolling in Stockholm's Royal College of Music, Gunnarsson auditioned for Hootenanny Singers, who were looking for a bass player for their Folkparks tour. This was how he met Björn Ulvaeus and Benny Andersson.

A virtuoso at the service of others

Gunnarsson's talent and adaptability made him a valuable partner. So when Ulvaeus and Andersson started producing *Ring Ring*, Gunnarsson was invited to participate in the recording. Over the years, his precise, inventive playing style earned him a key place in ABBA's backing band, alongside Janne Schaffer and Ola Brunkert. While he shared bass parts with another bassist, Mike Watson, on some ABBA songs, Gunnarsson left his mark on classics such as *Waterloo, Dancing Queen, Knowing Me, Knowing You, Take a Chance on Me, Gimme! Gimme! Gimme!,* and *Lay All Your Love on Me.* "I consider myself a utility bassist, not a flash guy," he explained in *Bass Player* magazine in 2000. "I've never really practiced bass music; I try instead to work out on charts for other instruments—guitar, strings, sax, and so on. It gives you new views of the bass. To me, music is about a melody line on top, a bass line as the fundament, and the other parts filling the gap in between. It all begins with a good melody and a strong bass line."[61] After making a huge contribution to the ABBA legend and playing on all the group's albums, Rutger Gunnarsson passed away at the age of 69 on 8 May 2015.

The Mexican revolutionary Francisco "Pancho" Villa was Björn's inspiration for the lyrics to *Fernando*.

Overleaf: Although director Lasse Hallström complained of the low budget for *Fernando*, it became one of the band's best-known music videos.

FERNANDO

(Benny Andersson, Stig Anderson, Björn Ulvaeus/4'15)

Musicians

Anni-Frid "Frida" Lyngstad: lead vocals, backing vocals
Agnetha Fältskog: backing vocals
Benny Andersson: synthesizers, piano, backing vocals
Björn Ulvaeus: acoustic guitar, backing vocals
Lasse Wellander: electric guitar, mandolin?
Rutger Gunnarsson: bass
Ola Brunkert: drums
Jan Kling: flute

Recording

Metronome, Stockholm: 3 September, 10 October 1975

Technical team

Producers: Benny Andersson, Björn Ulvaeus
Sound engineers: Michael B Tretow, Janne Hansson
String arrangements: Sven-Olof Walldoff

Single

Swedish and UK version
A-side: *Fernando*/4'15
B-side: *Hey Hey Helen*/3'16
US version
A-side: *Fernando*/4'15
B-side: *Rock Me*/3'03
Released in Sweden by Polar Music: March 1976
(single ref.: POS 1224)
Released in the UK by CBS/Epic: April 1976 (single ref.: S EPC 4036)
Released in the USA by Atlantic: 4 September 1976
(single ref.: 45-3346)
Best chart ranking in Sweden: 2
Best chart ranking in the UK: 1
Best chart ranking in the USA: 13

Genesis

On 3 December 1975, the Swedish public broadcaster Sveriges Television aired *Mr Trendsetter*, a documentary about Polar Music boss Stig Anderson, who was also ABBA's manager and regular songwriter. In the program, the businessman is filmed going about his daily life, with work sessions in the studio, business lunches, and swimming in his private pool. But ABBA fans noticed one sequence in particular: Anderson is shown working on the words of a song for Frida called *Fernando*. The piece, developed under the working title *Tango*, was recorded for her album *Frida Ensam* in August 1975. It took Stig Anderson three months to write the Swedish version of the track, but when Benny and Björn decided to re-record it with Agnetha, they completed the English version much more quickly. Björn rewrote the lyrics while observing a clear night sky on the island of Viggsö, drawing on the song's title and the drum rolls in the intro to tell the story of two Mexican men recalling their fight for freedom alongside Federal Army general Francisco "Pancho" Villa, hero of the Mexican revolution (1910–1920). In early 1975, when ABBA had to choose a single to keep fans happy while they waited for the next album to be released, *Fernando* won out, with *Dancing Queen* set aside for the fourth album. A good decision, as *Fernando* shot to the top of the British charts as soon as it was released. It also appeared on the Australian and New Zealand versions of the *Arrival* album.

Production

On 10 October 1975, ABBA called in flautist Jan Kling, who had already worked on the recording of *Frida Ensam* and on Ted Gärdestad's third LP, *Upptåg* ("Antics"), the previous year. Metronome's in-house sound engineer, Janne Hansson, was at the controls that day. "I recorded that flute, played by Jan Kling, and it was a little scary for me," the technician later remarked. "It was the beginning of the song, and this flute went out of tune, so I had to punch in, punch out, until it was right."[62]

Flutes of all kinds, be they transverse, recorders, or panpipes, had been all the rage since Simon & Garfunkel's 1970 hit *El Condor Pasa*. In 1976, when a journalist from *Popshop* magazine asked Björn Ulvaeus about the similarities in the arrangements between *Fernando* and *(Fly Away) Little Paraquayo*, a 1974 hit by the Dutch band George Baker

Selection, he replied: "[...] it's purely a coincidence. We did listen to this song at the time, but to be honest I had completely forgotten about it already."[47] In 1979, it was Boney M.'s turn to wheel out flutes, guitars, and mandolins for their song *El Lute*, which also bears a striking resemblance to *Fernando*.

FOR ABBA ADDICTS

In the summer of 1976, ABBA recorded another version of *Fernando*, renamed *National Song*, to be used for five Australian TV commercials for Japanese electronics company National (later renamed Panasonic). The lyrics were duly rewritten to extol the virtues of the brand, and the four band members sang about how much they loved National. Sacrilege for fans, but a guaranteed source of income for ABBA.

WHEN I KISSED THE TEACHER

(Benny Andersson, Björn Ulvaeus/3'00)

Musicians
Agnetha Fältskog: vocals, backing vocals
Anni-Frid "Frida" Lyngstad: vocals, backing vocals
Benny Andersson: synthesizers, piano, backing vocals
Björn Ulvaeus: acoustic guitar, backing vocals
Janne Schaffer: electric guitar
Rutger Gunnarsson: bass
Ola Brunkert: drums
Malando Gassama: percussion

Recording
Metronome, Stockholm: 14 June 1976

Technical team
Producers: Benny Andersson, Björn Ulvaeus
Sound engineer: Michael B Tretow

1976

Genesis

On 5 November 1976, the day *Arrival* was released in the UK and USA, Swedish TV viewers were treated to a Channel 2 program devoted entirely to ABBA's career. Their first retrospective, *ABBA-Dabba-Dooo!!* presented the artists through interviews and films of their private life shot on Viggsö island. Along with several other ABBA songs, the program featured a never-before-seen video of the opening track from *Arrival*, *When I Kissed the Teacher*, in which Agnetha, Frida, Björn, and Benny take the roles of students sitting in front of their teacher, played on screen by the well-known Swedish actor and presenter Magnus Härenstam. The lyrics are about a young woman who fancies her teacher and decides to kiss him one day in the middle of a geometry lesson. The film was later used as a promotional video for the song which, despite its obvious commercial potential, was never released as a single.

Production

With the first bars borrowed from the intro to *Det Där Med Kärlek* ("That With Love") on Benny and Björn's 1970 album *Lycka* ("Happiness"), *When I Kissed the Teacher* is the perfect prelude to ABBA's new album. Recorded on 14 June 1976, it boasts extraordinary arrangements of cleverly structured and blended backing vocals which no longer just double-tracked (either in unison or harmonized) the main vocal line. ABBA would further develop this method and make it one of their hallmarks, featuring it in songs such as *Knowing Me, Knowing You* and *The Winner Takes It All*. Benny Andersson rarely gives away recording secrets, but in 1982 he spoke about the way ABBA's vocal tracks were laid down. "Only when we're sure that the backing track is spot on do we begin to think about the voices, and we have to build them up gradually by overdubbing until the harmonies are complete. We have to be careful to ensure that we don't end up with something which sounds amazing on record, but which can't be reproduced live—it would be very embarrassing to have to refuse to perform a song because we knew we simply couldn't match up to the recorded version."[63]

ABBA photographed by Ola Lager
during the famous Black & Hat
session, 1976.

Single

DANCING QUEEN

(Benny Andersson, Stig Anderson, Björn Ulvaeus/3'50)

Overleaf: The small room adjoining
Agnetha and Björn's house on
Viggsö island, where ABBA's most
famous songs would be composed.

Musicians

Agnetha Fältskog: vocals, backing vocals
Anni-Frid "Frida" Lyngstad: vocals, backing vocals
Benny Andersson: piano, synthesizers, Hohner Clavinet, backing vocals
Björn Ulvaeus: electric guitar, backing vocals
Anders Glenmark: electric guitar
Janne Schaffer: electric guitar
Rutger Gunnarsson: bass
Roger Palm: drums
Malando Gassama: shaker
Martin Bylund: violin
Anders Dahl: violin
Gunnar Michols: violin
Claes Nilsson: violin
Bertil Orsin: violin
Lars Stegenberg: violin
Sixten Strömvall: violin
Harry Teike: violin
Kryztof Zdrzalka: violin
Åke Arvinder: viola
Lars Brolin: viola
Håkan Roos: viola
Hans-Göran Eketorp: cello
Åke Olofsson: cello
Bertil Andersson: double bass

Recording

Glen Studio, Stocksund: 4 to 5, 27 August 1975
Metronome, Stockholm: 10 September 1975
KMH studios, Stockholm: 3 December 1975

Technical team

Producers: Benny Andersson, Björn Ulvaeus
Sound engineer: Michael B Tretow
String arrangements: Sven-Olof Walldoff

Single

A-side: *Dancing Queen*/3'51
B-side: *That's Me*/3'16
Released in Sweden by Polar Music: 16 August 1976
(single ref.: POS 1225)
Released in the UK by CBS/Epic: 16 August 1976 (single ref.: S EPC 4499)
Released in the USA by Atlantic: 16 August 1976 (single ref.: 45-3372)
Best chart ranking in Sweden: 1
Best chart ranking in the UK: 1
Best chart ranking in the USA: 1

1976

Genesis

July 1975. Stig Anderson and his daughter Marie were enjoying the peace and quiet of their chalet on Viggsö, where the other members of ABBA also had holiday homes, when Björn Ulvaeus and Benny Andersson turned up at the door, carrying a cassette player. Although the two songwriters didn't usually record their sessions on Viggsö ("What we do here is come up with melodies that stick in your head," Ulvaeus explained. "If you can't keep them in your head, they're probably not that great."[64]), that day's composition seemed like a good one. "It was Björn and Benny on piano and guitar," recalled Stig's daughter, now Marie Ledin. "They were clowning around [really]. They played the song and it was so good. It sounded awful, but I really liked it…It was the most incredible song."[65]

Birth of an anthem

Sensing the potential of their new composition, Ulvaeus and Andersson assembled a crack team of musicians at Glen Studio on 4 August to lay the track down on tape. The impressive rhythmic base is provided by drummer Roger Palm and bassist Rutger Gunnarsson, accompanied by Benny on piano and Anders Glenmark and Michael Areklew on guitar; in the control room Bjorn directs the ensemble alongside Michael B Tretow. After two days' work, the backing tracks were finished and the song had a working title, *Boogaloo*, in reference to the 1960s American music trend that was great for dancing. Exhausted but euphoric, Benny and Björn returned home with the cassettes of the instrumental. "[…] I was so excited, I just could not rest," Björn recalled. "Agnetha was asleep and I just had to share it with someone, so I drove all over Stockholm looking for someone to play it to. Finally I ended up at my sister's house. I played it over and over again to her."[3] "I loved it from the beginning when Benny brought home the backing track […]," Frida recalled. "It was so beautiful I started to cry. I mean, even without lyrics or voices on it, it was outstanding."[7]

Stig Anderson quickly set to work to produce lyrics worthy of this highly promising song. Reprising a theme from the 1972 track *Nina, Pretty Ballerina*, he sketched out a portrait of a young woman who loves to hit the dancefloor at night. "It's about an ordinary girl. She only lives actually when she's in the disco, dancing," Björn Ulvaeus would later explain.[66]

This was a universal theme at the time, as disco music had taken over the world a few months earlier and disco lyrics were often about a love for dancing and how good it

On set for *ABBA w Studio 2* in Warsaw, 7 October 1976.

Countless cover versions of *Dancing Queen* have been performed on stages the world over since 1976. The most astonishing is undoubtedly the one played by Kirk Hammett and Robert Trujillo from Metallica at the Ericsson Globe in Stockholm on 7 May 2018, as part of their daily sequence of incongruous covers called *Rob & Kirk's Doodle*. That evening, the ultimate disco hit was enjoyed by 33,000 Swedish metalheads.

is for the morale. ABBA knew this was the direction they wanted to take and they planned to release the track as a single quickly while fans were still awaiting their next album. In the end, it was *Fernando* that was chosen as a single in March 1976, as the team at Polar Music felt that a ballad was more appropriate after the release of *Mamma Mia* several months earlier. The group kept *Dancing Queen* on ice and used it a few months later as the first single from their fourth album, *Arrival*. Promoted with a video filmed at Stockholm's famous Alexandra's nightclub, it was released to great fanfare on 16 August and within days catapulted the group to global superstardom, topping the charts in over 15 countries, including Australia, the USA, the UK, and the USSR. The song would be ABBA's biggest hit, but it would forever label them as a disco band, even though their discography was built around music that was far more complex than it appeared.

Production

Disco music was a massive craze in the mid-1970s, but it is important to remember that it was a passing trend. It emerged in 1974 and died a brutal death in 1979, reviled, hated, and ultimately boycotted by many radio programmers. In August 1976, however, when *Dancing Queen* was released, disco was still all over the airwaves, steamrolling everything in its path. In fact, it was one of the foundational tracks of disco that inspired Ulvaeus and Andersson for the song's cadence. When the two men went to Glen Studio on 4 August 1976, they brought with them George McCrae's single *Rock Your Baby*, which had been a big hit at the end of 1974. They left the cover on the console and played the record throughout the day over the control room speakers. "We used that for the guide of the swing, for the feel of the swing to 'Ah, that's the way we should put it in a bass track,'"[67] explained Michael B Tretow. The team also drew inspiration from the powerful playing of drummer Richard Finch on McCrae's hit to make *Dancing Queen* swing. An eminent master of rhythm with KC and The Sunshine Band (Finch played drums, percussion, and bass for the band at the

1976

time!), here he hits his hi-hat cymbals like nobody else, prompting Tretow and the other musicians to get together one last time, on 3 December, to add some hi-hat openings to the drum parts. These can be heard between the bars of the famous synth intro, itself inspired by Delaney & Bonnie's 1971 release *Sing My Way Home*.

The guitar rhythm, played by Björn and based on original backing tracks on which Michael Areklew, Anders Glenmark, and Janne Schaffer had already laid down six-string guitar tracks, emerged from Viggsö, with *Dancing Queen* becoming the first song Ulvaeus wrote with the help of an electric guitar. Benny Andersson recalled that this was not something Björn usually did on Viggsö, where he played acoustic guitar. But on this occasion the two songwriters had taken a little electric amplifier to their island retreat. "That automatically creates a different style of playing, [and] allows you to experiment with different sounds," Benny explained.[35] With its catchy melody and irresistible rhythm, *Dancing Queen* would become one of the most famous songs in the history of modern music.

MY LOVE, MY LIFE

(Benny Andersson, Stig Anderson, Björn Ulvaeus/3'52)

Musicians

Agnetha Fältskog: lead vocals, backing vocals
Anni-Frid "Frida" Lyngstad: backing vocals
Benny Andersson: synthesizers, piano, backing vocals
Björn Ulvaeus: backing vocals
Janne Schaffer: electric guitar
Rutger Gunnarsson: bass
Ola Brunkert: drums
Martin Bylund: violin
Anders Dahl: violin
Gunnar Michols: violin
Claes Nilsson: violin
Leandr Pfeiler: violin
Lars Stegenberg: violin
Bo Söderström: violin
Harry Teike: violin
Snorri Thorvaldsson: violin
Bernt Nylund: violin
Per-Erik Olsson: violin
Kryztof Zdrzalka: violin
Åke Arvinder: viola
Lars Arvinder: viola
Alm Nils Ersson: viola
Niels Heie: viola
Håkan Roos: viola

Recording

Metronome, Stockholm: 20, 30 August 1976

Technical team

Producers: Benny Andersson, Björn Ulvaeus
Sound engineer: Michael B Tretow
String arrangements: Rutger Gunnarsson

Genesis

Paris as the backdrop to a love affair was Björn Ulvaeus's inspiration when he wrote the lyrics to *Monsieur, Monsieur*, which he and Benny Andersson recorded at Metronome on 19 July 1976 with Rutger Gunnarsson, Lasse Wellander, and Ola Brunkert. In the song, Agnetha laments her imminent departure from the French capital and sings in the choruses: "This is my last night in France/Monsieur, Monsieur/So tonight is our last chance/Monsieur, Monsieur." Dissatisfied with this version, ABBA ultimately ditched it, stored away the theme of a Parisian romance (which would be exhumed in 1980 for *Our Last Summer*), and re-recorded the song on 20 August with a new title: *My Love, My Life*, about a relationship break-up. Meanwhile, the *Monsieur, Monsieur* demo was broadcast on 27 December 1976 during a radio interview Agnetha Fältskog gave to Ulf Elfving on the Sveriges Radio P3 program *A För Agnetha*.

Production

As with many other ABBA songs, the Bolin grand piano at Metronome studios is the main instrument, guiding Agnetha and Frida during the vocal takes. To give the track substance, sound engineer Michael B Tretow recorded it with three AKG C414 condenser microphones, his favorites. "Piano is the secret,"[62] he said of the instrument that appears in most of ABBA's songs. The vocal parts on *My Love, My Life* are also testament to the quality of Tretow's work, especially when he used the hidden room behind the studio for some of the Metronome sessions. Built entirely in concrete, the room gives the takes a natural reverb that is the envy of sound engineers the world over. Janne Hansson, who became sound engineer at Metronome when Tretow left in 1974, talked in 2021 about the importance of this hidden room: "It's completely empty except for the microphones that are connected to the control room. A lot of musicians know that when they record their vocals in this room, they will attain a certain reverb. And, of course, it's very prominent on the ABBA records."[62]

DUM DUM DIDDLE

(Benny Andersson, Björn Ulvaeus/2'53)

Musicians
Agnetha Fältskog: vocals, backing vocals
Anni-Frid "Frida" Lyngstad: vocals, backing vocals
Benny Andersson: synthesizers, piano, backing vocals
Björn Ulvaeus: acoustic guitar, backing vocals
Lasse Wellander: electric guitar
Rutger Gunnarsson: bass
Ola Brunkert: drums

Recording
Metronome, Stockholm: 19 July 1976

Technical team
Producers: Benny Andersson, Björn Ulvaeus
Sound engineer: Michael B Tretow

1976

Genesis

Some sessions in the studio are more prolific than others. Monday 19 July 1976 was a red-letter day: it was when ABBA recorded the backing tracks to *Tiger*, *My Love, My Life*, the very disco number *Funky Feet* (which would be given to Svenne & Lotta because it was too similar to *Dancing Queen*), and also an untitled pop song whose vocals were recorded a few days later. The day before the vocals sessions, Björn Ulvaeus was faced with an insoluble problem: he couldn't think of any lyrics for the track. He stayed up until five o'clock in the morning trying to write some words, which he was fully expecting Benny Andersson to reject the next day. "I'd been working all night trying to come up with a decent lyric. And I thought, 'Well, I'd better take in something to prove that I've been working.' I showed them this song, thinking they'd say, 'Oh, no! We can't do that!'"[3] Unfortunately, the song *Dum Dum Diddle*, about a young woman who is jealous of her boyfriend's relationship with his violin, met with Benny's approval, was recorded by Agnetha and Frida, and slotted into fourth position on the *Arrival* tracklist.

Production

Although Björn later admitted that he hates *Dum Dum Diddle* (as does Frida), the song has a catchy melody and the lyrics sit fairly well with ABBA's other lightweight songs, such as *Ring Ring (Bara Du Slog En Signal)*, *Sitting in the Palmtree*, and *Bang-A-Boomerang*. Carried by Frida and Agnetha's clearly complementary voices, the song is a playful diversion in the middle of an album where Benny and Björn's trademark melancholy takes up a lot of space. "Our two voices together create a very special sound," Frida said in 2021. "Together we had a register of three octaves, more or less. Agnetha is a soprano and I'm a mezzo-soprano. I can go much lower, while she can go much higher."[62] "Frida and Agnetha, however high they sing the notes, they never yell or shout," Benny added in a later interview. "I don't know what it is, but they sound controlled at the same time as they hit those unbelievably too-high notes. It's kind of special."[68]

Above: On set for *ABBA w Studio 2*, 7 October 1976.
Overleaf: ABBA photographed during the famous Kimono session, 1976.

Image used for the cover of the single *Knowing Me, Knowing You* in February 1977.

Overleaf: On set filming the music video for *Knowing Me, Knowing You*, directed as ever by Lasse Hallström.

Single

KNOWING ME, KNOWING YOU

(Benny Andersson, Stig Anderson, Björn Ulvaeus/4'02)

Musicians
Anni-Frid "Frida" Lyngstad: lead vocals, backing vocals
Agnetha Fältskog: backing vocals
Benny Andersson: synthesizers, backing vocals
Björn Ulvaeus: acoustic guitar, backing vocals
Janne Schaffer: electric guitar
Lasse Wellander: electric guitar
Rutger Gunnarsson: bass
Ola Brunkert: drums
Malando Gassama: percussion

Recording
Metronome, Stockholm: 23 March, 24 May 1976

Technical team
Producers: Benny Andersson, Björn Ulvaeus
Sound engineer: Michael B Tretow

Single
A-side: *Knowing Me, Knowing You*/4'02
B-side: *Happy Hawaii* (early version of *Why Did It Have to Be Me?*)/4'22
Released in the UK by CBS/Epic: 16 February 1977
(single ref.: EPC 4955)
Released in the USA by Atlantic: May 1977 (single ref.: 3387)
Best chart ranking in the UK: 1
Best chart ranking in the USA: 14

1976

HEADPHONES AT THE READY
Every chorus of *Knowing Me, Knowing You* contains one of ABBA's best-known hallmarks: A-HA. Some enterprising ABBA fans compiled a list of songs in which this vocal feature appears: *Honey, Honey* (00'10), *Hey Hey Helen* (2'10), *So Long* (0'20), *Money, Money, Money* (00'57), *Hole in Your Soul* (1'41), *Voulez-Vous* (00'54), *Angeleyes* (00'01), *The King Has Lost His Crown* (1'26), *You Owe Me One* (1'03), and *Just a Notion* (00'20).

Genesis
Although this track is not the first in the ABBA repertoire to talk about love, in particular the pain of a break-up (think *Disillusion, SOS,* or *Mamma Mia*), here Björn Ulvaeus addresses the subject from the viewpoint of an adult couple confronted with images of children playing in the family home and the painful memories of a family life that is long gone. At this point, the relationship between Björn and Agnetha was on shaky ground. While the former, despite being an attentive father and loving husband, was focusing most of his attention on developing ABBA, his wife was increasingly reluctant to embark on tours or even to travel to promote the records. Even though ABBA toured very little over the years and Björn and Agnetha were still very much pulling their weight in the band, they did not see eye to eye on this subject. After their marriage broke down in 1979, Björn found himself having to justify the lyrics of *Knowing Me, Knowing You* and other songs that explicitly deal with relationship break-ups (*The Winner Takes It All, One of Us*). He maintained that he hadn't been thinking specifically about himself and Agnetha when he wrote *Knowing Me, Knowing You*, but instead imagining the echoing steps of a man walking round a house he had moved out of, looking at the few bits and pieces that were left behind, and remembering the past.

Production
Knowing Me, Knowing You was the first song to be recorded during the *Arrival* sessions in March 1976 (*Dancing Queen* having been committed to tape long before then), and is one of the album's key tracks, propelling it to the top of the world's charts. Initially called *Number One, Number One*, the song works in large part because of the harmonic division into minor-chord verses and major-chord choruses. The layering of guitars is also important, and gives the track—which has an almost disco rhythm (with its hi-hat openings that had already been used on *Dancing Queen*)—an equally rock texture. "There's a melody guitar and a harmony guitar, not doubled, plus two electric power-chord guitars playing the same thing," explained electric guitarist Lasse Wellander, "plus some acoustic guitars. It's very thought-through."[44]

MONEY, MONEY, MONEY

(Benny Andersson, Björn Ulvaeus/3'05)

Musicians
Anni-Frid "Frida" Lyngstad: lead vocals, backing vocals
Agnetha Fältskog: backing vocals
Benny Andersson: synthesizers, piano, marimba, backing vocals
Björn Ulvaeus: electric guitar, backing vocals
Anders Glenmark: electric guitar
Rutger Gunnarsson: bass
Ola Brunkert: drums, kettledrum
Mats Glenngård: violin
Malando Gassama: tambourine

Recording
Metronome, Stockholm: 17 to 18, 24, 31 May, 1 June 1976

Technical team
Producers: Benny Andersson, Björn Ulvaeus
Sound engineer: Michael B Tretow

Single
A-side: *Money, Money, Money*/3'05
B-side: *Crazy World*/3'47
Released in the UK by CBS/Epic: 1 November 1976
(single ref.: S EPC 4713)
Released in the USA by Atlantic: October 1977 (single ref.: 3434)
Best chart ranking in the UK: 3
Best chart ranking in the USA: 56

Genesis

It is on public record that the visual universe and the music from Bob Fosse's 1972 film *Cabaret* heavily influenced Freddie Mercury in the songs he composed for Queen from 1974 onwards (*Killer Queen, My Melancholy Blues*). *Cabaret*, starring Liza Minnelli in fishnet stockings and a top hat, was an international blockbuster, and its impact was also felt in Sweden, where our friends from ABBA decided to compose a song in the style of the film. Writing words for music composed by Benny Andersson, Björn Ulvaeus planned to call the track *Gypsy Girl*, a title he'd had in mind for some time. He then decided against it, took a blank page, and started over. He next considered basing the chorus on three words that had been going round in his head for months: "Money, Money, Money." He didn't want to use this as a title, however, because, after the 1973 oil crisis, too many artists were singing about the evils of money (not least Minnelli herself with *Money, Money* in *Cabaret*). He presented Benny with an initial version of the lyrics, which the latter didn't appear to like much. "It was originally called *Been and Gone and Done It*," Andersson later commented. "I said, 'Do you think this is really the best you can do?'"[3] Ulvaeus got back to work and ended up writing a text about a young woman who dreams of becoming rich through means other than work. "We worked a full three months on *Money, Money, Money*, before we were really satisfied," said Andersson. "More than a dozen concepts were thrown in the waste-paper basket…"[10] It isn't easy to find a way into the song, due to its angst-ridden atmosphere—which can be blamed mainly on the descending chord progression in the intro, reminiscent of the one in Queen's *Death on Two Legs (Dedicated to…)*—and its burlesque feel, a double nod to the composer Paul Williams (the final part of *The Hell of It* on the *Phantom of the Paradise* soundtrack in 1974 and the track *Bugsy Malone* from the 1976 film of the same name, directed by Alan Parker). It nevertheless became one of the group's biggest hits, despite not being released as a single in Sweden. "It's my favorite," said Benny Andersson in 1977. "Of all the things we've done, that one is the best ever."[69] Symptomatic of an era when carefree, lighthearted fun would soon be replaced by worldly worries, *Money, Money, Money* proved once again that ABBA loved to surprise their audiences and managed to hit the mark with every one of their musical experiments.

The members of ABBA photographed by Peter Bischoff for the cover of the *Money, Money, Money* single.

Overleaf: Very 1970s-style framing through the lens of Peter Bischoff.

Production

When the song still had the working title *Gypsy Girl*, Björn Ulvaeus decided to add a violin track to develop the theme of the girl in question. With this in mind he called in Mats Glenngård, violinist in the Swedish group Kebnekajse, whose first solo album, *Kosterläge*, had been recorded by Michael B Tretow in 1972. Once the *Gypsy Girl* idea had been dropped in favor of *Money, Money, Money*, only a few violin tracks were kept in the final mix, noticeable mainly at 00'36. The instruments at the core of this unusual hit are cleverly layered, as is evidenced by Rutger Gunnarsson's spectacular bass line, which inspired the marimba line and is interwoven into Anders Glenmark's discreet guitar riffs. Behind the legendary and slightly angst-inducing melody of *Money, Money, Money* lies an artistic revolution that ABBA would fully embrace from 1980 on *Super Trouper*, when they began using synthesizers instead of piano as the central instrument in their music.

HEADPHONES AT THE READY

Benny Andersson had recorded the descending piano chord that precedes each chorus of *Money, Money, Money* several months earlier. When he contributed—along with Björn, Agnetha, and Frida—to Michael B Tretow's first album *Let's Boogie*, Benny placed this line at 1'45 and 2'29 of the song *Sandwich*.

THAT'S ME

(Benny Andersson, Stig Anderson, Björn Ulvaeus/3'15)

Musicians
Anni-Frid "Frida" Lyngstad: lead vocals, backing vocals
Agnetha Fältskog: backing vocals
Benny Andersson: synthesizers, piano, Polymoog 203a, ARP Solina String Ensemble, backing vocals
Björn Ulvaeus: backing vocals
Janne Schaffer: electric guitar
Rutger Gunnarsson: bass
Ola Brunkert: drums
Malando Gassama: shaker

Recording
Metronome, Stockholm: 23 March, June, July 1976

Technical team
Producers: Benny Andersson, Björn Ulvaeus
Sound engineer: Michael B Tretow

Genesis

So who is this Carrie and why is she "not the kind of girl you'd marry"? In a 1982 interview, Benny Andersson revealed his fondness for literature, in particular a certain genre: "I'm a science-fiction fan and have been for many years. [...] My favorite authors are Nevil Shute, Harry Harrison, John Steinbeck..."[70] In the same interview, Björn Ulvaeus talked about his passion for science-fiction films, so it's highly likely that the two men had enjoyed Stephen King's first novel, *Carrie*, published in April 1974. It tells the story of a young girl who is bullied by her mother and her classmates and decides to take revenge. The book was a bestseller and was swiftly followed by a film adaptation by the master of horror, Brian De Palma. *Carrie*'s huge success is unlikely to have escaped the notice of Björn Ulvaeus when he was writing the lyrics of *That's Me*.

Production

Determined to embrace the disco style, Benny and Björn gave *That's Me* a much faster tempo than *Dancing Queen*, closer to the 120 bpm of 1976 and 1977 hits such as Donna Summer's *I Feel Love*, Cerrone's *Supernature*, and Chic's *Everybody Dance* than hits from 1974 and 1975 which still had a certain funkiness about them and didn't exceed 110 bpm—George McCrae's *Rock Your Baby*, *That's the Way (I Like It)* by KC and The Sunshine Band, *Jive Talkin'* by the Bee Gees. Just as Chic's then-bassist Bernard Edwards had done, Rutger Gunnarsson lit up the track with a powerful guitar line, which, along with the one on *Dancing Queen*, contributed to his status as a legend. In Japan, the artistic directors of Discomate, ABBA's distributors there, sought and obtained Stig Anderson's authorization to release *That's Me* as a single instead of *Knowing Me, Knowing You*. "Let's be fair, I'm sure they know their own market best," Anderson said to *Billboard Magazine*. "We'll make an exception in this case and let them bring out a special release against the usual international run of the thing."[71]

Benny hiding behind his piano during the filming of *ABBA w Studio 2*, Warsaw, 7 October 1976.

Björn playing (in playback) his acoustic guitar on the set of *ABBA w Studio 2*, 7 October 1976.

WHY DID IT HAVE TO BE ME

(Benny Andersson, Björn Ulvaeus/3'20)

Musicians

Björn Ulvaeus: vocals, electric guitar, backing vocals
Agnetha Fältskog: vocals, backing vocals
Anni-Frid "Frida" Lyngstad: vocals, backing vocals
Benny Andersson: piano, backing vocals
Janne Schaffer: electric guitar
Rutger Gunnarsson: bass
Ola Brunkert: drums
Lars O Carlsson: saxophone

Recording

Metronome, Stockholm: 27 August, 3 to 7 September 1976

Technical team

Producers: Benny Andersson, Björn Ulvaeus
Sound engineer: Michael B Tretow

1976

Genesis

On 26 April 1976, Benny Andersson and Björn Ulvaeus presented their musicians Rutger Gunnarsson, Lasse Wellander, and Roger Palm with a track inspired by the diverse influences in the music of the great Fats Domino, who combined rock'n'roll and rhythm and blues with panache. There were touches of *Ain't That a Shame* and *Blueberry Hill* in the composition the two men introduced that day at Metronome studios under the working title *Why Did It Have to Be Me?* Andersson was dissatisfied with the raw feel of the first demo recorded at the session and suggested transforming the track by adding the sound of waves crashing against the shore to give it a more summery feel. Stig Anderson then chipped in with the title *Hawaii*, and guitarist Janne Lindgren was brought in on 14 May to add a track played on a six-string steel guitar, on which a bottleneck is slid along the strings to change the notes. Last but not least, Agnetha and Frida added their vocals to the song (now called *Happy Hawaii*) about the adventures of a young woman who flies to Honolulu to forget a painful break-up. Once recording was complete, the team realized they had reached their quota of seaside songs with *Sitting in the Palmtree, Hasta Mañana,* and *Tropical Loveland,* and so they went back to the drawing board and turned *Happy Hawaii* into the more country-sounding *Memory Lane.*

Production

On 27 August 1976, Benny and Björn changed their minds again and decided to revert to the first version of the track. The Fats Domino spirit was back in the studio at Metronome as the definitive version of *Why Did It Have to Be Me?* was recorded. Saxophonist Lars O Carlsson was brought in to add a rock'n'roll score to the track. Carlsson was also a vocalist who had first met ABBA when he was invited to contribute some backing vocals on *Vill Du Låna En Man* ("Do You Want to Borrow a Man?") and *Aldrig Mej* ("Never Miss"), two tracks on Anni-Frid's album *Frida Ensam*, recorded the previous year. Carlsson became a regular fixture with ABBA, accompanying the group on their 1977 tour and playing on *ABBA–The Album* the same year, *Voulez-Vous* in 1979, and *Super Trouper* in 1980.

TIGER

(Benny Andersson, Björn Ulvaeus/2'55)

Musicians
Agnetha Fältskog: backing vocals
Anni-Frid "Frida" Lyngstad: backing vocals
Benny Andersson: synthesizers, piano, backing vocals
Björn Ulvaeus: backing vocals
Lasse Wellander: electric guitar
Rutger Gunnarsson: bass
Ola Brunkert: drums

Recording
Metronome, Stockholm: 19 to 20, 23 July 1976

Technical team
Producers: Benny Andersson, Björn Ulvaeus
Sound engineer: Michael B Tretow

Genesis

On 7 October 1976, three members of ABBA, Björn, Frida, and Benny, landed at Chopin Airport in Warsaw, Poland. They would spend three days promoting their fourth album prior to its impending release. Journalists from the television channel TVP1 interviewed Björn on the plane and were told that his wife Agnetha had already landed: as parents of a young daughter, the two artists avoided traveling in the same aircraft, to ensure that one of them would survive in the event of an accident. The real reason was quite different, as Agnetha was petrified of flying and avoided air travel where possible. But the group were back together again in Poland, where they recorded a TV special called *ABBA w Studio 2*, in which they performed almost all of *Arrival*, with the exception of *Dum Dum Diddle*, *That's Me*, and *Why Did It Have to Be Me?* One of the numbers presented in the program, which aired on 13 November, was a rock song called *Tiger*, featuring a sequence in which Agnetha and Frida ended up batting away inflatable cushions that should have floated into the audience but were instead making a nuisance of themselves on stage.

Production

In 1976, Benny Andersson described the methodology he and Björn Ulvaeus used to compose songs together. "Usually, I come up with the melody and Björn with the lyrics. In the beginning, we work separately. While Björn—who's best at speaking English—is writing the words, I'm simply jingling away on my keyboard, at which only my dog Zappa is allowed to listen in. As soon as I like a melody, I'm singing some dummy lyrics to it in the vein of 'the pigs have crooked legs and a curly pig-tail.' Very often, children's songs give me an idea as well. When this work is roughly done, I play it to Björn, who then writes a decent lyric to it. It often takes hundreds of hours of work before an ABBA song is completely finished."[10]

When ABBA arrived in Warsaw, they appeared shocked by the poverty of the Polish people and the scars left by the bombardments of the Second World War. "We don't have the right to disappoint these people," Benny said at the time, "because they are the ones that buy our records…"[72] "I knew that Poland was a poor country," Agnetha added, "but I didn't know that it was this bad…"[72] A few hours later, during a press conference with 300 journalists in the city's Novotel hotel, the four artists were asked about their personal lives, a subject they tended to avoid: "What are you actually doing when you are not on the road, not composing or working in the studio?" Björn shot back point-blank, "We are counting our money…"[9]

Above: ABBA in Stockholm, April 1976.
Overleaf: Agnetha and Frida surrounded by balloons on the set of *ABBA w Studio 2*.

ARRIVAL

(Benny Andersson, Björn Ulvaeus/3'00)

Musicians

Agnetha Fältskog: backing vocals
Anni-Frid "Frida" Lyngstad: backing vocals
Benny Andersson: synthesizers, Polymoog 203a, backing vocals
Björn Ulvaeus: backing vocals
Martin Bylund: violin
Anders Dahl: violin
Gunnar Michols: violin
Bo Söderström: violin
Harry Teike: violin
Bernt Nylund: violin
Lars Arvinder: viola
Alm Nils Ersson: viola

Recording

Metronome, Stockholm: 30 August, 12 to 13 September 1976

Technical team

Producers: Benny Andersson, Björn Ulvaeus
Sound engineer: Michael B Tretow
String arrangements: Rutger Gunnarsson

Genesis

After *Intermezzo No. 1* on *ABBA* in 1975, Benny Andersson here delivers another track that has backing vocals but no lyrics, evidence of his fondness for operatic productions. In the intimacy of Metronome studios on the evening of 30 August 1976, Benny and Michael B Tretow recorded a track with obvious folk overtones, inspired by the Swedish music that the former so loves. He called it *Ode to Dalecarlia* in homage to a Swedish province known for its traditional music. The backing vocals were added in mid-September, but at that point the song was not included on the tracklist for the upcoming album, because Benny felt it did not fit in with the others that had already been recorded. When the band did the photo shoot for the album cover at Barkarby airfield, the shot of the helicopter with the four of them on board inspired photographer Ola Lager to suggest that they called the album *Arrival*. Andersson liked the name, and also used it for this composition, which concludes the album. Mike Oldfield did a grandiose, over-the-top, and poignant cover version of *Arrival* on his 1980 album *QE2,* and in 1983 Frida recorded it twice: the first time as a duet with B A Robertson for *ABBAcadabra, A Musical Adventure,* and then with Daniel Balavoine for the French version, *Belle.*

Production

Benny Andersson used a brand new instrument to record the ethereal textures of *Arrival.* The Polymoog 203a had been designed by the American company Moog Music in 1975 from the ashes of an ambitious three-unit synthesizer project called the Constellation, comprising the polyphonic Apollo, the monophonic Lyra, and the bass synth and pedalboard Taurus. Production of the Lyra was abandoned, but the Apollo was built, renamed Polymoog, and sold well from the outset. Benny used it on *Arrival* and *That's Me* in 1975. Its Strings, Piano, Organ, Harpsichord, Funk, Clavi, Vibes, and Brass presets enabled him to layer synth pads in his compositions, a process he further developed in 1978 when he acquired the legendary Yamaha GX-1 synthesizer, which changed the feel of ABBA's music.

HAPPY HAWAII

(Benny Andersson, Stig Anderson, Björn Ulvaeus/4'23)

Musicians
Anni-Frid "Frida" Lyngstad: lead vocals, backing vocals
Agnetha Fältskog: backing vocals
Benny Andersson: synthesizers, piano, backing vocals
Björn Ulvaeus: electric guitar, backing vocals
Lasse Wellander: electric guitar
Janne Lindgren: steel guitar
Rutger Gunnarsson: bass
Ola Brunkert: drums

Recording
Metronome, Stockholm: 26 April, 14, 24 May 1976

Technical team
Producers: Björn Ulvaeus, Benny Andersson
Sound engineer: Michael B Tretow

Single *Knowing Me, Knowing You*
A-side: *Knowing Me, Knowing You*/4'02
B-side: *Happy Hawaii* (early version of *Why Did It Have to Be Me?*/4'22
Released in the UK by CBS/Epic: 16 February 1977
(single ref.: EPC 4955)
Released in the USA by Atlantic: May 1977 (single ref.: 3387)
Best chart ranking in the UK: 1
Best chart ranking in the USA: 14

Genesis
Few ABBA songs have undergone as many transformations as *Happy Hawaii*. After the track was recorded in April 1976, it was stored on the shelves at Polar Music and totally re-recorded twice, the first time for an American version, the second as a Fats Domino-style rock 'n' roll number, similar to the very first demo, which was called *Why Did It Have to Be Me?* The latter ultimately nudged *Happy Hawaii* off the tracklist for *Arrival* and it ended up as the B-side of *Knowing Me, Knowing You* in February 1977—not a bad place to be, since the single made it into the Top 10 around the world. One of the few ABBA outtakes, *Happy Hawaii* had its own promotional video commissioned by Australian production company Reg Grundy Organization in 1976, when the project to make a cartoon series based on ABBA hits was mooted. This was intended to be similar to the *Jackson Five* cartoon series about the adventures of the Jackson brothers between 1971 and 1972, but was soon abandoned and never came to fruition. In the end, all that fans got to see was a video of *Happy Hawaii* on the DVD of the 2006 deluxe edition of *Arrival*.

Production
At Benny Andersson's request, European steel-guitar pioneer Janne Lindgren added a Hawaiian touch to the song. The members of ABBA already knew Lindgren, as he had been involved in the production of *Frida Ensam* in 1975 and was also in the band Nashville Train, which released an album of country-style covers in 1977 called *Abba Our Way*. The song seemed ideally suited for different versions and was also covered in 1980 by German singer Manuela, who sang it in her mother tongue with lyrics by Robert Jung. Once again, we prefer the original to the copies, so let's go surfing in Honolulu with Agnetha and Frida!

Janne Lindgren (left) behind his pedal-steel MSA Super Sustain II Vintage XL, with guitarist Hasse Rosén.

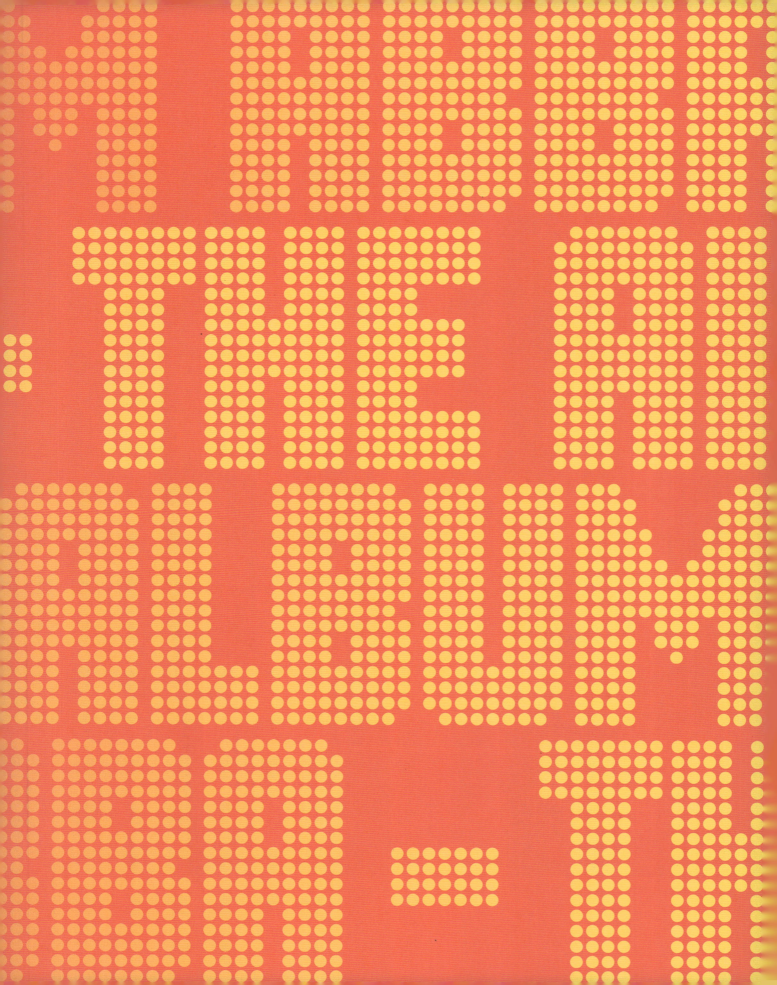

ABBA-THE ALBUM

Eagle • Take A Chance On Me • One Man, One Woman •
The Name Of The Game • Move On • Hole In Your Soul •
"The Girl With The Golden Hair" – 3 Scenes From A Mini-Musical
A. Thank You For The Music / B. I Wonder (Departure) / C. I'm A Marionette

Released in Sweden by Polar Music: 12 December 1977 (album ref.: POLS 282)
Released in the UK by CBS/Epic: January 1978 (album ref.: EPC 86052)
Released in the USA by Atlantic: January 1978 (album ref.: SD 19164)
Best chart ranking in Sweden: 1
Best chart ranking in the UK: 1
Best chart ranking in the USA: 14

FOR ABBA ADDICTS

There are no photographs of ABBA at any private parties during their Australian and European tours. Bosse Norling, their charismatic tour manager, banned photographers from taking pictures of these events because, in his words, "The world's most beautiful people don't sweat!"[55]

ABBA AROUND THE WORLD

1977

When ABBA returned to Sweden in March 1977, they had already sold 12 million albums and 27 million singles worldwide, the second biggest record sales after The Eagles with the 1976 compilation *Their Greatest Hits (1971–1975)*. "When you look at the international sales figures it really makes your head spin," the group's manager Stig Anderson said at the time. "[…] In Holland we have already surpassed The Beatles. In America *Waterloo* is number seven in the charts and as soon as we have some time we will go over there to do a couple of television shows."[26] Inevitably, this kind of success brought with it phenomenal pressure for Agnetha, Frida, Benny, and Björn, who wanted to do even better and surprise their audiences. "We feel that we have to come up with something different," said Ulvaeus. "So many people have been talking about 'the forthcoming album must be sort of equivalent to [The Beatles'] *Sgt. Pepper* album,' and it puts a lot of pressure on us, sure."[73] The fans were clamoring for new ABBA material, so the band set themselves two objectives: to release their new album before the end of 1977 and to make a film of their Australian tour.

Taking the box office by storm

Before ABBA left for Australia, they brought on board filmmaker Lasse Hallström to film their concerts. The original plan was to provide material for Polar Music to put together a television program aimed at promoting the band in Europe, but the project took a different turn when Hallström decided to add a story to the images and create a feature film with concert footage slotted in, rather than a simple documentary. He came up with a storyline about a radio presenter called Ashley Wallace desperately trying to get an interview with ABBA when they came to Australia. Post-production work on the film, scheduled for release in late 1977, kept the band busy once they returned to Sweden, where many extra scenes were shot. Overdubs for the soundtrack were also recorded at Bohus studios in Kungälv in September, to iron out the imperfections in the live takes. Alongside this time-consuming task, Benny and Björn were writing and recording the new album, which they'd begun in the spring and which the press and fans were eagerly awaiting.

Experimenting with a musical

On 31 May, the artists and their loyal sound engineer Michael B Tretow took up residence at Marcus Music studios in Solna, a northern suburb of Stockholm. The studio, owned by Marcus Österdahl, a Swedish musician and entrepreneur who had achieved success in the early 1960s with his group The Telstars, was at the time the only one that could accommodate ABBA for long enough to record their album. Two songs (*The Name of the Game* and *Eagle*) were quickly committed to tape, and subsequent sessions gave the musicians time to record their new productions. These included three that had been performed to audiences during their recent tour: *Thank You for the Music*, *I Wonder (Departure)*, and *I'm a Marionette*.

This trio of songs, which together would constitute the mini-musical *The Girl with the Golden Hair* that appears at the end of the album, is an important feature in ABBA's discography, as it marks Ulvaeus and Andersson's first foray into the world of musicals, a genre that they would embrace successfully after the group took a break in 1982. Other tracks,

Happy atmosphere at the
ABBA—The Album
sessions.

Overleaf: On stage in
1977 during the Europe
and Australia tour.

Shortly before the release of *ABBA—The Album*, Frida hit the headlines in the Swedish press. Andrea Buchinger, a 15-year-old German fan, had read a biography of the singer in *Bravo* magazine and realized that her uncle, Alfred Haase, was Frida's biological father. The meeting between Haase and his daughter was splashed over the papers, accompanied by carefully choreographed photos. But the reconciliation was short-lived: Frida preferred to cut all ties with her father, believing that it was too late for any real connection.

1977

notably the emotional *Move On*, incorporated the American influences from the trip the two songwriters and their team (including Michael B Tretow and Hans "Berka" Bergkvist, Stig Anderson's right-hand man) made to Los Angeles in May 1977. The purpose was to visit recording studios and meet people from the record industry in preparation for the construction of Polar Music Studios, which would shortly provide ABBA with premises commensurate with their ambitions.

Songs with American influences

Despite the pressure and chaos engendered by the band's huge number of projects, ABBA managed to release their fifth album on 12 December 1977, at the same time as *ABBA—The Movie* first appeared in Swedish and Australian cinemas. When the album came out, press and fans alike were surprised by the absence of the innocent, lighthearted music characteristic of previous records. Openly inspired by the ethereal and melodic pop of Fleetwood Mac and The Eagles, who were battling it out for the top spot on the *Billboard* charts with their respective albums *Rumours* and *Hotel California*, ABBA seemed to have made it a point of pride to distance themselves from disco, taking their listeners on a journey into folk (*Eagle, Move On*), rock (*Hole in Your Soul*), and pop (*The Name of the Game*), with the latter being a particular preference of Björn Ulvaeus and Benny Andersson. Although the songs

cited here are of undeniable quality, only *Take a Chance on Me* resembled the ABBA of before, when they were churning out a string of international hits. Despite its superb songs and the enthusiastic reception in Sweden, where it topped the charts for four weeks, *ABBA—The Album* lacks artistic coherence and, notwithstanding the timeless classic *Thank You for the Music*, the final triptych, *The Girl with the Golden Hair*, even risks losing the listener. While the success achieved by *ABBA—The Album* can hardly be described as modest (after all, by this time ABBA was one of the best-selling bands on the planet), fans who bought it were a little more circumspect in their response, as they had undoubtedly been hoping for a host of easy-listening hits. For Ulvaeus and Andersson, this was an eye-opener and a sign that they needed to change the way they worked. The album had been recorded in a hurry and the songwriters wouldn't make that mistake again.

In 1978, for the first time, there would be no recording schedule, with the band preferring to concentrate on their new priorities: building Polar Music Studios for Ulvaeus and Andersson, and the birth of Agnetha and Björn's second child, Peter Christian, on 4 December 1977. Central to ABBA's aims over the next two years was observing the rapid evolution of the music scene and producing an album that was obviously coherent. They would soon return bigger, better, and ready to win back their audiences.

Lasse Hallström, who filmed the music videos for all of ABBA's singles, except *Chiquitita*, *On and On and On*, *The Day Before You Came*, and *Under Attack*.

Overleaf: Filming some of the scenes from *ABBA–The Movie* in room 819 of Stockholm's Sheraton hotel.

Agnetha was heavily pregnant by the time the overdubs for the *ABBA–The Movie* soundtrack were recorded in September 1977, so she didn't travel to Bohus studios in Kungälv. Frida therefore supplied Agnetha's harmonizations and backing vocals.

ABBA–THE MOVIE: ABBA IN PANAVISION

When ABBA's European and Australian tour got underway on 29 January 1977, the band took with them Lasse Hallström, who had produced all their videos since *Waterloo* in 1974 and was tasked with filming their life on the road so that he could later compile the footage into a promotional video or television program. Equipped with a 16mm camera, Hallström joined the tour and even filmed ABBA's concert at London's Royal Albert Hall on 14 February. Just as the team was preparing to fly to Australia on 3 March, Hallström received a call from the Reg Grundy Organization, offering to provide him with a 35mm Panavision camera and suggesting he should turn his film into a story. Hallström wrote the synopsis of what would become *ABBA–The Movie* on the flight to Sydney: Ashley Wallace, a radio presenter played by actor Robert Hughes, spends the whole Australian tour desperately trying to land an interview with the group. The final film incorporated footage from the concerts and the band's daily life in Australia, along with extra scenes shot in Sweden to flesh out the plot. These included a sequence where Benny and Björn were seen reading the American papers in their hotel room in Perth, which was in fact filmed at the Sheraton in Sweden. Although the filming was fairly chaotic (the director, like his character, frequently found himself being barred from entering the concerts by over-zealous bodyguards and unable to contact the band), *ABBA–The Movie*, like Richard Lester's films *A Hard Day's Night (1964)* and *Help! (1965)*, starring The Beatles, is a thrilling insight into the band on the road, especially as ABBA rarely performed on stage after that tour. "If you regard it as a document of what ABBA was, this film is incredibly good. It shows a lot of what ABBA represented: energy,"[74] Benny Andersson said in the bonus section of the *ABBA–The Movie* DVD. Lasse Hallström would go on to a brilliant career as a director, with *Mitt Liv Som Hund/My Life as a Dog* (1985), *What's Eating Gilbert Grape* (1993), *Chocolat* (2001), and many other great films to his name.

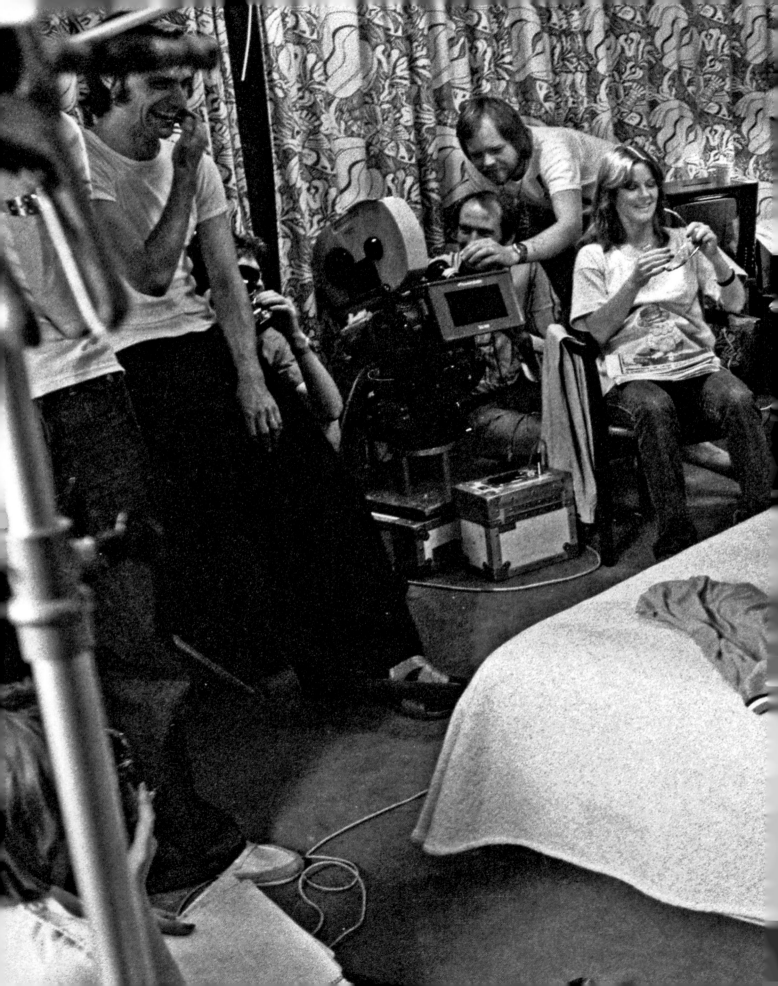

Single

EAGLE

(Benny Andersson, Björn Ulvaeus/5'51)

Musicians

Agnetha Fältskog: vocals, backing vocals
Anni-Frid "Frida" Lyngstad: vocals, backing vocals
Benny Andersson: synthesizers, backing vocals
Björn Ulvaeus: acoustic guitar, backing vocals
Janne Schaffer: electric guitar
Lasse Wellander: electric guitar
Rutger Gunnarsson: bass
Ola Brunkert: drums
Malando Gassama: percussion

Recording

Marcus Music, Solna: 1 to 2, 12 June 1977

Technical team

Producers: Björn Ulvaeus, Benny Andersson
Sound engineer: Michael B Tretow

1977

Single

A-side: *Eagle*/3'36
B-side: *Thank You for the Music*/3'48
Released in Sweden by Polar Music: 18 May 1978
(single ref.: POS 1237)
Released in the USA by Atlantic: April 1978 (single ref.: 3469)
Best chart ranking in Sweden: did not make the charts
Best chart ranking in the USA: did not make the charts

HEADPHONES AT THE READY

For the intro to their 1981 hit *Don't You Want Me*, British band The Human League claim to have been inspired by the intro to *Eagle*, borrowing the sounds Benny Andersson had created with his Polymoog 203a.

Genesis

After the band returned to Sweden in March 1977, Benny and Björn worked on the post-production of *ABBA–The Movie*. In addition to the numerous scenes that had to be filmed in Stockholm, the director, Lasse Hallström, asked them to write two new songs with lyrics adapted to the film script. While the first, *The Name of the Game*, contains a few sporadic references to the script, the same cannot be said for the second, *Eagle*, whose lyrics refer to a best-selling book Björn Ulvaeus had just finished reading: *Jonathan Livingston Seagull* by Richard Bach, an allegorical story about a bird's quest to fly high and find freedom. *Eagle* was released as a single in a number of European countries in May 1978, but only as a limited edition in Sweden, where it didn't even make the charts. For some reason, in the USA too the single—with *Thank You for the Music* on the B-side—was withdrawn from sale immediately after release and Atlantic reused its catalog number, 3469, for one of their other singles, *Everybody Dance* by Chic.

Production

When recording got underway at Marcus Music studios in Solna, Benny and Björn spent the first few days experimenting with new sound textures, influenced by their trip to Los Angeles in early May 1977. The results are clearly audible in the first bars of *Eagle*, which opens the album. Benny, who once again used his Polymoog 203a synthesizer to add ethereal pads to the track, was supported by guitarist Janne Schaffer's effects on his Morley Echo pedal—already heard on 1974's *So Long*—to simulate the cry of seagulls above the waves, as well as using the picking technique popularized by Brian May of Queen several years before. Sound engineer Michael B Tretow explained: "They were played by Janne Schaffer, who gets the basic sound by plucking one string both ways, i.e., up and down very quickly, while running down the fretboard with the left hand."[75] During concerts, ABBA's other regular guitarist Lasse Wellander treated audiences to a spectacular solo, making *Eagle* one of his favorite ABBA songs to perform on stage.

Richard Bach, the American author who wrote the best-selling novel *Jonathan Livingston Seagull*.

The rhythm of his daily run was Björn Ulvaeus's inspiration for the melody of *Take a Chance on Me*.

Overleaf: ABBA in 1977.

Single

TAKE A CHANCE ON ME

(Benny Andersson, Björn Ulvaeus/4'05)

Musicians

Agnetha Fältskog: vocals, backing vocals
Anni-Frid "Frida" Lyngstad: vocals, spoken voice, backing vocals
Benny Andersson: synthesizers, backing vocals
Björn Ulvaeus: acoustic guitar, backing vocals
Lasse Wellander: electric guitar
Rutger Gunnarsson: bass
Roger Palm: drums, tambourine

Recording

Marcus Music, Solna: 3, 15, 17 August 1977
Metronome, Stockholm: 18, 24 October 1977

Technical team

Producers: Björn Ulvaeus, Benny Andersson
Sound engineer: Michael B Tretow

Single

A-side: *Take a Chance on Me*/4'05
B-side: *I'm a Marionette*/3'54
Released in the UK by CBS/Epic: January 1978
(single ref.: S EPC 5950)
Released in the USA by Atlantic: 22 April 1978 (single ref.: 3457)
Best chart ranking in the UK: 1
Best chart ranking in the USA : 3

Genesis

Björn Ulvaeus has revealed in interviews that he is a keen runner and likes to go running every day in the forests near his home in Lidingö. "I'll never stop until I'll die,"[76] he said in the *ABBA in Concert* documentary in 1980. Björn didn't just exercise for health reasons—he was also inspired by his running cadence when he wrote the song that became one of ABBA's biggest hits. "When I'm in the middle of writing a lyric, I think about it when I run. [...] I was running around my neighborhood [...] and it was like a rhythm, you know: 'Taka-tch, taka-tch.'"[76] The words to accompany the rhythm came to him instantly: "Take a chance," perfect for a new composition whose backing tracks he had already recorded with Benny Andersson and the ABBA musicians on 3 August 1977. "For this particular song," he said in 2008, "there was no image, no scenario, there was only the title phrase, and I constructed the lyric around that."[35] Once the famous riff for the chorus, "Take-a-chance, Take-a-take-a-chance-chance," was recorded, Ulvaeus added the "on me" to the track and wrote the lyrics for the song about a young woman making advances to a man she has fallen in love with.

Production

The demo, with the working title *Billy Boy*, had a very conspicuous piano line, as featured in the first few minutes of *ABBA Undeleted*, an excellent medley over 23 minutes long that was made up of studio takes that ABBA had rejected and that came free with the 1994 box set *Thank You for the Music*. It was probably to make the song sound more up to date that Benny Andersson decided to replace the piano with various synth tracks. With a drum pattern similar to *Dancing Queen* and its obvious commercial potential, *Take a Chance on Me* is a departure from the experimental feel of the rest of *ABBA–The Album* and gives audiences another eminently danceable hit. The directors of Atlantic, ABBA's US distributors, made the right decision when they placed huge quantities of the single in record stores: it instantly boosted album sales stateside.

1977

ONE MAN, ONE WOMAN

(Benny Andersson, Björn Ulvaeus/4'25)

Musicians

Anni-Frid "Frida" Lyngstad: lead vocals, backing vocals
Agnetha Fältskog: vocals, backing vocals
Benny Andersson: synthesizers, piano, backing vocals
Björn Ulvaeus: acoustic guitar, backing vocals
Lasse Wellander: electric guitar
Rutger Gunnarsson: bass
Roger Palm: drums
Martin Bylund: violin
Tullo Galli: violin
Inge Lindstedt: violin
Gunnar Michols: violin
Claes Nilsson: violin
Bertil Orsin: violin
Lars Stegenberg: violin
Sixten Strömvall: violin
Harry Teike: violin
Kryztof Zdrzalka: violin
Lars Arvinder: viola
Niels Heie: viola
Håkan Roos: viola
Bo Söderström: viola
Hans-Göran Eketorp: cello
Olle Gustafsson: cello

Recording

Marcus Music, Solna: 18 June, 9 November 1977

Technical team

Producers: Björn Ulvaeus, Benny Andersson
Sound engineer: Michael B Tretow
String arrangements: Rutger Gunnarsson

Genesis

It would be impossible to calculate how many songs have been written about break-ups, a classic theme in all types of contemporary music from pop and rock to variety and other diverse styles around the world. But when ABBA sang about break-ups, as they did in 1976 with *Knowing Me, Knowing You* and in 1977 with *One Man, One Woman*, the lyrics took on a more personal meaning, as it was, of course, common knowledge that the band consisted of two couples. Here, Frida sings about a relationship falling apart and a couple who are unable to talk through their issues. Doors slam, the silence is deafening and their love is disappearing over the horizon. However, the two protagonists seem prepared to fight to save their relationship and the end of the song brings renewed hope. Although Agnetha and Björn had just welcomed their second child, Peter Christian, into the world, their relationship was heading for the rocks. History tells us that their marriage had started to crumble a few months earlier and their subsequent separation was big news in the music press in 1978. It was also central to many ABBA songs between 1979 and 1982. Prophetically, as keen observers of the group had already spotted with *Knowing Me, Knowing You*, Björn described the end of his relationship with Agnetha in *One Man, One Woman*.

Production

While Benny Andersson's Polymoog 203a synthesizer is as omnipresent on the track as on the rest of the album, the piano also plays a major role in this song. Despite his attraction to electronic instruments, Andersson has always proclaimed his affection for his second favorite instrument, after the accordion, describing it years later as more "real" than electronic equipment: "[…] it doesn't have the fine adjustment like with a violin where you can decide exactly where you want to put your finger to make the notes, but otherwise the piano has everything: it's a rhythmic instrument, it's melodic, and the grand piano in particular looks great."[35]

1977

Above: Benny and Frida on a flight to Warsaw, 7 October 1976.
Overleaf: On stage at Brøndby Hallen, near Copenhagen, January 1977.

Single

THE NAME OF THE GAME

(Benny Andersson, Stig Anderson, Björn Ulvaeus/4'54)

Musicians
Agnetha Fältskog: vocals, backing vocals
Anni-Frid "Frida" Lyngstad: vocals, backing vocals
Benny Andersson: synthesizers, backing vocals
Björn Ulvaeus: acoustic guitar, backing vocals
Lasse Wellander: electric guitar
Rutger Gunnarsson: bass
Ola Brunkert: drums
Malando Gassama: percussion

Recording
Marcus Music, Solna: 31 May 1977

Technical team
Producers: Björn Ulvaeus, Benny Andersson
Sound engineer: Michael B Tretow

Single
A-side: *The Name of the Game*/4'53
B-side: *I Wonder (Departure)* (live)/4'27
Released in Sweden by Polar Music: 17 October 1977
(single ref.: POS 1234)
Released in the UK by CBS/Epic: 17 October 1977
(single ref.: S EPC 5750)
Released in the USA by Atlantic: 24 December 1977
(single ref.: 3449)
Best chart ranking in Sweden: 2
Best chart ranking in the UK: 1
Best chart ranking in the USA: 12

1977

Genesis

When ABBA returned to Sweden after their Australian tour, filmmaker Lasse Hallström asked Benny and Björn to provide two new songs for the scenes he still had to shoot in Stockholm. One of them was about a dream the radio presenter Ashley Wallace has in which he is a psychoanalyst listening to his patient—Agnetha Fältskog—reveal her feelings for him. Setting the words to a track he and Andersson had recorded in May 1977, Ulvaeus wrote the lyrics for *The Name of the Game*, which at the time had the working title *A Bit of Myself.* It was Stig Anderson who came up with the definitive name for the song, whose first lines "I've seen you twice, in a short time/ Only a week since we started/It seems to me, for every time/ I'm getting more open-hearted" are the words Agnetha speaks to her therapist in the film. Shortly before the release of *ABBA–The Album,* Polar Music still couldn't decide which track would be the new single. For a while they considered the rock number *Hole in Your Soul,* but in the end they chose this mid-tempo ballad, reflecting the more adventurous direction the band wanted to take. "It's a bit more unusual than our earlier material…," Frida said later. "There's some form of development."[73]

Although not one of the band's best-known songs, *The Name of the Game* was very well received on its release, even reaching number one in the UK charts. Then in 1997, it became one of only two songs that Andersson and Ulvaeus allowed to be sampled by other artists. In this case the group concerned was Fugees, who used it in segments of *Rumble in the Jungle,* a track recorded for the soundtrack of the Leon Gast documentary *When We Were Kings,* about the Muhammad Ali/ George Foreman fight on 30 October 1974. In 2008, Benny Andersson admitted he had been very flattered that this "incredibly hip American band" had wanted to use an ABBA song dating from 20 years earlier. "I think they are a great band and Lauryn Hill is a fabulous singer. Once we had agreed to them using the bass line, they could use it however they wanted: I didn't feel any sense of possessiveness."[35]

Production

With a pattern based on a synth riff reminiscent of *I Wish* on Stevie Wonder's 1976 album *Songs in the Key of Life, The Name of the Game* joins *My Mama Said* and *Man in the Middle* on the podium of ABBA songs with a genuine funk groove.

Above: Frida and Agnetha recording *ABBA—The Album* in 1977.
Overleaf: Benny Andersson reviewing his performance in the Polar Music offices, July 1977.

However, the track quickly morphs into a ballad with highly effective choruses, carried by the singing of Frida and Agnetha, who, for once, split the song according to their respective vocal ranges. The piece is mainly sung in two voices, with Agnetha concluding the verses and Frida the choruses, for which Benny and Björn provide a vocal counterpoint. "The girls' voices are essential to the sound, of course, because they had these extremely compatible voices," explained Michael B Tretow. "Agnetha was very punchy and Frida had this hi-fi quality to it. Because it was both very bright and very soft bassy in itself."[67]

MOVE ON

(Benny Andersson, Stig Anderson, Björn Ulvaeus/4'42)

1977

Musicians

Agnetha Fältskog: lead vocals, backing vocals
Anni-Frid "Frida" Lyngstad: vocals, backing vocals
Benny Andersson: synthesizers, Fender Rhodes, piano, backing vocals
Björn Ulvaeus: spoken voice, acoustic guitar, electric guitar, backing vocals
Lasse Wellander: electric guitar
Rutger Gunnarsson: bass
Ola Brunkert: drums
Lars O Carlsson: flute
Malando Gassama: congas, percussion

Recording

Marcus Music, Solna: 4 to 5, 8 August, 10, 15 October 1977

Technical team

Producers: Björn Ulvaeus, Benny Andersson
Sound engineer: Michael B Tretow

Genesis

Although our four artists have always said that Sweden is their home, their repertoire also clearly shows that they hanker after far-flung destinations. After the invitation to join Frida on her paradise island in 1975's *Tropical Loveland*, the memories of Mexico in 1976's *Fernando*, and vacations in the USA's most exotic state in 1977's *Happy Hawaii*, Agnetha sings about the benefits of travel and a change of scenery in this, the juiciest morsel on *ABBA—The Album*. Inspired by Richard Bach's novel *Jonathan Livingston Seagull*, Björn Ulvaeus had written about freedom on the album's first track, *Eagle*, and for *Move On* he returned to the subject. This invitation to travel (seeking out the sun, perhaps?) would soon crop up again, notably on the band's 1980 album *Gracias por la Musica*, which consisted of tracks re-recorded in Spanish, and in the musical *Mamma Mia!*, set on the beaches of Kalokairi, a fictional Greek island.

Production

Instrumentally, the song is heavily influenced by the ethereal folk feel of Fleetwood Mac's album *Rumours*, a colossal worldwide hit that left its mark on Benny Andersson. "I thought they were wonderful. *Rumours* would be one of my top ten albums of all time; I know I played it hundreds of times after it came out."[73] It was undoubtedly his attraction to the compositions of Stevie Nicks, Christine McVie, and Lindsay Buckingham that led Andersson to incorporate American sounds, midway between folk and country, into the album, as is demonstrated by Mats Rosén's steel-guitar contribution. Rosén, a Swedish honky-tonk specialist, had previously appeared on albums by Red Jenkins and Country Masarna, two worthy representatives of Scandinavian Americana, a popular music trend at the time. Production of *Move On* took a different direction after Rosén's scores were dropped and Lars O Carlsson's flute was added on 15 October. This more Latino sound perfectly suits Björn's lyrics about travel, freedom, and personal development.

ABBA decided to
have some of their
instruments painted
white for various tours.

ABBA standing next to Benny and Frida's Maserati Merak SS AM 122, 1976.

Overleaf: Benny and Björn with guitars belonging to the latter, respectively an Ovation Breadwinner and a Gibson Les Paul Deluxe, in the Polar Music offices.

HOLE IN YOUR SOUL

(Benny Andersson, Björn Ulvaeus/3'41)

1977

Musicians
Agnetha Fältskog: vocals, backing vocals
Anni-Frid "Frida" Lyngstad: vocals, backing vocals
Björn Ulvaeus: vocals, electric guitar, backing vocals
Benny Andersson: synthesizers, piano, Fender Rhodes, backing vocals
Lasse Wellander: electric guitar
Rutger Gunnarsson: bass
Ola Brunkert: drums
Malando Gassama: congas, percussion

Recording
Marcus Music, Solna: 3 August 1977

Technical team
Producers: Björn Ulvaeus, Benny Andersson
Sound engineer: Michael B Tretow

Genesis

Although too often referred to as a disco group, ABBA have always managed to blur the genres by incorporating pop, or even rock, tracks into their albums, as with the explosive *Hole in Your Soul*. The British punk movement was at its height in 1977 and Benny Andersson steered well clear of it, aware that the message it conveyed was totally incompatible with the spirit of ABBA. "That was like a stone crusher zooming by outside the window, nothing more," he explained in the liner notes for the deluxe edition of *ABBA–The Album*, released as a CD in 2007. "I just couldn't get into it. Not even the energy of it, because there was an enormous energy. I think I was too old even then."[73]

Production

Hole in Your Soul rose from the ashes of *Get on the Carousel*, the fourth and last song in the mini-musical *The Girl with the Golden Hair*, with which ABBA concluded each concert on their 1977 tour. *Hole in Your Soul* retains the energy, rock'n' roll color, and part of the structure of *Get on the Carousel*, notably the melody in the chorus originally sung by Lena Andersson, Lena-Maria Gårdenäs-Lawton, and Maritza Horn, the backing vocalists on the tour. In *Hole in Your Soul*, Frida and Agnetha recorded this melody, which appears on the bridge at 1'43, with great verve. Fans would probably have loved to hear *Get on the Carousel* in its entirety after *I'm a Marionette* on *ABBA–The Album*. Fortunately, a large section of the live version appears in all its glory on the 50th minute of the *ABBA–The Movie* DVD. There has never been a studio recording of the song.

"THE GIRL WITH THE GOLDEN HAIR" – 3 SCENES FROM A MINI-MUSICAL – THANK YOU FOR THE MUSIC

(Benny Andersson, Björn Ulvaeus/3'48)

Musicians
Agnetha Fältskog: lead vocals, backing vocals
Anni-Frid "Frida" Lyngstad: backing vocals
Benny Andersson: synthesizers, piano, backing vocals
Björn Ulvaeus: backing vocals
Lasse Wellander: acoustic guitar, mandolin, backing vocals
Rutger Gunnarsson: bass
Roger Palm: drums, tambourine

Recording
Glen Studio, Stockholm: 21 June, September 1977

Technical team
Producers: Björn Ulvaeus, Benny Andersson
Sound engineer: Michael B Tretow

Single
A-side: *Thank You for the Music*/3'48
B-side: *Our Last Summer*/4'20
Released in the UK by CBS/Epic: 6 November 1983
(single ref.: A 3894)
Best chart ranking in the UK: 33

1977

Genesis

Benny Andersson and Björn Ulvaeus first thought of writing a musical in 1970, when their manager Stig Anderson sent them a promotional edition of the *Jesus Christ Superstar* concept album written by Tim Rice and Andrew Lloyd Webber. The success of the subsequent rock opera, first performed on Broadway in 1971, encouraged the two Swedes to think about the idea again. They came up with a concept called *The Girl with the Golden Hair,* which became part of every performance on ABBA's 1977 tour. This mini-musical is based on a simple idea. A young woman tells the story of her meteoric rise in show business, from which she will not emerge unscathed. Performed at the close of every concert, *The Girl with the Golden Hair* consisted of four songs: *Thank You for the Music, I Wonder (Departure), I'm a Marionette*, and *Get on the Carousel.* Dressed in identical white outfits and blonde wigs, Frida and Agnetha put in an energetic performance, with each song introduced by British actor Francis Matthews, who played the role of narrator. Although this segment of the concerts was not without interest, audiences were not entirely convinced by it, as they had mostly come to hear the band's classics rather than musical experiments. Benny Andersson later admitted that including it hadn't been a great decision; he put this down to the band's not spending a lot of time on the road, and not being "in tune with what audience really wanted."[35]

Thank You for the Music was recorded for the first time on 2 June 1977, to be used on the new album, then re-recorded on 21 July in a version better suited to the ABBA universe. Agnetha Fältskog, as lead vocalist, sings candidly about the heroine's naivety and how she has always been pushed to achieve her dream of being a singer.

During the 1977 tour, every evening Agnetha and Frida assumed the role of *The Girl with the Golden Hair.*

An iconic image of the group, shot by Alex Henderson for the promotion of *ABBA–The Movie*.

The song became an ABBA classic, despite being released as a single only in Belgium, Holland, Germany, France, Austria, and Switzerland, as a double A-side with *Eagle* in May 1978. On 6 November 1983, it was released as a single in the UK to promote yet another CBS compilation, also called *Thank You for the Music*. As ABBA had dropped off the radar by then, the single reached only number 33 in the UK charts.

Production

Michael B Tretow wanted to give *Thank You for the Music* the music-hall feel he felt it deserved. So he added a choral effect to Benny Andersson's piano that very slightly varied the pitch of the notes, in the style of the honky-tonk pianos in American bars during the Great Depression that were slightly off-key due to lack of regular tuning. It is very effective, and in the track's overall mood listeners can easily discern an elegant nod to Bob Fosse's 1972 film *Cabaret*, or even the musical *Chicago* by Bob Fosse, Fred Ebb, and John Kander, which opened on Broadway in June 1975. Not Liza Minnelli this time, but Agnetha Fältskog absolutely singing her heart out. At the time of the recording, in September 1977, she was heavily pregnant and had been advised by doctors not to stand while she was working. So she did her takes lying down.

"THE GIRL WITH THE GOLDEN HAIR" – 3 SCENES FROM A MINI-MUSICAL – I WONDER (DEPARTURE)

(Benny Andersson, Stig Anderson, Björn Ulvaeus/4'33)

Musicians

Anni-Frid "Frida" Lyngstad: lead vocals, backing vocals
Agnetha Fältskog: vocals, backing vocals
Benny Andersson: piano, backing vocals
Björn Ulvaeus: acoustic guitar, electric guitar, backing vocals
Lasse Wellander: electric guitar
Rutger Gunnarsson: bass
Ola Brunkert: drums
Bengt Sundberg: horn
Bo Eriksson: oboe
Martin Bylund: violin
Anders Dahl: violin
Inge Lindstedt: violin
Gunnar Michols: violin
Claes Nilsson: violin
Bernt Nylund: violin
Lars Stegenberg: violin
Bo Söderström: violin
Harry Teike: violin
Snorri Thorvaldsson: violin
Kryztof Zdrzalka: violin
Lars Arvinder: viola
Niels Heie: viola
Örjan Högberg: viola
Håkan Roos: viola
Hans-Göran Eketorp: cello
Gloria Lundell: harp

Recording

Marcus Music, Solna: 2 August 1977
Europa Film, Stockholm: 8 September 1977

Technical team

Producers: Björn Ulvaeus, Benny Andersson
Sound engineer: Michael B Tretow
String arrangements: Rutger Gunnarsson

Genesis

I Wonder (Departure) is the second segment of the three-part *The Girl with the Golden Hair*. It tells the story of a girl who is hesitant about leaving the comfort of her small village to follow her destiny. Sung by Frida Lyngstad, the song is a poignant ballad that makes direct reference to the singer's youth, firstly when she left her native Norway for Sweden at the age of two, and then when she left her husband and two children, Hans and Ann Lise-Lotte, in 1969, to pursue her career as an artist. "We wanted a sad ballad and as always the melody came first," Björn Ulvaeus said. "I felt that it would provide the vehicle for explaining this girl's trepidation, the worry that surrounds any departure, the feeling of what's going to happen to me."[35] The live version of the song did well as the B-side of the single *The Name of the Game* when it was released in October 1977.

Production

To emphasize the lyrical side to this song, Benny and Björn decided to add string arrangements, which were more authentic than the modulations available on the various synthesizers Benny used at the time. Once again, it was bassist Rutger Gunnarsson who wrote the arrangements, supplying an effective score that gave the song the depth it needed in order to move listeners. The takes were recorded at Europa Film studios in Stockholm, under the watchful eye of the band, who had come over from Marcus Music, a few miles away in Solna, where they were busy finalizing the overdubs for the soundtrack to *ABBA–The Movie*.

Rutger Gunnarsson wrote one of his finest string scores for *I Wonder (Departure)*.

Overleaf: Rutger Gunnarsson and Benny Andersson on stage at the Ekeberg Idrettshall, Oslo, on 28 January 1977.

"THE GIRL WITH THE GOLDEN HAIR" – 3 SCENES FROM A MINI-MUSICAL –
I'M A MARIONETTE

(Benny Andersson, Björn Ulvaeus/3'54)

Musicians

Agnetha Fältskog: vocals, backing vocals
Anni-Frid "Frida" Lyngstad: vocals, backing vocals
Benny Andersson: synthesizers, piano, marimba, backing vocals
Björn Ulvaeus: backing vocals
Lasse Wellander: electric guitar
Rutger Gunnarsson: bass
Ola Brunkert: drums
Malando Gassama: percussion
Martin Bylund: violin
Tullo Galli: violin
Inge Lindstedt: violin
Gunnar Michols: violin
Claes Nilsson: violin
Bertil Orsin: violin
Lars Stegenberg: violin
Sixten Strömvall: violin
Harry Teike: violin
Kryztof Zdrzalka: violin
Lars Arvinder: viola
Niels Heie: viola
Håkan Roos: viola
Bo Söderström: viola
Hans-Göran Eketorp: cello
Olle Gustafsson: cello

Recording

Marcus Music, Solna: 1 August, 9 November 1977

Technical team

Producers: Björn Ulvaeus, Benny Andersson
Sound engineer: Michael B Tretow
String arrangements: Rutger Gunnarsson

Genesis

While the live version of *The Girl with the Golden Hair* ended with *Get on the Carousel,* in which the backing vocalists try to persuade the heroine to go into show business and she tries to get out of it, Andersson and Ulvaeus decided to end *ABBA–The Album* with *I'm a Marionette*, as they felt *Get on the Carousel* was not sufficiently well constructed for the album. In this third segment, our starlet loses control of her destiny, likening herself to a puppet whose every act and move are controlled by someone else. To illustrate this episode on stage, Frida and Agnetha, coached by their dance teacher Graham Tainton, moved around like puppets, although, in hindsight the choreography looks a bit clumsy. The director added his personal touch to the sequence, playing with special effects to repeat some of the actors' actions. Agnetha later told an amusing anecdote about it: "One evening Frida's wig was not on very tight and she did a dance move and her wig came off. We had our own hair underneath, in a sock, so poor Frida was on stage with her hair on her head in a big sock. We just laughed so much."[34]

Production

Benny Andersson has happily admitted that this is an unusual song. With choruses built around triplets supported by clashing cymbals, it clearly evokes a tragic finale to an opera, amplified by Rutger Gunnarsson's string arrangements, recorded on 9 November 1977. But the key sequence in the track is undeniably Lasse Wellander's guitar solo, executed at a tempo of almost 140 bpm and accentuated by Gunnarsson and Brunkert's rock-solid rhythm section. "I used a Fender '62 Strat on most of the songs in the studio and on the tours," Wellander explained. "But the pickups were very weak and there was more hum than sound sometimes. [...] I changed the bridge pickup to a stacked humbucker because the single coil was weak and there was always trouble with the distorted sound. I also played a Gibson ES-175 on some of the songs. For many years I used a Music Man amp, the small one, the 112HD. The Strat is now in the ABBA museum in Stockholm."[44]

THANK YOU FOR THE MUSIC (DORIS DAY MIX)

(Benny Andersson, Björn Ulvaeus/4'03)

Musicians

Agnetha Fältskog: lead vocals, backing vocals
Anni-Frid "Frida" Lyngstad: vocals, backing vocals
Benny Andersson: synthesizers, piano, backing vocals
Björn Ulvaeus: backing vocals
Janne Schaffer: acoustic guitar
Rutger Gunnarsson: bass
Ola Brunkert: drums

Recording

Marcus Music, Solna: 2 June

Technical team

Producers: Björn Ulvaeus, Benny Andersson
Sound engineer: Michael B Tretow

Genesis

On 2 June 1977, ABBA recorded the first version of *Thank You for the Music* as the intro to the musical *The Girl with the Golden Hair*, which would conclude *ABBA–The Album*. Benny Andersson was on piano, Janne Schaffer on acoustic guitar, Rutger Gunnarsson on bass, and Ola Brunkert on drums. This was a real jazz-ragtime track, redolent of the cabaret atmosphere of post-war clubs; Agnetha Fältskog, as lead vocalist, takes her inspiration from one of her idols, the American actress and singer Doris Day. Despite a great take in which Fältskog shines with perfect accuracy and stunning vocal effects (those amazing tremolos on the choruses…), the band didn't approve this version and so they re-recorded the song on 21 July. The original take re-emerged 17 years later in 1994 on the *Thank You for the Music* box set, entitled *Thank You for the Music (Doris Day Mix)*.

Production

As with classic songs in musicals, it's the piano that takes the lead on *Thank You for the Music (Doris Day Mix)*. The other musicians simply follow Andersson in that discreet and obliging manner of the best studio artists. Janne Schaffer, who plays acoustic guitar on the track, later talked about how he worked with Benny: "It was important to know my chord theory, because I played together with Benny all the time, trying to find the right things to fit his piano playing. Everything would start with his idea of how the melodies sounded and then how we added to it. I wouldn't say it was normal guitar chords and it took a bit of figuring things out, but I was used to working like that. You can hear a lot of heavy rock guitars in the first and second albums. We'd been listening to Deep Purple."[40] With its sparkling piano and affected vocals, this is a rare gem that is well worth (re)discovering, as it reveals an unvarnished and unadorned side to ABBA and showcases their undeniable talent.

VOULEZ-VOUS

As Good As New • Voulez-Vous • I Have A Dream • Angeleyes •
The King Has Lost His Crown • Does Your Mother Know • If It Wasn't For The Nights •
Chiquitita • Lovers (Live A Little Longer) • Kisses Of Fire

Released in Sweden by Polar Music: 23 April 1979 (LP ref.: POLS 292)
Released in the UK by CBS/Epic: 23 April 1979 (LP ref.: EPC 86086)
Released in the USA by Atlantic: 23 April 1979 (LP ref.: SD 16000)
Best chart ranking in Sweden: 1
Best chart ranking in the UK: 1
Best chart ranking in the USA: 19

For the cover of their most disco album, ABBA held a photo shoot in Alexandra's club in Stockholm.

Overleaf: A gala evening with Olivia Newton-John and Andy Gibb, whose single *Shadow Dancing* was making the whole world dance.

ABBA'S DISCO PHASE

1979

Even though Norway, Sweden, and even the UK warmly welcomed *ABBA–The Album*, sending it to the top of the charts, the group's members and their manager, Stig Anderson, had to be content with number 14 in the American charts. Since the success of the single *Take a Chance on Me* in the USA had not been enough to propel the record to the top of the *Billboard* chart, our friends decided at the start of 1978 to conquer that country—the last bastion of resistance to their international success—once and for all. Their first action was to postpone the release of the film *ABBA–The Movie* in the USA, in order to make it coincide with their visit in the spring. "We are intending to wait a little while before releasing the film in the States," Frida explained at the time, "because we have still a lot of work to do making new friends in America. America is a hard place to crack especially as it is so big, but obviously we would love to do as well there as everywhere else. We are all hoping that this visit will help us along a bit as far as America is concerned."[77]

Working closely with their US distributor Atlantic, ABBA arranged to travel to Los Angeles in May, in a blaze of publicity. A gigantic hoarding was even installed on Sunset Boulevard, announcing that ABBA was now the group that had sold the most albums in the whole history of recorded music. Repeating to anyone who would listen that ABBA had outdone The Beatles in this respect (a claim that was quickly challenged by specialists), Atlantic succeeded in getting the attention of the press, which began to take an interest in the group. The magazine *Creem*, which specialized in heavy rock, described them in these terms: "The Beach Boys Meets Kraftwerk By Way Of The Honeys,"[21] and ABBA were even

invited on to the show *Olivia!*, presented by the actor and singer Olivia Newton-John, then fresh from the success of her hits *If You Love Me, Let Me Know,* and *Have You Never Been Mellow*, released in 1974 and 1975. The episode, which was shot on 8 May 1978 and broadcast nine days later on ABC, offered ABBA a high degree of exposure, as they appeared with Andy Gibb—younger brother of Barry, Robin, and Maurice Gibb of The Bee Gees, and the star of the moment thanks to the success of his album *Shadow Dancing*. Alongside Olivia Newton-John (whom ABBA had beaten in the 1974 Eurovision Song Contest, where she had represented the UK with her song *Long Live Love*), Agnetha, Frida, Björn, and Benny performed several songs, including *Take a Chance on Me* and *Fernando*, hoping to benefit from the program's 30 million viewers to revive sales of *ABBA–The Album*. "The whole thing was a beautiful experience," Benny said about shooting *Olivia!* "It was one of the best shows we've ever done. [...] Of course, we've done the usual quota of TV talk shows in America, but this one with Olivia was an important step for us."[78]

Fältskog and Ulvaeus break up

After this promotional marathon, the group returned to Stockholm to work on a new album that would finally win over the American public. Although they had already recorded two new songs at the end of April—*Lovers (Live a Little Longer)* and *Lovelight*—Benny and Björn struggled to find inspiration to bring the successor to *ABBA–The Album* into being. From May, the official opening of Polar Music Studios, the brand new recording complex that would henceforth enable them

The members of ABBA with Stig Anderson, their manager and the head of Polar Music, on the occasion of the opening of the Polar Music Studio, 18 May 1978.

Voulez-Vous is the first ABBA album on which Stig Anderson receives no credit as co-writer, for the group's manager was by then completely involved in running Polar Music and its satellite companies. "I don't miss writing lyrics," he said at the time. "It was extremely demanding. Granted it contributed to the success of the business, but it isn't the kind of burden you want to carry for long a period of time."[1]

to work at their own pace, offered the two composers renewed creativity. There, they recorded another new song, *Summer Night City*, a potential disco hit that was very much of its time. Even though Benny and Björn composed most of their new songs in the basement of Agnetha and Björn's house in Lidingö, they worked relentlessly at Polar Music Studios, in the company of their faithful sound engineer, Michael B Tretow.

But the euphoria of finally owning their own studio was soon obscured by Björn and Agnetha's relationship problems which, during the summer of 1978, came to overshadow the creative process within the group. The couple went through a profound crisis, whose outcome seemed ever more uncertain. In October they decided to seek couples' therapy with the psychologist Hakan Lonnbak, whom Agnetha also consulted separately, thus giving rise to rumors of a liaison between the singer and her therapist. Despite all their efforts to save their marriage, in the autumn the two singers saw that it was disintegrating, and decided to separate. Although their divorce was not announced until the following January, from the end of 1978 Agnetha Fältskog and Björn Ulvaeus were no longer a couple. "Björn and I thought that we couldn't go on as a married couple any longer," Agnetha explained in 1980. "It was a joint decision. We both didn't take the first step. The end of a marriage doesn't have to mean the end of a group as well [...]. You can't spend eight years together, have two children together, without still having some feelings for each other. The only thing that I can say is that our music had absolutely nothing to do with our marital problems."[79]

Above: When he was not playing his 12-string Ovation Balladeer 1751, Björn remained faithful to his favorite make of guitar, Ibanez.
Opposite: Agnetha is interviewed by Michel Drucker on the show *Les Rendez-vous du dimanche* ("Sunday Meetings") in Paris, 12 April 1978.

Naturally, the separation was much talked about in January 1979, and the press became concerned about possible repercussions on ABBA's future. "There's absolutely no reason to worry about ABBA as a group," Björn declared during a press conference they held. "Our divorce only has private reasons. Agnetha and I simply couldn't live together any longer, although we've tried everything. The divorce was inevitable. As anyone can see, Agnetha and I will remain good friends."[80] Ironically, it was during this troubled period that Benny and Frida, who had been engaged for more than eight years, decided to get married. They tied the knot on 6 October 1978, in the small church at Lidingö—without telling anyone, not even Agnetha and Björn. They told their entourage about it the day after the secret wedding, during a large party that had been announced weeks earlier, but with no mention of any connection with the marriage.

The end of an era

Although ABBA's internal affairs were extremely painful, they interfered only temporarily with the progress of the album, which Björn and Benny were working hard to drive forward. Despite the terrible welcome that *Summer Night City* got from American radio stations, which discouraged Atlantic from releasing it as a single, the group continued with the production of their sixth album at Polar Music Studios. When their new single, *Chiquitita*, came out on 16 January 1979, they were once again struggling with a lack of inspiration. This forced them to postpone the release of the LP, for which they had so far recorded only five songs: *Chiquitita*, *Lovelight*, *Lovers (Live a Little Longer)*, *Dream World*, and *Summer Night City*. "Perhaps the divorce has played a part in that, after all it isn't easy, but it wasn't the deciding factor," Björn told the German magazine *Bravo*. "The true reason: Benny and I thought that the songs we had composed were not the best. We know that the fans expect something special from us every time. That's why we decided to get together again to compose some more."[81]

Like a sign of the times, presaging the coming decade during which the power of the media would be vastly increased, ABBA's affairs of the heart now caused more of a stir than any news about their new album. Immediately after Björn and Agnetha's divorce had been announced to the press, he revealed his relationship with Lena Källersjö, an advertising agent whom he had met at a new year's party thrown by Benny and Frida a few days earlier. "When Agnetha and I separated, I knew immediately that I would fall in love again,"

VOULEZ-VOUS

Björn explained. "I realized that I wasn't cut out for a bachelor's life. Despite all our problems we have done the right thing by getting divorced. We were both very selfish and this caused numerous arguments. Agnetha isn't jealous of my new girlfriend either. We often go out to dinner together. Lena and Agnetha get along great with each other."[82] Some time later, however, it was claimed that Björn was in a relationship with Liz Mitchell, lead singer of the group Boney M., something he quickly denied. "Liz Mitchell is really a wonderful woman. A real sport, intelligent, pretty and always in good spirits. I spent a couple of wonderful evenings with her in Leysin, but there absolutely isn't anything more serious between us. Liz has her fiancé that she is very fond of and soon will be married to."[83] As for Agnetha, she was soon seen in the company of Lars-Erik Ericsson, an ice hockey player with the Stockholm team AIK, whose exploits were reported by the press after his team won the Ahearne Cup in 1977. Their break-up a few months later saddled Agnetha with the image of a young single mother for many long years, in the eyes of the press. Her romantic distress was frequently noticed by ABBA watchers in the group's songs, even though she did not write them. A page had turned for ABBA, who now would have to develop without their image of a group built around two stable couples—perfect representatives of pop music for all the family, without any rough edges.

The last days of disco

The group's (very showbiz) troubles did not interfere with the release of their sixth album, which came out on 23 April 1979. The cover photograph, taken by Ola Lager in Alexandra's nightclub in Stockholm (where the clip of *Dancing Queen* had been shot three years earlier) made a clear statement: the year 1979 would be a year of disco—or not. In it, Benny is wearing a tuxedo, Björn a bright white shirt, and Agnetha and Frida elegant evening dresses. All four look ready to dance all night, despite their impassive expressions. From the first bars of the album, disco sounds gush from the stereo, introduced by the strings of *As Good as New*, whose arrangements, by Rutger Gunnarsson, immediately won praise as the finest string arrangements of the disco era. Potential hits come thick and fast on this danceable, melodious record—for example, *As Good as New*, *Voulez-Vous*, *Angeleyes*, and *If It Wasn't for the Nights*.

Above: Benny Andersson at his Yamaha CP80 keyboard, on stage at the Auditorium Theatre in Chicago, 30 September 1979.
Opposite: Lasse Wellander's solo in *Does Your Mother Know* was one of the high points of concerts in 1979.

But although it features remarkable songs, *Voulez-Vous* falls down on account of its lack of originality, which until then had been ABBA's unique feature. Certainly, *I Have a Dream* and *Chiquitita* recall the group's *schlager* influences, but the desire to reach out to a young audience eager to dance is far too obvious when you listen to the record, which labelled ABBA for ever as a "disco group"—even though their music is considerably more complex than that, as their subsequent albums clearly proved.

Although *Voulez-Vous* was another hit (especially in Japan, where it got an ecstatic welcome), its release coincided with the end of the disco era, for that style of music provoked controversy in the USA, where it was accused of putting out pointless messages, and of being artistically poor, even mediocre. On 12 July 1979, initiated by Steve Dahl, a disc jockey at the local WLUP-FM radio station, "Disco Demolition Night" was held at the Comiskey Park stadium in Chicago. Dahl asked his listeners to bring their records in order to treat them to a collective explosion in the interval between two

baseball matches between the Chicago White Sox and the Detroit Tigers. The event marked the end of this musical trend, which had been a colossal success all over the world, and whose hits had for years provoked the ire of rock fans. It must be said that, between 1977 and 1979, an overabundance of disco hits resulted in thousands of songs—to name but a few: *Stayin' Alive* by The Bee Gees, *I Feel Love* by Donna Summer, *Dance, Dance, Dance (Yowsah, Yowsah, Yowsah)* by Chic, and *You Make Me Feel (Mighty Real)* by Sylvester—flooding the airwaves to the point of nauseating listeners. It was against this background that in April 1979 ABBA released their most danceable album, displaying the power of their compositions but, inevitably, already appearing somewhat dated.

Joy and sorrow at Wembley Arena

The year 1979 also saw ABBA's last tour. The group, whose members had for several years declared their aversion to life on the road, nevertheless decided to embark on their biggest tour to date. In June, Polar Music issued a press release

Agnetha performs *I'm Still Alive*, which ABBA never recorded in the studio.

Overleaf: Although it was exhausting for the group, the 1979 tour marked the peak of ABBAmania.

FOR ABBA ADDICTS

Every evening during the tour of the USA and Europe, Agnetha sang a song that had never been heard before: *I'm Still Alive*, which she had written herself and whose lyrics, by Björn, described the difficulty of recovering from a break-up. This was the first in a long series of songs that implicitly alluded to the separation of Agnetha Fältskog and Björn Ulvaeus.

1979

announcing that ABBA would visit the USA, Canada, and Europe between 13 September and 15 November. Although they did not finish the tour, the six sell-out concerts the group performed at the Wembley Arena in London from 5 to 10 November 1979 bore witness to the progress they had made since starting out. The show was meant to be celebratory, but each evening concluded with the poignant *The Way Old Friends Do*, an anthem to reconciliation that had echoes of the recent separation of Björn and Agnetha. "It was momentous and successful, but for me it was awful," Agnetha said in 1997. "Björn and I had separated and I had torn myself away from the children. I just wanted to be home, home, home. But I had no choice. Björn and I were agreed about doing this tour together, despite the divorce, so we had to form a new relationship with each other and work together in a new way. It was an unfamiliar situation for all four of us—an ordeal by fire. I had no one to talk to. So I mourned alone."[59]

On 15 October 1979, as ABBA continued their tour, their new single, *Gimme! Gimme! Gimme! (A Man after Midnight)*, was released. Although it eventually became a cult song, it reached only number 16 in the Swedish charts on its release, and did not even make the *Billboard* chart in the USA. The decade that was drawing to a close seemed to mark the end of an era for the group, yet their worldwide success had never been so great.

POLAR MUSIC STUDIO:
THE ROLLS-ROYCE OF
RECORDING STUDIOS

From 1977, the tireless Benny Andersson and Björn Ulvaeus needed to face up to an insoluble problem: the various recording studios in Stockholm and its suburbs were constantly fully booked, which forced them to rush from one to another, according to their availability. The two artists and their manager, Stig Anderson, quickly decided to embark on the construction of their own recording complex, which was to become Polar Music's flagship and ABBA's work tool. In an interview with *ABBA Magazine* in 1978, Benny explained the reasons behind this project: "In the past we have often been held up with recording, because we have not been able to get studio time. [...] We are now well used to most of the Swedish studios, but having to wait for a studio to become free when you are in a hurry to finish an album is a considerable nuisance [...], so we decided recently to build our studio so that we could record, mix, and so on whenever we wanted to do so."[84] The three Polar Music associates then agreed to use the revenue from the sales of *ABBA–The Album* to launch their project, which they entrusted to the American architect Tom Hidley, who had already designed The Record Plant in Los Angeles. They allocated a budget of some US\$500,000 to the project, with which Hidley soon parted company because of a disagreement: the control room, located in the center of the 2,700-square-foot (250-square-meter) structure, featured a panoramic pane of glass that did not meet the acoustic standards of the buildings he usually designed.

ABBA's Xanadu

When Polar Music Studios opened its doors in May 1978, it was one of the best-equipped complexes in the world, and had finally cost more than US\$1 million to build. It consisted of five rooms, which allowed Lennart Östlund, the establishment's factotum and also the assistant recording engineer on all projects except ABBA's albums, to separate recording sections from each other. In the central room, up to 40 musicians could play together, such as the orchestra conducted by Rutger Gunnarsson in *As Good as New* or the children's choir of the International School of Stockholm in *I Have a Dream*. Each musician had their own set of headphones with an individual mixing console, allowing them to create their own balance between instruments. The control room featured the last word in consoles, a Harrison 40/32 with Allison 65K automation, two 24-track tape recorders, and Altec 604 monitoring speakers. Under the management of recording engineer Leif Mases, Polar Music Studios quickly attracted foreign artists, including the British group Led Zeppelin, who came to record some parts of their eighth studio album, *In Through the Out Door*, in November 1978. The most "Swedish" part of the album is the legendary keyboard solo in *All My Love*, played by John Paul Jones on his brand-new Yamaha GX-1 synthesizer. In addition to ABBA, many international artists recorded at Polar Music Studios, including Genesis, The Ramones, and Roxy Music. Despite its importance in Swedish musical culture, the complex sadly closed in 2004.

Above: With its glass giving visibility into all its cubicles, Polar Music Studio was, in 1978, the ultimate of its kind.
Overleaf: The inauguration of Polar Music Studio on 18 May 1978, with Michael B Tretow, left, and Stig Anderson, center.

SUMMER NIGHT CITY

(Benny Andersson, Björn Ulvaeus/3'34)

Musicians

Agnetha Fältskog: vocals, backing vocals
Anni-Frid "Frida" Lyngstad: vocals, backing vocals
Björn Ulvaeus: vocals, backing vocals
Benny Andersson: synthesizers, piano, chimes, backing vocals
Lasse Wellander: electric guitar
Rutger Gunnarsson: bass guitar
Ola Brunkert: drums
Rolf Alex: drums (hi-hat overdubs)
Claes Nilsson: violin
Anders Dahl: violin
Bertil Orsin: violin
Martin Bylund: violin
Harry Teike: violin
Sixten Strömvall: violin
Kryztof Zdrzalka: violin
Tullo Galli: violin
Gunnar Michols: violin
Håkan Roos: viola
Örjan Högberg: viola
Olle Gustafsson: cello
Åke Olofsson: cello

Recording

Metronome, Stockholm: 29 to 30 May 1978
Polar Music Studios, Stockholm: 5 to 6 June 1978

Technical team

Producers: Björn Ulvaeus, Benny Andersson
Sound engineer: Michael B Tretow
String arrangements: Rutger Gunnarsson

Single

A-side: *Summer Night City*/3'34
B-side: Medley: *Pick a Bale of Cotton—On Top of Old Smokey—Midnight Special*/4'15
Released in Sweden by Polar Music: 6 September 1978
(single ref.: POS 1239)
Released in the UK by CBS/Epic: 6 September 1978
(single ref.: S EPC 6595)
Best chart ranking in Sweden: 1
Best chart ranking in the UK: 5

Genesis

For ABBA, 5 June 1978 was a red-letter day: the day they settled into Polar Music Studios, where they would record their next three albums. They recorded two songs that day: *Lovers (Live a Little Longer)* and *Summer Night City*. The latter was an ode to partying and to Swedish summer nights, and it was quickly decided to release it as a single, for its disco potential guaranteed a new hit for the group. But nothing went according to plan. First of all, the song caused controversy in the UK when BBC programmers thought they heard the words "Fucking in the moonlight" at 1'36, although Ulvaeus maintained he had sung "Walking in the moonlight." Even though the singer denied it, he can unquestionably be heard singing the words "Love-making in a park" at 1'08—another phrase that did not impress the British radio station's bosses. Despite having released the single, Epic did not promote it, and *Summer Night City* reached only number 5 in the British charts—a failure from ABBA's point of view, because it was their worst sales figure for a record since *SOS* in 1975. In the USA, the song was not even released. For consolation, it was necessary to look at the charts in Japan, a country where ABBA now enjoyed huge popularity, partly thanks to exhaustive work on the part of their Japanese distributor, Discomate.

Production

Production of *Summer Night City* proved to be a headache for Andersson, Ulvaeus, and Tretow, who spent more than a week on mixing it. Dissatisfied with the end result, the two composers decided not to include it on the tracklist of the forthcoming album. Although its release as a single in September, and its live version—performed every evening during the subsequent tour—pleased the fans, these did not bear comparison with the complete version, which was unveiled only in 1994 with the release of the box set *Thank You for the Music*. Indeed, the song initially included a 43-second introduction that showcased Rutger Gunnarsson's string arrangements, on which the crystal-clear voices of Benny, Agnetha, and Frida were overlaid. Since this section was deemed far too long for a single, it was removed from the final mixing.

The clip of *Summer Night City* showed Stockholm in summer, when the sun sets for only a few hours each day.

Agnetha and Frida dress colorfully for a photo shoot on 21 August 1978.

AS GOOD AS NEW

(Benny Andersson, Björn Ulvaeus/3'22)

1979

Musicians

Agnetha Fältskog: lead vocals, backing vocals
Anni-Frid "Frida" Lyngstad: backing vocals
Benny Andersson: synthesizers, piano, backing vocals
Björn Ulvaeus: backing vocals
Janne Schaffer: electric guitar
Rutger Gunnarsson: bass guitar
Ola Brunkert: drums
Anders Dahl: violin
Lennart Fredriksson: violin
Inge Lindstedt: violin
Gunnar Michols: violin
Claes Nilsson: violin
Lars Stegenberg: violin
Sixten Strömvall: violin
Bo Söderström: violin
Harry Teike: violin
Kryztof Zdrzalka: violin
Lars Arvinder: viola
Niels Heie: viola
Håkan Roos: viola
Hans-Göran Eketorp: cello
Olle Gustafsson: cello
Bertil Andersson: double bass
Bo Hellman: double bass

Recording

Polar Music Studios, Stockholm: 14, 27 March 1979

Technical team

Producers: Björn Ulvaeus, Benny Andersson
Sound engineer: Michael B Tretow
String arrangements: Rutger Gunnarsson

Genesis

Listening to *As Good as New* makes it clear beyond any doubt that disco left its mark on Benny Andersson and Björn Ulvaeus during 1978. The Bee Gees, who were riding high on the international success of the soundtrack to *Saturday Night Fever*—released in November 1977, and featuring six of their songs—had an influence on ABBA, which the four members openly acknowledged. "I think the influence affects everyone, because I haven't experienced anything similar since The Beatles," Agnetha Fältskog explained in 1978. "Whether or not their sound is commercial, it doesn't bother me. I love their disco sound because I feel it so much, most of the things you hear in disco have no melody."[85]

Production

While the first disco hits, which appeared in 1973 and 1974, showcased the authentic sound and mellow voices of their performers, most of whom had come from soul music or funk, a second wave, originating in Europe, soon featured massive use of synthesizers, like Giorgio Moroder's productions for Donna Summer (*Need-A-Man Blues, I Feel Love*). From 1976, and until 1979, the big names in the genre decided also to enhance their productions with string arrangements, as on *Love in C Minor* by Cerrone (1976), *Wasted* by Donna Summer (1976), *(Funny) Bone* by Chic (1978), and *Mission to Venus* by Silver Convention (1978). Determined to make ABBA a part of this fashionable artistic trend, Benny Andersson and Björn Ulvaeus gave Rutger Gunnarsson—whose talents as an arranger had been revealed in *One Man, One Woman* and *I Wonder (Departure)*—the task of writing the string score for *As Good as New*. Although the bass guitarist's virtuosity had already been well proven on *Dancing Queen*, his creative genius was again immortalized from the first bars of *Voulez-Vous*, where the violins are incisive and create a tension that soon leads to the unstoppable groove that he produces once again, endowing the song with a slap bass line worthy of Chic's Bernard Edwards. As for Janne Schaffer, he plays funk chords on his Fender Telecaster, which has a crystal-clear sound. The whole amounts to absolute perfection, and for fans the dance-floor beckons.

Single

VOULEZ-VOUS

(Benny Andersson, Björn Ulvaeus/5'11)

Musicians

Agnetha Fältskog: vocals, backing vocals
Anni-Frid "Frida" Lyngstad: vocals, backing vocals
Benny Andersson: synthesizers, backing vocals
Björn Ulvaeus: acoustic guitar backing vocals
Janne Schaffer: electric guitar
Malando Gassama: percussion
Halldor Pálsson: saxophone
Johan Stengård: saxophone
Nils Landgren: trombone

Recording

Polar Music Studios, Stockholm: February and March 1979

Technical team

Producers: Björn Ulvaeus, Benny Andersson
Sound engineer: Michael B Tretow

Single

UK version
A-side: *Angeleyes*/4'20
AA-side: *Voulez-Vous*/5'11
US version
A-side: *Voulez-Vous*/4'20
B-side: *Angeleyes*/5'11
Released in the UK by CBS/Epic: 2 July 1979 (single ref.: S EPC 7499)
Released in the USA by Atlantic: 2 July 1979 (single ref.: 3609)
Best chart ranking in the UK: 3
Best chart ranking in the USA: 80

HEADPHONES AT THE READY

Listening closely to the arrangements in *Voulez-Vous* reveals a lot about ABBA's influences. The rhythm of Schaffer's guitar (audible at 0'18) is a nod to *You Should Be Dancing* by The Bee Gees (at 0'11), while the discreet saxophone line recorded by Johan Stengård between 1'36 and 1'43 is borrowed from the vocal line in *Nature Boy*, sung by Nat King Cole in 1948 and now a jazz standard.

Genesis

In January 1979, Benny and Björn flew to the Bahamas, where they hoped to find inspiration for ABBA's new album. "Mind you, it is getting somewhat more difficult to come up with new material," Benny remarked at the time. "You need outside inspirations."[21] "We must have read something about other bands going away to write and work in various exotic places and decided to follow their example," Björn added.[35] The Bahamas sounded attractive, particularly at that time of year, and the two friends moved into a small villa, where they worked using a grand piano. They also discovered the Florida sound, which then reigned supreme in American disco and flooded the airwaves as far as the Bahamas. "We wrote, listened to the radio and wrote some more," Björn recalled. "It's not that you take things from the radio, that's not it, but you get a kick out of hearing something good."[86] They wrote four songs during that stay: *If It Wasn't for the Nights, Kisses of Fire, Does Your Mother Know*, and *Voulez-Vous*. The last of these dealt with seduction on nightclub dancefloors, and its title was inspired by the sensual quality of the French language, which Björn had noticed in *Je t'aime… moi non plus*, sung by Serge Gainsbourg and Jane Birkin in 1969. As they were an hour's flight time from Miami, Andersson and Ulvaeus decided to go and work in Criteria Studios, where some disco masterpieces had been recorded, including *Main Course* (1975) and *Children of the World* (1976) by The Bee Gees, as well as classics such as *Hotel California* by The Eagles (1976) and *Rastaman Vibration* by Bob Marley and The Wailers (1976).

Production

At Benny and Björn's request, Michael B Tretow jumped on the first plane and joined them in Miami to help them in their quest for the ultimate in production. The two artists were offered the services of the musicians from the group Foxy, then fresh from the success of their single *Get Off*, released in 1978. Ish Ledesma and George Terry were on electric guitar, Arnold Paseiro on bass guitar, Joe Galdo on drums, and Paul Harris at the piano. Although the musicians' expertise created an unheard-of groove, Benny and Björn soon became disenchanted by this unsettling collaboration. "There was nothing wrong with them, they were good, but it wasn't our band, you know?" Benny explained. He and Björn were used

to a certain way of working with their regular musicians: "I'd play the piano, Björn would play the guitar, we would sing them the song with rubbish lyrics and I would write down the harmonies on a sheet of paper so they knew what they were doing."[53] Getting new musicians to understand what they wanted turned out to be too much of a challenge. Since 1979, legend has it that, once the backing tracks had been recorded, ABBA and their musicians added overdubs to the song at Polar Music Studios. This makes *Voulez-Vous* the only ABBA song to have been recorded outside Sweden —something that Benny Andersson denied in 2022, to widespread surprise. He maintained that, when he and Björn got back to Stockholm, they brought Rutger Gunnarsson and the other regulars back into the studio to redo the track, and the result is what is heard on the record. "But the original was done in Florida. I think the [American musicians are] credited still, because they were in it from the beginning. [The first version] should be somewhere on a roll of tape."[53]

Single

I HAVE A DREAM

(Benny Andersson, Björn Ulvaeus/4'44)

1979

Musicians

Anni-Frid "Frida" Lyngstad: lead vocals, backing vocals
Agnetha Fältskog: backing vocals
Benny Andersson: synthesizers, backing vocals
Björn Ulvaeus: acoustic guitar, backing vocals
Janne Schaffer: Danelectro Coral Sitar
Rutger Gunnarsson: bass guitar
Ola Brunkert: drums
Choir of the Stockholm International School: choir

Recording

Polar Music Studios, Stockholm: March 1979

Technical team

Producers: Björn Ulvaeus, Benny Andersson
Sound engineer: Michael B Tretow
Choir conductor: Kerstin Feist

Single

Swedish version
A-side: *I Have a Dream*/4'44
B-side: *Take a Chance on Me* (live version)/4'25
UK version
A-side: *I Have a Dream*/4'44
B-side: *Take a Chance on Me* (recorded live at Wembley)/4'25
Released in the UK by CBS/Epic: December 1979
(single ref.: S EPC 8088)
Best chart ranking in the UK: 2

FOR ABBA ADDICTS

It will never again be possible to remix the various vocal takes of *I Have a Dream*. For when he was given the task of recording *Estoy Soñando*, the Spanish version of the song, on 30 August 1979 at the Metronome studios, the recording engineer Janne Hansson asked on which tape he should record the vocal take. He was told to erase the original take, on the grounds that the song had already been released and it was of no importance—with the result that the original tracks recorded by Agnetha and Frida were lost for good.

Genesis

As they were now trying to find their way in the world of disco, the members of ABBA presented their audience with a U-turn to which they alone held the secret. This was a return to their love of *schlager*, revealed in the third track of *Voulez-Vous* with this simple, effective ballad whose melodious verses once again highlight the talent of the composers Andersson and Ulvaeus. The song was the last to be recorded for the album during March 1979. Benny then worked on the lyrics, which he finished one evening before going to a party he was holding with Frida in their house in Lidingö. When he arrived, the group announced to the assembled guests that ABBA had just finished a new song, and urged them to join them in singing once Benny was seated at his piano. This gave them the idea of inviting some guests to sing the finale of the song with them in the studio. In order to do this, Björn called on the children's choir of the International School of Stockholm (renamed Stockholm International School a few years later), conducted by Kerstin Feist.

Production

The recording session took place at the end of March; the 28 pupils and their teacher went to Polar Music Studios, having rehearsed using a tape the group had sent to them in advance. Since the United Nations had proclaimed 1979 as International Year of the Child, ABBA decided, on each date of their North American and European tour, to invite a choir from the country they were visiting to join them for the finale. As well as being anything but a disco song, *I Have a Dream* has the distinctive feature that it is inspired by Greek music, largely thanks to the use of a Coral Sitar, an electric guitar made by Danelectro in 1967, which produced a sound very like that of an Indian sitar, but also like that of the traditional Greek bouzouki. Janne Schaffer played this instrument, formerly heard on *I Was Made to Love Her* by Stevie Wonder (1967), *Didn't I (Blow Your Mind This Time)* by the Delfonics (1969), and *Do It Again* by Steely Dan (1972). Schaffer brought out his Coral Sitar again in 2020, when he recorded a few lines for the song *Painting Black*, which appeared in 2023 on the album *#lovestorm* by the German group Groenalund.

Above: The children of the International School of Stockholm would never forget their day spent with ABBA.
Overleaf: Every evening on their 1979 tour, ABBA invited children from the host city to join them in singing *I Have a Dream*.

Single

ANGELEYES

(Benny Andersson, Björn Ulvaeus/4'20)

Musicians

Anni-Frid "Frida" Lyngstad: vocals, backing vocals
Agnetha Fältskog: vocals, backing vocals
Benny Andersson: synthesizers, piano, backing vocals
Björn Ulvaeus: backing vocals
Janne Schaffer: electric guitar
Mike Watson: bass guitar
Ola Brunkert: drums
Anders Dahl: violin
Martin Bylund: violin
Gunnar Michols: violin
Claes Nilsson: violin
Bernt Nylund: violin
Lars Stegenberg: violin
Sixten Strömvall: violin
Bo Söderström: violin
Harry Teike: violin
Lars Arvinder: viola
Niels Heie: viola
Håkan Roos: viola
Thomas Sundkvist: viola

Recording

Polar Music Studios, Stockholm: 26 October, 8 November 1978

Technical team

Producers: Björn Ulvaeus, Benny Andersson
Sound engineer: Michael B Tretow
String arrangements: Anders Eljas

Single

A-side: *Angeleyes*/4'20
AA-side: *Voulez-Vous*/5'11
Released in the UK by CBS/Epic: 2 July 1979
(single ref.: S EPC 7499)
Best chart ranking in the UK: 3

1979

Genesis

Some songs have a history fraught with difficulties. So it was with *Angeleyes*, which Benny and Björn had been trying to bring to life for several months, without success. The song, in which Agnetha and Frida sing together, advises a young woman to beware of the angelic eyes of a young lad whose reputation precedes him. During the recording of *Voulez-Vous*, Björn had revealed in the pages of *ABBA Magazine*: "The only thing I can say so far is that this album is going to be much happier than the previous ones. They have been a little sad recently."[87] This proves to be the case on listening to the first few songs on the album, which are perfectly of their time. Both a disco song *par excellence* and a remarkable one, *Angeleyes* is one of ABBA's most important numbers, and was showcased in the movie *Mamma Mia! Here We Go Again*, directed by Ol Parker in 2018.

Production

With its lively chorus and dance rhythm, *Angeleyes* had everything of a potential ABBA hit about it, but unfortunately it proved impossible for Michael B Tretow to mix it to a standard equal to the quality of its writing: the song just didn't sound as modern as the rest of the album. "It's back to the Sixties and also the tune is in a strange key; it's somehow both too low and too high," Benny Andersson explained in 2010. "But I like it better now—it sounds like it was made ten years earlier, but that doesn't matter today when a further 30 years have passed."[86] No one knows what fans will think about it in 2040, but in 2022 a sped-up version of the song created a sensation online after a user on TikTok, @_theaea, posted it on their personal page. Several hundred thousand views later, thanks to this indigestible version, the song enjoyed renewed popularity with the younger generation. Here is a message for those new fans: listen, instead, to the original version of *Angeleyes*, which is unquestionably one of the best tracks on the album *Voulez-Vous* and does not need to be sped up in order to be appreciated for its true worth.

Above: Fleetwood Mac (1975–1987 line-up) were one of the biggest influences on Björn and Benny.
Overleaf: Lindsey Buckingham, Christine McVie, Mick Fleetwood, Stevie Nicks, and John McVie of Fleetwood Mac, 1977.

THE KING HAS LOST HIS CROWN

(Benny Andersson, Björn Ulvaeus/3'30)

Musicians

Anni-Frid "Frida" Lyngstad: lead vocals, backing vocals
Agnetha Fältskog: backing vocals
Benny Andersson: Fender Rhodes, piano, synthesizers, backing vocals
Björn Ulvaeus: acoustic guitar, backing vocals
Lasse Wellander: electric guitar
Rutger Gunnarsson: bass guitar
Rolf Alex: drums
Jan Risberg: oboe
Martin Bylund: violin
Gunnar Michols: violin
Claes Nilsson: violin
Lars Stegenberg: violin
Sixten Strömvall: violin
Bo Söderström: violin
Harry Teike: violin
Snorri Thorvaldsson: violin
Kryztof Zdrzalka: violin
Lars Arvinder: viola
Niels Heie: viola
Håkan Roos: viola
Kjell Bjurling: cello
Olle Gustafsson: cello
Miroslav Jovic: cello

Recording

Polar Music Studios, Stockholm: 17 to 18 August, 7, 18 to 22 September 1978

Technical team

Producers: Björn Ulvaeus, Benny Andersson
Sound engineer: Michael B Tretow
String arrangements: Anders Eljas

Genesis

In September 1978, Charlie Bates, the new editor in chief of *ABBA Magazine*, published by Polar Music for fans, was invited to meet the group's members, who were then in the midst of recording sessions for their forthcoming album. At Polar Music Studios, the young journalist met his idols, who were doing vocal takes for the song *Just a Notion*. Although this was not retained for *Voulez-Vous*, and would spend the next 40 years languishing in the ABBA archives before finally being resuscitated for the album *Voyage* in 2021, the second song recorded at that time was kept for the album. This was *The King Has Lost His Crown*, in which Frida sings of the misfortunes of a man who once had irresistible charm but who now seems to have lost the ability to win women's hearts. The singer mocks this king without a throne or a crown, this Don Juan who has lost his power to seduce.

Production

In this song more than ever, the allusion to the music of The Bee Gees is unquestionable. After performing an artistic U-turn with their album *Main Course*, released in 1975, which gave prominence to soul, funk, and disco, the Gibb brothers and their producer Arif Mardin had found the recipe for a new kind of success. Their songs, often built around a strong chorus and gentle verses (*Wind of Change, You Stepped into My Life, Love You Inside Out*) are recognizable among a thousand others. Their brother Andy Gibb's hit *Shadow Dancing*, released in 1978, followed the same formula. In 2022 Benny Andersson revealed how ABBA had been inspired by the way The Bee Gees transformed themselves, having had hits such as *Massachusetts* in the 1960s, but then taking "a totally different approach."[53] In order to give *The King Has Lost His Crown* an aesthetic similar to that of The Bee Gees' songs, Björn and Benny entrusted the string arrangements to Anders Eljas, who had played keyboard on their 1977 tour. The latter acquitted himself in masterly fashion in this song, as well as in *If It Wasn't for the Nights* and *Angeleyes*.

Single

DOES YOUR MOTHER KNOW

(Benny Andersson, Björn Ulvaeus/3'13)

1979

Musicians
Björn Ulvaeus: lead vocals, backing vocals
Anni-Frid "Frida" Lyngstad: backing vocals
Agnetha Fältskog: backing vocals
Benny Andersson: Yamaha GX-1, synthesizers, piano, backing vocals
Lasse Wellander: electric guitar
Mike Watson: bass guitar
Ola Brunkert: drums
Lars O Carlsson: saxophone
Kajtek Wojciechowski: saxophone

Recording
Polar Music Studios, Stockholm: 6 February, 27 March 1979

Technical team
Producers: Björn Ulvaeus, Benny Andersson
Sound engineer: Michael B Tretow

Single
A-side: *Does Your Mother Know*/3'13
B-side: *Kisses of Fire*/3'16
Released in the UK by CBS/Epic: April 1979 (single ref.: S EPC 7316)
Released in the USA by Atlantic: May 1979 (single ref.: 3574)
Best chart ranking in the UK: 4
Best chart ranking in the USA: 19

Björn Ulvaeus was the protagonist in this frenzied pop number.

Genesis

The idea for the theme of *Does Your Mother Know* came to Björn Ulvaeus while he was engrossed in reading a newspaper. He'd been reading, he explained later, about "predatory older men using younger women"[35] and decided to reverse the idea, focusing on a man who recognizes that a girl is too young for him and asks her if her mother knows that she is out. In May 1979, ABBA decided to release the song as a single, the first since *Rock'n'Roll Band* in July 1973 on which the lead voice was not Agnetha's or Frida's, but Björn's. Why? Because of the song's subject, which drove its writer to sing the vocal tracks himself (even though the two women provide masterly backing vocals), but also because of a balance ABBA sought in their albums. "We thought a good balance would be if I had the lead vocal on one or two tracks on each album," Ulvaeus said. "Just for variety."[7] The song's title was written separately from the lyrics, but appealed to Ulvaeus, who thought it fitted the words perfectly. *Does Your Mother Know* was to be one of the high points of ABBA's American and European tour in 1979. Every evening, Ulvaeus, wearing his close-fitting blue outfit, made an impression performing on stage, as did the group's two guitarists, Lasse Wellander and Mats Ronander. Their solos, which do not feature on the studio version, resembled a heroic duel, with Agnetha and Frida encouraging them each time by gripping their legs, like fans clinging to their idol.

Production

When Polar Music Studios hosted the British band Led Zeppelin in November 1978, all eyes were on this brand new recording complex capable of rivalling the greatest studios in the UK, even the world. The band who wrote *Stairway to Heaven* recorded some tracks for their forthcoming album, *In Through the Out Door*, including *All My Love*, whose keyboard solo would provoke much press comment. The group's bass guitarist and keyboard player, John Paul Jones, had brought with him the all-new Yamaha GX-1 synthesizer, capable of producing sounds never heard before. There were only a very few in existence, the first ones having already been sold to Stevie Wonder, Keith Emerson, and John Paul Jones himself. Benny Andersson was invited to try out this new instrument, and was immediately spellbound by its many functions; he asked Lennart Östlund, Polar Music's in-house

recording engineer, if he could find him one quickly, despite the exorbitant price of 380,000 kroner—equivalent to $43,000 (£34,000) today. Yamaha's manager in Gothenburg referred Östlund to "two Japanese guys in Hamburg,"[62] who had one synthesizer available. Having initially said that Benny could buy it, they then offered to give it to him if he would agree to appear seated at the keyboard in an advertisement for the brand. Andersson, however, preferred to pay for it, and a few months later received the instrument, which he nicknamed his Dream Machine. The Yamaha GX-1, which the following year would change the group's overall sound, was used for

the very first time on 27 March 1979, when Benny Andersson decided to replace the introduction written and played by Mike Watson with a synthesized bass guitar sound from his Dream Machine. Hearing the result, Östlund said, "[...] we realized that the synthesizer had already been repaid with this."[62] The drums track, played by Ola Brunkert, was inspired by the playing of Carmine Appice, Rod Stewart's drummer, whom Brunkert had heard in concert at Granby Halls, Leicester, England, in December 1978.

"Benny asked me to do some solo drum bars for the intro," Brunkert recalled, "and then I remember what Appice had

Every evening, Björn gave his all in performing *Does Your Mother Know* on stage.

Overleaf: Abba's last tour left a bitter taste for the group's members, who were frequently harassed by uncontrollable fans.

done."[31] With its 1960s sound and fake disco quality, the song delighted fans and the press, who praised its qualities, witness the Danish *Hitkrant*: "A thumping guitar/drums intro and sure enough, a lead vocal by Björn, something we don't get to hear very often. But then the familiar voices of both ladies come in and it's clear for us to hear: top-drawer pop music. ABBA have once again surpassed themselves."[88]

HEADPHONES AT THE READY

The post-chorus of *Does Your Mother Know*, sung by Agnetha and Frida between 1'04 and 1'18, is a section borrowed from *Dream World*, a song the group recorded in September 1978 but did not finally retain on the tracklist of *Voulez-Vous*.

The athletic Björn Ulvaeus
by the swimming pool at
the Sunset Marquis hotel,
Los Angeles, in 1979.

Overleaf: Michael B
Tretow, Björn Ulvaeus, and
Benny Andersson at work at
Polar Music Studio in 1978.

IF IT WASN'T FOR THE NIGHTS

(Benny Andersson, Björn Ulvaeus/5'13)

1979

Musicians

Anni-Frid "Frida" Lyngstad: vocals, backing vocals
Agnetha Fältskog: vocals, backing vocals
Benny Andersson: synthesizers, piano, backing vocals
Björn Ulvaeus: backing vocals
Janne Schaffer: electric guitar
Mike Watson: bass guitar
Ola Brunkert: drums
Malando Gassama: percussion
Anders Dahl: violin
Martin Bylund: violin
Gunnar Michols: violin
Claes Nilsson: violin
Bernt Nylund: violin
Lars Stegenberg: violin
Sixten Strömvall: violin
Bo Söderström: violin
Harry Teike: violin
Lars Arvinder: viola
Niels Heie: viola
Håkan Roos: viola
Thomas Sundkvist: viola

Recording

Polar Music Studios, Stockholm: 25 to 27 October,
4 to 8 November 1978

Technical team

Producers: Björn Ulvaeus, Benny Andersson
Sound engineer: Michael B Tretow
String and brass arrangements: Anders Eljas

Genesis

Like *Voulez-Vous, Kisses of Fire*, and *Does Your Mother Know*, *If It Wasn't for the Nights* was written by Benny and Björn during their trip to the Bahamas in January 1979. With its introduction carried along by Anders Eljas's string arrangements, it suggests that the two men, determined to soak up the disco music that came from Miami via the radio, had also not escaped the influence of German music, whose chief ambassadors at the time were Frank Farian and Michael Kunze. The latter, whose most famous achievement was the success of the all-female trio Silver Convention, had produced the song *San Francisco Hustle* for them in 1976. Its introduction is very similar to that of *If It Wasn't for the Nights*. Although Andersson and Ulvaeus were totally involved in their quest for the ultimate disco song, this new direction nevertheless asked artistic and moral questions of them. "I have to say, I was just a little reluctant to us doing disco songs," Benny explained, "simply because everybody else was doing it. My feeling was, 'Wouldn't it be more fun to do something that everybody else isn't doing?'"[86]

Production

As with *Voulez-Vous*, Björn and Benny worked on *If It Wasn't for the Nights* with musicians from the group Foxy and producer Tom Dowd at the Criteria Studios in Miami during January 1979. Communication was difficult, and the project ended in failure. Benny later recalled[35] that although the Americans understood in principle what was required, they didn't really get what *If It Wasn't for the Nights* was about until Björn played it for them on his guitar. It was not until ABBA reconvened at Polar Music Studios in Stockholm with their session musicians Ola Brunkert, Mike Watson, and Janne Schaffer that the song finally came to life. Björn wrote the lyrics immediately afterwards, during a night when he was thinking about the failure of his marriage to Agnetha, even though at the time he was already in a relationship with Lena Källersjö, with whom he would spend the next 42 years (the couple broke up in 2022).

Overleaf: ABBA shot the clip
of *Chiquitita* during their visit to
Switzerland in February 1979,
while recording the show
ABBA in Switzerland.

Single

CHIQUITITA

(Benny Andersson, Björn Ulvaeus/5'26)

1979

Musicians
Agnetha Fältskog: lead vocals, backing vocals
Anni-Frid "Frida" Lyngstad: backing vocals
Benny Andersson: synthesizers, piano, backing vocals
Björn Ulvaeus: acoustic guitar, banjo, backing vocals
Lasse Wellander: acoustic guitar
Rutger Gunnarsson: bass guitar
Ola Brunkert: drums

Recording
Polar Music Studios, Stockholm: 13 to 21 December 1978

Technical team
Producers: Björn Ulvaeus, Benny Andersson
Sound engineer: Michael B Tretow

Single
A-side: *Chiquitita*/5'26
B-side: *Lovelight*/3'46
Released in Sweden by Polar Music: 16 January 1979
(single ref.: POS 1244)
Released in the UK by CBS/Epic: January 1979
(single ref.: S EPC 7030)
Released in the USA by Atlantic: 1979 (single ref.: 3629)
Best chart ranking in Sweden: 2
Best chart ranking in the UK: 2
Best chart ranking in the USA: 29

Genesis
The United Nations had proclaimed 1979 as International Year of the Child, and on the evening of 9 January the Music for UNICEF Concert: A Gift of Song was held at the UN headquarters in New York. A constellation of artists had come to sing for the occasion, and footage of the evening was to be broadcast the following day on the American television network NBC. ABBA were part of the prestigious list of guests, alongside Rita Coolidge, Kris Kristofferson, Olivia Newton-John, Andy Gibb, Earth, Wind & Fire, Rod Stewart, Donna Summer, The Bee Gees, and John Denver. While everyone else present performed their most danceable disco song, ABBA that evening chose a totally anachronistic number, *Chiquitita*, which reconnected with their beloved *schlager*. Although they gave a dazzling performance in the concert, it was the depth of their involvement in the event that elevated them far above the other guest artists: they offered the entire earnings from *Chiquitita* to UNICEF, as envisaged by the concept of the program.

Production
The song proved to be a headache for its creators, who recorded several versions before finding the perfect formula. Björn Ulvaeus had to rewrite the lyrics three times before he was completely satisfied with them. "I heard *Chiquitita* as a rock song, a pop song, a ballad, and a symphony song," Lennart Östlund, then employed by Polar Music Studios, said.[62] ABBA's members were caught off guard by the song's success, as Björn explained to *ABBA Magazine* in 1979: "It seems that the Spanish people have taken *Chiquitita* in their hearts. The demand has been so great that we are translating the lyrics and releasing a Spanish version there soon. You know Spanish is a beautiful language. There are so many words of one syllable only, which is very different from English."[89] With its lyrics translated by the Argentine writers Buddy and Mary McCluskey, what had initially been entitled *In the Arms of Rosalita* reached number one in the Argentine charts on its release in April 1979—a success of such magnitude that it prompted the group to embark on the production of *Gracias por la Música* ("Thank You for the Music"), an album sung in Spanish, which would be released a year later.

Agnetha

Björn

BA ABBA

Benny

Frida
(Anni-Frid)

ABBA® ABB

LOVERS (LIVE A LITTLE LONGER)

(Benny Andersson, Björn Ulvaeus/3'28)

1979

Musicians

Anni-Frid "Frida" Lyngstad: lead vocals, backing vocals
Agnetha Fältskog: backing vocals
Benny Andersson: synthesizers, piano, backing vocals
Björn Ulvaeus: backing vocals
Lasse Wellander: electric guitar
Rutger Gunnarsson: bass guitar
Ola Brunkert: drums
Malando Gassama: percussion
Claes Nilsson: violin
Anders Dahl: violin
Bertil Orsin: violin
Martin Bylund: violin
Harry Teike: violin
Sixten Strömvall: violin
Kryztof Zdrzalka: violin
Tullo Galli: violin
Gunnar Michols: violin
Håkan Roos: viola
Örjan Högberg: viola
Olle Gustafsson: cello
Åke Olofsson: cello

Recording

Marcus Music, Solna: 25 April 1978
Glenstudio, Stockholm: 22 to 24 May 1978
Polar Music Studios, Stockholm: 5 to 6 June 1978

Technical team

Producers: Björn Ulvaeus, Benny Andersson
Sound engineer: Michael B Tretow
String arrangements: Rutger Gunnarsson

Genesis

Before flying to Los Angeles for a marathon promotion that would start with a photo session on Sunset Strip under a banner that read: "ABBA, the group who have sold the most records in the history of recorded music," the band and their musicians recorded the backing tracks for a new song at Marcus Music in Solna, where most of *ABBA–The Album* had been recorded. The song's title, *Lovers (Live a little Longer)*, had come to Björn while he was reading a newspaper article reporting on some scientific research which had established that loving someone and making love led to an increased lifespan. Although he had only the title when he started the creative process, lyrics came to him quickly, and it was Frida who recorded the vocal lines in this most funky of tracks, as Björn had done in *Man in the Middle* and Agnetha in *My Mama Said* in 1974.

Production

Bass guitarist Rutger Gunnarsson excelled as much in his mastery of his instrument as in the string arrangements he wrote for this song. Alternating with Anders Eljas in the sessions for *Voulez-Vous*, Gunnarsson played the most delicate and discreet parts, which proved the most enduring in the long term. On drums for *Lovers (Live a Little Longer)*, Ola Brunkert played with finesse, demonstrating his ability to adapt to all the musical styles his employers wanted to tackle. "I am a session musician, and that is what I like doing most," he explained in 1979. "I don't ever feel envious that I am not one of the stars in the limelight. Björn and Benny deserve that sort of attention because they are both very good players. I respect that a lot. Playing with ABBA is the most enjoyable part of my job as a session man."[90] In order to give the drums' sound that controlled power, Michael B Tretow tried several recording approaches, without ever holding back the musicians' creative urge. "Michael never miked the drums the same way twice," Brunkert added. "There was always a new type of microphone he wanted to try out, or something like that. With most other engineers these things would quickly become a routine. They would place the mikes in a sort of boring way, and it turned out fine, but Michael would come up with anything and everything."[91]

Michael B Tretow, right, in the mobile recording studio used for the concerts at Wembley Arena, in London, in November 1979.

KISSES OF FIRE

(Benny Andersson, Björn Ulvaeus/3'16)

1979

Musicians

Agnetha Fältskog: lead vocals, backing vocals
Anni-Frid "Frida" Lyngstad: backing vocals
Benny Andersson: synthesizers, piano, backing vocals
Björn Ulvaeus: backing vocals
Lasse Wellander: acoustic guitar
Rutger Gunnarsson: bass guitar
Ola Brunkert: drums

Recording

Polar Music Studios, Stockholm: 7 to 13 February 1979

Technical team

Producers: Björn Ulvaeus, Benny Andersson
Sound engineer: Michael B Tretow

Genesis

After the allusion to sex in the open air in *Summer Night City*, and the description of looks charged with sexual tension in *Voulez-Vous*, Björn Ulvaeus now wrote lyrics in which a woman describes the carnal pleasure her partner gives her. What was happening to ABBA, formerly loved for their pretty little songs, which delighted young and old? "I guess we have become a bit bolder," Björn said by way of explanation. "Three years ago I probably would have felt myself that *Kisses of Fire* was a bit too physical. I simply wouldn't have written lyrics like that three years ago. But as the years go by you feel more liberated, acquire more confidence—dare to be yourself."[86] Composed during Andersson and Ulvaeus's stay in the Bahamas, *Kisses of Fire* emphasized their attraction to disco music, which they drank in while sipping margaritas.

Production

Although composed under the idyllic conditions of a villa in the Bahamas, *Kisses of Fire* demonstrates Benny and Björn's seriousness: whether in their cabin on Viggsö, in the basement at Lidingö, or on the above-mentioned paradise island, they subjected themselves to iron discipline when working on the group's songs. "For the past 50 years, I have always been very disciplined," Benny explained years later. "Sit down at the piano and wait for something to happen. I can't walk in the street and suddenly go, 'Oh, this is a good melody line.' I need to sit and play rubbish and all of a sudden I'm not for maybe ten seconds. Something sticks with me and I'll feel, 'Oh, a good four bars here.' So I keep those. When that happens, inspiration comes. The other part is just sweat."[92] The last track on *Voulez-Vous*, in its second verse *Kisses of Fire* unleashes a passage on the synthesizer that uses the Arpeggiator function, which plays chords as arpeggios and which Benny Andersson would soon use in many songs. The keyboard player is slipping us a hint, as if warning us of the artistic revolution that awaited ABBA's fans.

GIMME! GIMME! GIMME! (A MAN AFTER MIDNIGHT)

(Benny Andersson, Björn Ulvaeus/4'45)

Musicians

Agnetha Fältskog: lead vocals, backing vocals
Anni-Frid "Frida" Lyngstad: backing vocals
Benny Andersson: synthesizers, backing vocals
Björn Ulvaeus: backing vocals
Lasse Wellander: electric guitar
Rutger Gunnarsson: bass guitar
Ola Brunkert: drums
Åke Sundqvist: percussion
Martin Bylund: violin
Anders Dahl: violin
Lennart Fredriksson: violin
Gunnar Michols: violin
Claes Nilsson: violin
Bernt Nylund: violin
Bertil Orsin: violin
Lars Stegenberg: violin
Sixten Strömvall: violin
Bo Söderström: violin
Harry Teike: violin
Lars Arvinder: viola
Niels Heie: viola
Eduard van der Kwast: viola
Håkan Roos: viola
Kjett Bjurling: cello
Olle Gustafsson: cello
Lars O. Carlsson: saxophone
Halldor Pálsson: saxophone
Christer Danielsson: trombone

Recording

Polar Music Studios, Stockholm: 9 to 10, 28 to 31 August 1979

Technical team

Producers: Björn Ulvaeus, Benny Andersson
Sound engineer: Michael B Tretow
String and brass arrangements: Rutger Gunnarsson

Single

A-side: *Gimme! Gimme! Gimme! (A Man after Midnight)*/4'45
B-side: *The King Has Lost His Crown*/3'30
Released in Sweden by Polar Music: 15 October 1979
(single ref.: POS 1256)
Released in the UK by CBS/Epic: October 1979 (single ref.: S EPC 7914)
Best chart ranking in Sweden: 16
Best chart ranking in the UK: 3

Genesis

Gimme! Gimme! Gimme! (A Man after Midnight) is a hymn. In it, ABBA are at their disco peak, and it is undoubtedly one of the group's best-known songs, along with *Dancing Queen* and *The Winner Takes It All*. Although this statement is universally recognized, it is worth taking a step back and understanding the context in which it was offered to the public at the time of its release as a single in 1979. Its backing tracks were recorded on 9 August of that year, and its working title was *Man after Midnight*. ABBA soon tried to erase its disco quality in favor of a more rock aesthetic, and Björn wrote its lyrics, in the process renaming the song *Been and Gone and Done It.* "It took quite a long time. Every song was tried out in different fashions, different ways, to play it, with a different arrangement and then looking for a little thing here, a little thing there to add," Michael B Tretow explained in 1994, in the documentary *Thank You ABBA*.[93] Eventually, during the sessions at the end of August, the group returned to their original idea, giving the song—finally entitled *Gimme! Gimme! Gimme! (A Man after Midnight)*—all the disco qualities it deserved. But Benny remained frustrated by this decision, even admitting later that the direction the group had taken was a mistake, and that he preferred songs such as *Money, Money, Money* or *Chiquitita*. In the lyrics of *Gimme! Gimme! Gimme! (A Man after Midnight)*, Björn once again evoked the sensuality of the songs of Donna Summer, as he had done with *Summer Night City, Lovers (Live a little Longer)*, and *Kisses of Fire,* giving the leading role to Agnetha, who here demands a man who will make her forget her troubles. The song was released in Scandinavia, but made it no higher than number 16 in the Swedish charts. It was not even released in the USA, where just one promotional version came out. With the year 1980 fast approaching, ABBA felt the winds of change, and when *Gimme! Gimme! Gimme! (A Man after Midnight)* came out to general indifference, they clearly saw that the disco era was drawing to a close. It was not until 1992, when the group once again found favor in the eyes of the public thanks to the release of the compilation *ABBA Gold–Greatest Hits*, that the song was appreciated for its true value and became a classic.

Production

Although the song opens with piano and guitar arpeggios played by Benny Andersson and Lasse Wellander respectively, it is the ensuing synthesizer motif that is its signature. This bears a disconcerting resemblance to that in *Bul Bul Efendi,* a song by the Indonesian duo Benyamin Sueb and Ida Royani

Above: A recording session for *Gimme! Gimme! Gimme! (A Man after Midnight)*, one of ABBA's most famous songs.
Overleaf: ABBA reach out to fans on their 1979 tour.

released in 1978, and is played by Benny on an Arp Odyssey synthesizer that marvelously accompanies Rutger Gunnarsson's bass guitar line, playing notes an octave apart, alternating, in quavers. This is the most disco of all ABBA's hits, supported by Gunnarsson's majestic string arrangements, which were decidedly behind all the group's greatest songs. The backing vocals that come in each post-chorus firmly place the song in its time, with a nod to The Bee Gees, who were specialists in head-voice counterpoint. In 2005, Madonna and the producer Stuart Price worked on *Hung Up*, a remix of *Gimme! Gimme! Gimme! (A Man after Midnight)*, which they presented to Björn and Benny in the hope of obtaining their permission to release it. Andersson and Ulvaeus refused to agree until they had heard Madonna's version, so, reluctant to transmit it over the internet. she sent what Benny described as "her right-hand woman" to Sweden with a CD. "We listened to it in my room here," he added, "and I thought it was bloody great. So, we said, 'OK', and split the copyright."[53]

DREAM WORLD

(Benny Andersson, Björn Ulvaeus/3'35)

Musicians
Agnetha Fältskog: vocals, backing vocals
Anni-Frid "Frida" Lyngstad: backing vocals
Benny Andersson: synthesizers, backing vocals
Björn Ulvaeus: acoustic guitar, backing vocals
Lasse Wellander: electric guitar
Rutger Gunnarsson: bass guitar
Ola Brunkert: drums
Lars Arvinder: viola
Niels Heie: viola
Bo Söderström: viola
Kjell Bjurling: cello
Olle Gustafsson: cello
Åke Olofsson: cello

Recording
Polar Music Studios, Stockholm: 27 to 29 September 1978

Technical team
Producers: Björn Ulvaeus, Benny Andersson
Sound engineer: Michael B Tretow
String arrangements: Rutger Gunnarsson

Box set *Thank You for the Music*
Released in Europe and the UK by Polar Music—Polydor: 31 October 1994 (CD box set ref.: 523 472-2)
Released in the USA by Polar Music—Polydor: 31 October 1994 (CD box set ref.: 314 523 472-2)
Best chart ranking in the UK: 17
Best chart ranking in the USA: did not make the charts

Genesis
Dream World was written and recorded at the end of September 1978, and mixed on the very day Benny and Frida were married—Friday 6 October—as well as the day after the wedding, when the couple were welcoming some 20 guests that evening to announce their secret marriage. Despite its pleasant melody, the song failed to convince its authors. "*Dream World* is one of those examples where we took it in the studio and we worked with it and found out that it didn't work," Björn explained. "Or we thought it didn't work at that time. Usually we wouldn't get that far—we would just have the fragments, but not the whole song."[7] "We thought it was quite fun," Benny added, "but the verses are a bit daft, a bit square, and it has no real chorus."[86] ABBA kept only the sequences sung at 1'04 and 2'11, which became the post-choruses in *Does Your Mother Know*. *Dream World* gathered dust at Polar Music until 1994, when Michael B Tretow dug it out to add it to the track listing of the landmark box set *Thank You for the Music*, which brought together classic and rarely heard songs by the group.

Production
Once past the surprising introduction played by Benny Andersson on a Polymoog synthesizer, which imitates the music of a fairground, the song is remarkable for its impeccable production and meticulous mixing, which reveal Michael B Tretow's mastery of Polar Music Studios. It was with the album *Super Trouper*, for which the recording would start five months later, that Tretow produced his masterpiece, offering ABBA the most accomplished production of his career. "Then, I had everything together," he recalled in 1994. "We have bounced from studios to studios in the previous years, making recording of bits and pieces everywhere, and then we got the Polar Studio in 1978. I thought I had the control of the studio."[93]

Michael B Tretow, without whom ABBA might never have tasted success.

LOVELIGHT

(Benny Andersson, Björn Ulvaeus/3'47)

Musicians
Agnetha Fältskog: vocals, backing vocals
Anni-Frid "Frida" Lyngstad: vocals, backing vocals
Benny Andersson: synthesizers, piano, backing vocals
Björn Ulvaeus: acoustic guitar, backing vocals
Lasse Wellander: electric guitar
Rutger Gunnarsson: bass guitar
Ola Brunkert: drums

Recording
Marcus Music, Solna: 24 April 1978

Technical team
Producers: Björn Ulvaeus, Benny Andersson
Sound engineer: Michael B Tretow

Single *Chiquitita*
A-side: *Chiquitita*/5'26
B-side: *Lovelight*/3'46
Released in Sweden by Polar Music: 16 January 1979
(single ref.: POS 1244)
Released in the UK by CBS/Epic: January 1979
(single ref.: S EPC 7030)
Released in the USA by Atlantic: 1979 (single ref.: 3629)
Best chart ranking in Sweden: 2
Best chart ranking in the UK: 2
Best chart ranking in the USA: 29

Genesis
In the spring of 1978, Björn Ulvaeus informed readers of *ABBA Magazine* that six songs for the group's next album had already been recorded: *Summer Night City*, *Lovers (Live a Little Longer)*, *Lovelight*, and three others that were as yet untitled. Recorded on 24 April 1978 at Marcus Music, Marcus Österdahl's studio in Solna, *Lovelight* had everything needed for a potential disco hit—catchy choruses, a tempo of 120 bpm, and a subject dear to ABBA: romantic passion. But the verses did not sound right to the group, who finally decided not to include it on *Voulez-Vous*. Two different mixings of *Lovelight* exist. The first (nicknamed "Original Version") appeared as the B-side of the *Chiquitita* single, but also on the compilation *The Love Songs* released by Pickwick Music in 1989, on the 1999 reissue of the compilation *More ABBA Gold–More ABBA Hits*, and on the deluxe edition of *Voulez-Vous*, released in 2010. The second mixing, which is more sparkling and modern, appeared on the original edition of *More ABBA Gold–More ABBA Hits* (1993), the box set *Thank You for the Music* (1994), the 1997 remastered edition of *Voulez-Vous* (which also includes *Summer Night City*), the uncut *The Complete Studio Recordings* of 2005, and the 2008 edition of the box set *Thank You for the Music*.

Production
The production of *Lovelight*, which is in the same vein as that of *Angeleyes*, *If It Wasn't for the Nights*, and *Kisses of Fire*, showcases the vocal aerobatics of Agnetha and Frida, which were written to make dancers in nightclubs sing. Its effective choruses are less subtle than those in the group's most "pop" songs, such as *Take a Chance on Me*, *Thank You for the Music*, or *Mamma Mia*. Here, it is more a repeat of the formula for *Dancing Queen*, and even though *Voulez-Vous* and its outtakes are appealing, especially in their irresistible choruses, listening to *Lovelight* provokes a sense of *déjà vu*. Benny and Björn's artistic re-evaluation during 1979 allowed ABBA to reinvent themselves spectacularly, switching from the fashion for disco to the nascent craze for synth-pop in the blink of an eye. This is the hallmark of a great producer: to be able to reinvent oneself without ever betraying the authenticity that is dear to fans.

Above: Lasse Wellander and Agnetha during rehearsals for the 1979 to 1980 tour.
Overleaf: A moment's relaxation for the unstoppable ABBA in 1979.

SÅNG TILL GÖREL
ABBA & STIKKAN

(Benny Andersson, Björn Ulvaeus, Stig Anderson/3'50)

Musicians
Agnetha Fältskog: vocals, backing vocals
Anni-Frid "Frida" Lyngstad: backing vocals
Benny Andersson: drums, percussion, accordion, piano, synthesizers, vocals, backing vocals
Björn Ulvaeus: drums, percussion, acoustic guitar, mandolin, vocals, backing vocals
Stig "Stikkan" Anderson: vocals, backing vocals

Recording
Polar Music Studios, Stockholm: 7 June 1979

Technical team
Producers: Björn Ulvaeus, Benny Andersson
Sound engineer: Michael B Tretow

Offered by Polar Music: 21 June 1979

Genesis

Although she had been in the shadow of Stig Anderson for almost ten years, Görel Johnsen was the other person who had ensured that Polar Music was firing on all cylinders. Having begun her career as Stikkan's secretary, Görel was soon offered the job of vice-president, especially because the people with whom the record company had dealings in other countries gave her due credit and respected her. When the time came to celebrate her 30th birthday, in 1979, the members of ABBA, who were deeply indebted to her, joined forces with Stig to record a new song for Görel, which they performed on the day of her party, 21 June. "I remember it was on a boat," Görel recalled, "and suddenly someone said, 'You have to stand over here', and then ABBA and Stikkan started to sing. I didn't understand anything of what was going on, but it was magic. I recall just dancing. And the only one thing that really struck me—I couldn't quite understand how they could have arranged this without me!"[62]

Production

Recorded in the utmost secrecy by Benny and Björn at Polar Music Studios on 7 June 1979, *Sång Till Görel* ("Song for Görel") was performed by the four members of ABBA, but also by Stikkan himself. In pure *schlager* style, with bass drum, accordion, and mandolin, the song is typical of the folk tunes that Benny liked so much and which he sang, accompanying himself on the accordion, at the Midsommar festivities that were held every year towards the end of June. About 200 maxi singles with *Sång Till Görel* were pressed, to be handed out to guests at the 30-year-old's party, making this record one of the most sought-after by ABBA collectors. In 2023 one was offered on the specialist website Discogs, at a price of €3,900 (about $4,200/£3,300)! Görel Johnsen (Görel Hanser from 1980, when she married the photojournalist Anders Hanser) could enjoy her precious copy of the record, which she treasured. "I do play the record from time to time to encourage myself…" she said in 2021.[62]

SUPER TROUPER

Super Trouper • The Winner Takes It All • On And On And On • Andante, Andante •
Me And I • Happy New Year • Our Last Summer • The Piper • Lay All Your Love On Me •
The Way Old Friends Do

Released in Sweden by Polar Music: 3 November 1980 (album ref.: POLS 322)
Released in the UK by CBS/Epic: 3 November 1980 (album ref.: EPC 10022)
Released in the USA by Atlantic: 3 November 1980 (album ref.: SD 16023)
Best chart ranking in Sweden: 1
Best chart ranking in the UK: 1
Best chart ranking in the USA: 17

1980

THE ROAD
TO SYNTH-POP

The success of the *Chiquitita* single in South America—where it topped the charts in Argentina, El Salvador, Venezuela, and Mexico—persuaded ABBA to give their fans a greatest hits album in Spanish. In January 1980, Frida and Agnetha began recording the vocal tracks for the ten songs on the album *Gracias por la Música* ("Thank You for the Music"), scheduled for release in spring of that year. Benny and Björn, who were not involved in the project, decided to fly to Barbados in search of inspiration for new songs, as they had done with their creative pilgrimage to the Bahamas in January 1979. The two men rented a house that Benny and Frida had visited the previous year when Paul McCartney had been staying there. "Frida and I were on our way to Barbados on holiday in the summer of 1978," Benny explained, "and in Heathrow Airport we met up with Paul and Linda McCartney. They said, 'We're also going to Barbados, come on over to our house.'"[94] The rental property where the songwriters stayed was the height of luxury and provided them with every comfort to write the first songs for ABBA's new album. Despite the fabulous setting, Andersson and Ulvaeus knew they had to work their socks off to come up with songs good enough to top the charts in Europe and America. "Those two have to see to it that we don't run dry. The existence of the group depends on their creativity," Frida said in March 1980. "That responsibility for our repertoire never and nowhere leaves them alone. And we just have to wait and see whether there actually will be something new or we will see the well run dry tomorrow. There's a tremendous pressure upon the both of them."[95]

After ten days' work, Benny and Björn began to feel homesick and returned to Sweden with only two new songs completed: *Happy New Year* and *On and On and On*. They went over to Björn's cabin in Viggsö and continued writing in their usual surroundings, with a view of the Baltic Sea and the Stockholm archipelago. Agnetha, meanwhile, had stopped going to the little island cottage she had once shared with Björn. "I will leave ABBA's island in the Stockholm archipelago for good," Agnetha said to the Swedish women's magazine *VeckoRevyn* in May 1979. "But the others will continue to be there just like before. The island never really meant that much to me. It's nice to be there when the weather is nice. But that's not always the case and then you only feel isolated. You have to depend on boats to get there and back and I only drive them into the bridge. I just cannot learn how to dock the boat."[96]

The writing sessions on Viggsö were prolific and recording of ABBA's new album began at Polar Music Studio on 4 February 1980. In addition to the five songs that had already been written—*Andante, Andante, The Piper,* and *Elaine,* along with *Happy New Year* and *On and On and On*—another song with music composed by Agnetha, and which she had performed during their 1979 tour, was also considered for recording and inclusion on the upcoming album. As Björn explained at the time: "[…] *I'm Still Alive* will be on the next LP. It is a welcome departure for us, to have a number on an Abba record that wasn't written, in part at least, by Benny or myself."[97]

The recording sessions were arduous but effective, with Michael B Tretow now fully up to speed with the band's new structure and able to get the best out of it to give the new album a modern sound, polished to perfection. "The studio

Björn Ulvaeus and his son,
Peter Christian, at the
Midsommar festival on
the island of Viggsö
in 1980.

has made a tremendous difference to the way we work," Björn said during recording; "no longer do we have to get so much of the new material prepared before we enter the recording rooms. Now we can virtually take as long as we want in the creative process—all day over an intro sequence, for instance."[98]

One last lap

In March, ABBA flew to Japan, where they would embark on their last ever tour. Although the concerts had been scheduled several months in advance and proved hugely successful (tickets for the 11 dates sold out in record time), the tour, which kicked off on 12 March at Tokyo's Budokan arena and ended at the same venue on 27 March, taking in Koriyama, Fukuoka, Osaka, and Nagoya along the way, confirmed the four Swedes' aversion to life on the road. Once again, there was public hysteria and they couldn't leave their hotel rooms, even to use hotel pools, because the fans were everywhere. Although the tour was a triumph, it marked the end of ABBA's desire to conquer the world: they were no longer prepared to pay the price for this kind of success. At the time, Agnetha was very open about the difficulties she experienced when appearing in public: "For the time being, we will have to carry the consequences of the profession that we have chosen. That sense of responsibility keeps us going. The public doesn't always realize that. They see us as four glamorous characters on stage: slick music, beautiful voices, sexy show. Many people think that we're off in some kind of fairy tale world afterwards until the next time. They forget about the traveling, the hours spent in the studio on recordings, rehearsing, getting to bed at three o'clock at night and getting up at seven, packing and unpacking of suitcases, being away from home for weeks. That's just plain hard work."[95]

Back in Sweden, ABBA continued recording their new album and committed a number of tracks to tape, including *The Winner Takes It All*, which would become one of their best-known songs. The song alluded to Agnetha and Björn's separation and was destined to be a hit. Both it and the upcoming album were the start of a new era for ABBA, in which the lighthearted tracks of the *Waterloo* era seemed to have been replaced by bleaker songs that in many ways suited the new decade.

A (short-lived) circus act

ABBA's seventh album was released on 3 November 1980. With its exceptional songs and a production quality they had never achieved before, *Super Trouper* was an instant hit. Preceded by *The Winner Takes It All*, itself an international hit, the album was a worldwide triumph. The cover, designed by Rune Söderqvist, shows the band in the middle of a troupe of circus performers. Söderqvist, the group's stylist and designer who had created the ABBA logo, the legendary *Greatest Hits* cover from 1975, and the sets for the 1979 tour, originally wanted to do a photo shoot at Piccadilly Circus in central London, where the foursome would be surrounded by crowds of passers-by and a troupe of circus performers and their menagerie. In late September 1980, a delegation consisting of Söderqvist, Thomas Johansson (the band's tour manager), Harvey Goldsmith (a well-known British promoter), and John Spalding (ABBA's British publisher) went to the West End Central Police Station at 27 Savile Row to request authorization for the photo shoot. "We were in there for two hours," Johansson later said. "Of course we wanted to make a video film of it all, for use by the TV companies to link up with the new single. The police said they would allow us to set up all the gear and everything but they would have to have shut off

the area to traffic and that meant doing it at 3 a.m. on a Sunday morning. They also drew our attention to a law which says there should be no outside entertainers, animals or whatever, within a three-mile radius of Charing Cross. We tried everything to get round that. We said that we could use stuffed animals and even mentioned that people dress funnily nowadays so maybe they could turn a blind eye to the clowns! They wouldn't take it, though."[99]

With the authorities in London unwilling to play ball, the team ultimately decided to hold the event in Stockholm's Europa Film Studios on 3 October 1980. Two circus troupes were hired for the occasion, but as they were rivals, one left before the photo shoot began. So various members of the band's entourage, including Polar Music vice-president Görel Hanser and singer Tomas Ledin, were pulled in and dressed up as circus performers. The party atmosphere at the shoot gave the team an idea for a name for the album. "It's kind of strange how the name 'Super Trouper' came, because we didn't have an idea at all what to call the album," Björn explained. "We actually started out making this photo for the sleeve. […] Seeing the spotlight coming up and down on us, it looked very much like one of the spotlights that we use on tour. They're very very big ones. They're called Super Troupers. And that's where it came from."[100]

1980s, here we come

Super Trouper was one of ABBA's biggest hits. Its synth-pop sounds (despite no drum machines being used on the record) differentiated it from past disco experiments and placed the band firmly in the new decade. Alongside its many timeless numbers (*The Winner Takes It All*, *Super Trouper*, *Lay All Your Love on Me,* etc.), the album also introduced a kind of darkness we never thought we'd hear in ABBA's music. Benny

On the set of the German TV program *Show Express*, 27 November 1980. The show was shot in Sweden following kidnap threats directed at ABBA.

Andersson's Polymoog and Yamaha GX-1 synthesizers are more prominent than ever in the mix, blocking out Janne Schaffer and Lasse Wellander's guitars, which had once been highlights, and the album's most upbeat songs do little to conceal the inevitable outcome of the ABBA adventure, which everyone was now dreading. When, in March 1980, a *Viva* journalist asked Agnetha and Frida about the possibility of the band splitting up, Frida's answer left us in no doubt. "Do you want an honest answer? The question is whether we will be able to quit. I think all four of us are still enjoying what we're doing, but we do find it more and more difficult to be ABBA. We've been in the music business for fifteen years now. […] We're not that youthful, glittery bunch that we were six years ago anymore. Meanwhile, we've been through a lot. As women, we've matured, developed and especially got older as well. We look at life in a different way and then it becomes less fun to be ABBA. Because we actually have to switch off ourselves for that. Because we are the 'property' of so many millions."[95]

Shooting the clip of *Estoy Soñando*, the Spanish version of *I Have a Dream*.

Overleaf: ABBA on the legendary stage of the Nippon Budokan in Tokyo, March 1980.

GRACIAS POR LA MÚSICA, A GIFT FOR SPANISH-SPEAKING FANS

On 28 May 1979, the members of ABBA traveled to Roma Studios in Madrid to film the TV program *300 Millones*, which was broadcast on Spain's RTVE1 channel as well as in many South American countries via satellite. In the days following the program's first airing in Europe, Chile, Uruguay, Paraguay, Bolivia, Peru, Ecuador, Colombia, Venezuela, Panama, Costa Rica, Nicaragua, El Salvador, Honduras, and Mexico succumbed to ABBA's charms, as the band ended the show with a Spanish version of their new single, *Chiquitita*. It was an instant hit and shot to the top of the charts in most of these countries, as the original version had done. From there, the germ of an idea grew and a few months later ABBA launched production of an album sung entirely in Spanish, aimed at winning over this new audience for good. *I Have A Dream* was the second song to benefit from a Spanish makeover; after being translated and renamed *Estoy Soñando,* it was recorded at the Metronome studio on 30 August 1979. Released as a single in Spain and other Spanish-speaking countries, it proved another success for ABBA, who in January 1980 left Michael B Tretow to produce the album, while Benny and Björn headed off to work on new material in Barbados.

Three helpers for the album

Polar Music called in Stockholm-based Argentinian journalist Ana Martinez del Valle to help Frida and Agnetha pronounce the lyrics translated by fellow Argentinians Buddy and Mary McCluskey, who had also translated *Chiquitita* and *I Have A Dream*. Martinez del Valle assisted the two singers with the vocal takes, which took place on 7 and 8 January 1980 and were also attended by the McCluskeys. Buddy and Mary explained to the women that Spanish only has five vowels, A, E, I, O, and U, which always sound the same. It was agreed that the tracks would be performed in neutral Spanish, with no Argentinian or Mexican dialect, so that they would work in other countries, such as Venezuela and Chile. "It was a great experience to work with ABBA," Mary McCluskey said. "They were so huge around the world, but they lived in a very simple way. [...] They lived a normal life just like any other citizen. We had long chats in their homes, and everything about them was admirable. They were very humble people, and they were great with us."[101]

Single

SUPER TROUPER

(Benny Andersson, Björn Ulvaeus/4'13)

Musicians
Anni-Frid "Frida" Lyngstad: lead vocals, backing vocals
Agnetha Fältskog: backing vocals
Benny Andersson: synthesizers, piano, glockenspiel, backing vocals
Björn Ulvaeus: acoustic guitar, backing vocals
Janne Schaffer: electric guitar
Mike Watson: bass
Per Lindvall: drums
Åke Sundqvist: percussion

Recording
Polar Music Studio, Stockholm: 3, 14 October 1980

Technical team
Producers: Björn Ulvaeus, Benny Andersson
Sound engineer: Michael B Tretow

Single
A-side: *Super Trouper*/4'13
B-side: *The Piper*/3'25
Released in Sweden by Polar Music: 25 November 1979
(single ref.: POS 1274)
Released in the UK by CBS/Epic: 25 November 1979
(single ref.: S EPC 9089)
Released in the USA by Atlantic: 25 November 1979
(single ref.: 3806)
Best chart ranking in Sweden: 11
Best chart ranking in the UK: 1
Best chart ranking in the USA: 45

HEADPHONES AT THE READY
Benny borrowed the few glockenspiel notes after his piano in the intro and before every verse from a track called *Lesson One* by popular 1950s' pianist Russ Conway.

Genesis
Although the album's title track, *Super Trouper*, struggled to win over American audiences when it was released as a single in November 1979, it was a total triumph in the UK, where it hit the top of the charts as soon as it came out. Frida, singing about the anguish of a singer in the limelight who is longing to return to her loved one, seems to appropriate the lyrics in a way she has never done before, possibly because the theme of the song coincided perfectly with her state of mind and her weariness with the constant touring, a sentiment that Agnetha shared. But the words to *Super Trouper*, a title that refers to the brand name of the spotlights made by the American company Strong Lighting, were written by Björn Ulvaeus, who at the time had the title in mind but little else. On this occasion, he admitted to having drawn on his own personal experience to write the song. "The previous year I had just met my current wife, Lena," Björn explained in 2011, "and she flew out to meet me when we were out on tour. So I found that this spotlight could be used as a vehicle in the lyrics."[94] "Having a good title was all very well," he added in another interview, "but it was something of a challenge having to write about some damned spotlight."[31]

Production
On 3 October 1980, Björn and Benny shut themselves away in Polar Music Studio with a specific aim: to write and record the last song for the new album, despite the sessions having ended a few days previously. "In fact we only had about a week to go in which to finish the LP," recalled Björn. "I said to Benny, 'We must write one more song,' so we sat down in the studio on the Wednesday and the Thursday and as we had the musicians booked for the Friday we were writing like mad to get it finished."[102] This was the first time the two friends had written an ABBA song under such conditions, and the urgency of the creative process for the *Super Trouper* album didn't give them time to call in their regular musicians, some of whom were already committed to other projects. This is why the drums on this track were recorded by Per Lindvall, a young session musician recommended by Janne Schaffer, who would pop up again 40 years later on *Voyage*. On bass, Mike Watson puts in a sparkling performance, taking inspiration for his score from a jazz bassist he had seen playing on stage at Ronnie Scott's club in London shortly before.

An alternative photograph taken by Lasse Larsson for the sleeve of the album *Super Trouper*.

Overleaf: Part of the extra footage for the clip of *Super Trouper,* shot in Europa Film studios, Stockholm, in October 1980.

Once his line was on tape, it was doubled by Benny on the Yamaha GX-1 and then reduced sharply in the mix. The song proved to be one of ABBA's most successful and was built around a straight rhythm, which is the only thing it has in common with the disco music the band had been playing a year earlier. Instead, the quartet deliver here a high-quality pop number with production that places the timeless melody front and center (removing the piano and guitar at the start of the choruses was a stroke of genius and works well). Indisputably melancholic, *Super Trouper* is absolutely wonderful and one of ABBA's many masterpieces.

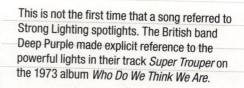

This is not the first time that a song referred to Strong Lighting spotlights. The British band Deep Purple made explicit reference to the powerful lights in their track *Super Trouper* on the 1973 album *Who Do We Think We Are.*

Single

THE WINNER TAKES IT ALL

(Benny Andersson, Björn Ulvaeus/4'55)

1980

Musicians

Agnetha Fältskog: lead vocals, backing vocals
Anni-Frid "Frida" Lyngstad: backing vocals
Benny Andersson: synthesizers, piano, backing vocals
Björn Ulvaeus: 12-string acoustic guitar, backing vocals
Lasse Wellander: acoustic guitar
Mike Watson: bass
Ola Brunkert: drums
Åke Sundqvist: percussion
Martyn Bylund: violin
Anders Dahl: violin
Gunnar Michols: violin
Bernt Nylund: violin
Bertil Orsin: violin
Lars Stegenberg: violin
Sixten Strömvall: violin
Harry Teike: violin
Niels Heie: viola
Håkan Roos: viola
Bo Söderström: viola
Olle Gustafsson: cello
Åke Olofsson: cello

Recording

Polar Music Studio, Stockholm: 2, 4, 6, 10, 12, 16 June 1980

Technical team

Producers: Björn Ulvaeus, Benny Andersson
Sound engineer: Michael B Tretow
String arrangements: Rutger Gunnarsson

Single

A-side: *The Winner Takes It All*/4'56
B-side: *Elaine*/3'39
Released in Sweden by Polar Music: 21 July 1980
(single ref.: POS 1272)
Released in the UK by CBS/Epic: 21 July 1980
(single ref.: S EPC 8835)
Released in the USA by Atlantic: 21 July 1980 (single ref.: 3776)
Best chart ranking in Sweden: 2
Best chart ranking in the UK: 1
Best chart ranking in the USA: 8

Genesis

ABBA's most famous song is also the saddest in their repertoire. It emerged from one of Benny and Björn's nocturnal work sessions on Viggsö island, starting on Saturday 31 May and continuing into 1 June 1980. They made a demo of the song using a drum machine and presented it to the band's musicians on Monday 2 June. "I will never forget the moment when *The Winner Takes It All* came together [...]," Björn Ulvaeus recalled in 2014. "We had this kind of folky hambo [a traditional Swedish dance] style verse and we also had this other bit that we thought was really good. Then we started playing the hambo half time—we left space in between the phrases of the hambo stuff and suddenly it was telling a story, suddenly it was like a French chanson. We played those two parts together and we knew, my God, this has got to be so good!"[103]

Once the backing tracks were laid down on tape, Ulvaeus worked on his lyrics one night in June, aided by a bottle of Scotch and the memories of his marriage to Agnetha. "As a matter of fact," he admitted in 2002, "I was quite drunk. And that's unusual, too, because it never works. Whenever you write drunk, whether it's music or lyrics, you look at it the next day and it's bullshit. But that was a good one. I remember presenting it to the girls, and there were tears, you know?"[3]

The Winner Takes It All openly alludes to the breakdown of Björn and Agnetha's marriage and he was asking her to perform the song as she was struggling to recover from the difficult split. "I went through a horrible, painful depression," Agnetha said later. "Knowing that I had to go further alone made me crazy. Björn always cared for everything, because we were very young when we met, and then, all of a sudden, I had to learn to stand on my own two feet. It touched me when he met Lena, and I cried when he re-married. I suffered. It was so strange that he had found someone else so soon."[5] Despite her pain, which is clearly audible in her performance, her vocal line on the piece, recorded with impeccable precision in a single take, provides ABBA with one of their most beautiful melodies.

The video for *The Winner Takes It All* was produced by Lasse Hallström, who was shooting some sequences for his fourth film, *Tuppen* ("The Rooster") in the small seaside town of Marstrand in the province of Bohuslän. The band traveled to Marstrand on 12 July to film the footage that would be used in the video, in which Agnetha acts her heart out as a woman

Françoise Pourcel, Mireille Mathieu, Anni-Frid "Frida" Lyngstad, and Björn Ulvaeus recording *Bravo tu as gagné*.

FOR ABBA ADDICTS

On 10 and 11 December 1980, the French singer Mireille Mathieu came to Polar Music Studio to record her own version of *The Winner Takes It All* (*Bravo tu as gagné* in French). Under the artistic direction of Alain Boublil and with lyrics by Charles Level, the French star was assisted by Björn, Frida, and Benny, who recorded backing vocals for the song. Benny provided the new piano tracks for this eminently forgettable reworking, which would nevertheless prove a huge hit for Mireille Mathieu, and put a few more royalties in the pockets of the two men who wrote *The Winner Takes It All*.

alone among her happy friends. The atmosphere on set was somewhat surreal that day, with Björn accompanied by his new wife and Agnetha by her new boyfriend, businessman Dick Håkansson. With the addition of images from the ABBA archive the video feels like the band's swansong, but it wasn't over yet.

Production

In June 1980, the editorial team from *ABBA Magazine*, the band's fanzine, was invited to Polar Music studio to see a song being recorded. *The Winner Takes It All* was being laid down on tape that day and the journalists enjoyed watching Benny Andersson record the song's famous keyboard lines on the studio's grand piano. Björn Ulvaeus was on 12-string acoustic guitar and Agnetha soon appeared, walking barefooted across the studio's wooden flooring. "It was fantastic to do that song because I could put in such feeling," she observed years later. "I didn't mind sharing it with the public. It didn't feel wrong. There is so much in that song. It was a mixture of what I felt and what Björn felt but also what Benny and Frida went through."[104] Rutger Gunnarsson once again did the string arrangements, giving *The Winner Takes It All* the last score of this kind in the ABBA catalog. After the session on 16 June 1980, the band stopped using violinists and cellists to add string layers to a song, preferring to emulate orchestral sounds with synthesizers. It wasn't until *Voyage* was recorded between 2017 and 2021 that real musicians returned to replace the synth modeling on Benny's Yamaha GX-1.

Single

ON AND ON AND ON

(Benny Andersson, Björn Ulvaeus/3'41)

Musicians

Agnetha Fältskog: vocals, backing vocals
Anni-Frid "Frida" Lyngstad: vocals, backing vocals
Benny Andersson: synthesizers, piano, backing vocals
Björn Ulvaeus: backing vocals
Janne Schaffer: electric guitar
Rutger Gunnarsson: bass
Ola Brunkert: drums
Åke Sundqvist: percussion
Lars O Carlsson: saxophone
Kajtek Wojciechowski: saxophone
Janne Kling: saxophone

Recording

Polar Music Studio, Stockholm: 12 February, 17, 20 April 1980

Technical team

Producers: Björn Ulvaeus, Benny Andersson
Sound engineer: Michael B Tretow

Single

A-side: *On and On and On*/3'41
B-side: *Lay All Your Love on Me*/4'31
Released in the USA by Atlantic: June 1981 (single ref.: 3826)
Best chart ranking in the USA: 90

Genesis

By June 1981, synth-pop and new wave were gradually making their way into the charts, with The Human League and their album *Dare* leading the charge, along with Prince's *Dirty Mind*, and Kim Wilde's hits. This wave of change was also felt in Sweden and didn't escape the notice of Benny Andersson and Björn Ulvaeus, even though the latter couldn't resist a dig at the new music genre: "I listen to everything new that's released on the market. In my opinion, some of this new wave stuff doesn't sound that new to me."[105] Inspired by these new synthetic sounds, *On and On and On* was produced in a similar fashion to other contemporary hits and would have been the start of a new era for ABBA had the band not decided to take a break two years later. Another inspiration behind the song's arrangements was The Beach Boys' number *Do It Again*, which had been a big hit for the Californian band in 1968. ABBA's backing vocals were based on those of The Beach Boys, a point not lost on their lead singer, Mike Love, who recorded two versions of *On and On and On*: in 1981 on his album *Looking Back with Love*, and again in 2019 on *12 Sides of Summer*. "I thought it was really fun that it came full circle," Benny Andersson said.[94]

Production

The year 1980 saw the advent of new musical instruments that would give artists infinite possibilities when it came to producing their tracks. In England, Queen discovered the LinnDrum machines, already used by Prince in the USA on his album *Controversy*, while, more generally, synthesizers began to replace violins and brass instruments in the studio. Suzanne Ciani, a pioneer in the field, was mocked when she demonstrated the use of electronic instruments on *The David Letterman Show* in August 1980, but she would go on to influence many musicians looking for less-organic sounds than those produced by traditional instruments. Benny Andersson was one such musician and when he first heard of this revolutionary instrument, in early 1980, he decided to use one with some ABBA songs: a Roland VP-330 vocoder popularized by the German band Kraftwerk and by David Bowie. It alters the pitch of a recorded note and can be heard in Agnetha's vocals at 00'36 of *On and On and On*.

Like Wendy Carlos, Suzanne Ciani was one of the pioneers of electronic music.

ANDANTE, ANDANTE

(Benny Andersson, Björn Ulvaeus/4'38)

1980

Musicians

Anni-Frid "Frida" Lyngstad: lead vocals, backing vocals
Agnetha Fältskog: backing vocals
Benny Andersson: synthesizers, piano, backing vocals
Björn Ulvaeus: mandolin, backing vocals
Lasse Wellander: electric guitar, mandolin
Rutger Gunnarsson: bass, mandolin
Ola Brunkert: drums

Recording

Polar Music Studio, Stockholm: 4, 8 February 1980

Technical team

Producers: Björn Ulvaeus, Benny Andersson
Sound engineer: Michael B Tretow

Genesis

Although ABBA's new songs were somewhat introspective, sharing with fans their relationship problems, songwriters Björn and Benny spoke of also wanting to write songs that their audiences would enjoy. "I'd like everybody to be entertained from what we're doing, from my music," Benny said in 1980. "That's the main goal for us."[100] Goal achieved with this ballad. Built around triplets, *Andante, Andante* is a somewhat sugary number that gives fans a chance to enjoy a slow dance. "I wanted some soft and beautiful lyrics for this song, that's all," Björn said. "I suppose I could have been inspired by the great romantic poets and maybe there is an element of John Donne in there."[106] With its erotic metaphors that remind us of Ulvaeus' flirtatious personality (*andante* refers to a slow tempo in music, as Frida sings, "Take it easy with me, please/ Touch me gently like a summer evening breeze"), *Andante, Andante* is a ballad that Frida has always loved. In 2018, she did a cover version accompanied by trumpet player Arturo Sandoval that appeared on his album *Ultimate Duets*.

Production

ABBA once again take us on a journey with this song, whose title is borrowed from the Italian. Perhaps inevitably, on 8 February 1980 Björn and Benny felt it necessary to add a mandolin score to the track; it was supplied by Lasse Wellander, Rutger Gunnarsson, and Björn himself. This is what makes ABBA unique. Despite their huge success and their millions of fans, they still come across as a band doing their own thing regardless of trends, and they see no problem with adding a track that sounds like something out of a cheap Italian rom-com to a perfectly produced new-wave album. A second version of *Andante, Andante* exists with a different mix and a few of the lyrics altered. It was included in the 2014 box set *The Singles*, a reissue of the 40 singles ABBA released during their career.

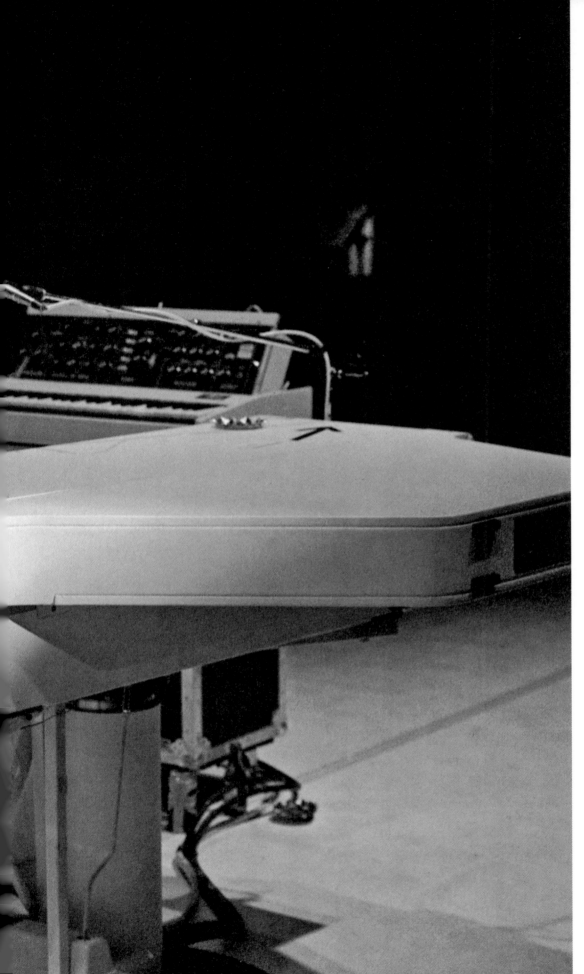

Frida imitated the voice of
Eartha Kitt when recording
Me and I.

Overleaf: Recording vocals
for *Our Last Summer,*
June 1980.

ME AND I

(Benny Andersson, Björn Ulvaeus/4'53)

1980

Musicians

Anni-Frid "Frida" Lyngstad: lead vocals, backing vocals
Agnetha Fältskog: vocals, backing vocals
Benny Andersson: synthesizers, backing vocals
Björn Ulvaeus: acoustic guitar, backing vocals
Lasse Wellander: electric guitar
Rutger Gunnarsson: bass
Ola Brunkert: drums
Åke Sundqvist: percussion

Recording

Polar Music Studio, Stockholm: 8 September 1980

Technical team

Producers: Björn Ulvaeus, Benny Andersson
Sound engineer: Michael B Tretow

Genesis

Produced by Björn Ulvaeus and Benny Andersson on Viggsö island during their August 1980 writing sessions, *Me and I* is the result of days and days of work, with the two songwriters waiting for inspiration to strike. "I'm a nine-to-five man," Andersson explained. "I have to sit here and wait for the good notes to sort of come from somewhere, and if I'm not here, they're not gonna come. It's like there's a dragon in a cave. You know it's in there but it's never coming out. So you have to sit outside and wait for it. If you sit there long enough, it's gonna come out but if you go home and take a nap, you'll never see it because that's when it's coming out."[107] This time, the dragon did indeed come out of hiding to inspire Benny to write *Me and I*, in which Frida sings about split personalities, the angel and the devil that live in some of us and that we generally get used to.

Production

Over the years, Björn Ulvaeus focused mainly on writing the lyrics to ABBA songs, leaving Benny Andersson to develop his many ideas for melodies and arrangements that increasingly involved electronic sounds produced by synthesizers. *Me and I* is one such song, mostly built around the infinite possibilities offered by Andersson's Yamaha GX-1, as well as the Roland VP-330 and its vocoder function, already used on *On and On and On* a few months earlier. "I love my synthesizers," he said at the time. "There's so many good things around these days, you can do anything. I prefer the grand piano, though, as an instrument, but as I don't write or read music, I use the synthesizers to add on the records what an orchestra would do otherwise."[100] As lead singer on the track, Frida deliberately disguises her voice, pronouncing the lyrics in the style of Eartha Kitt, the American singer of whom she is a great admirer. Agnetha had similarly paid tribute to Connie Francis on *Hasta Mañana* and to Doris Day on the first version of *Thank You for the Music.*

HAPPY NEW YEAR

(Benny Andersson, Björn Ulvaeus/4'37)

1980

Musicians

Agnetha Fältskog: lead vocals, backing vocals
Anni-Frid "Frida" Lyngstad: backing vocals
Benny Andersson: synthesizers, piano, backing vocals
Björn Ulvaeus: acoustic guitar, backing vocals
Janne Schaffer: electric guitar
Rutger Gunnarsson: bass
Ola Brunkert: drums

Recording

Polar Music Studio, Stockholm: 11 February 1980

Technical team

Producers: Björn Ulvaeus, Benny Andersson
Sound engineer: Michael B Tretow

Genesis

Similar to the topical Cold War theme that would be seen in their next album, *The Visitors*, ABBA in 1980 produced a ballad imbued with a certain anxiety, despite its festive name: *Happy New Year*. Agnetha sings about the end of a party, a metaphor for the end of the 1970s, the start of a new era, and whether or not there will be a happy ending. "The thought of what will come of this world in the future," Agnetha explains. "We don't know, none of us, what would come in, for example, 89 and that's what the song is about."[100] Björn and Benny wrote the song during their trip to Barbados, with the idea of using it in a musical, a project they had had in mind for some time. "We thought it would be a good framework," Andersson said: "A few people in a room, looking back on what has been, thinking about the future, that sort of thing."[108] The two friends were so excited about the project that they took the opportunity of a dinner they attended with the English comedian John Cleese, who was also on vacation in Barbados, to invite him to join them in the adventure. "He said, 'No!'" Andersson reported. "We didn't get any further with that idea. But we liked the song."[53] *Happy New Year* became an ABBA classic in Sweden, and since 2018 has been regularly re-released in time for the Christmas holidays.

Production

In February 1980, the magazine *Sound International* published an interview with Michael B Tretow in which the sound engineer revealed his studio secrets for the first time. Readers were able to discover some of the techniques applied to create the ABBA sound, such as the use of the famous Neumann U87 microphone to capture Björn's acoustic guitar, along with a pair of AKG C34s, one in front of the guitar and the second some distance away, to pick up the atmosphere of the room. Agnetha and Frida's vocals were recorded together, with the two singers facing one another on either side of an AKG C34. "For Benny and Björn, I use a U47 if they're doing tight harmonies," he said at the time. "If it is more of a 'choir' character we're after we usually record out in the big isolation room at Polar Studio with just one stereo mic hanging from the ceiling."[109]

Above: Once again, the break-up of Björn Ulvaeus and Agnetha Fältskog was portrayed in the video of *Happy New Year*.
Overleaf: Frida and Agnetha on the set of the clip of *Happy New Year*, 8 November 1980.

The vocal line in *Our Last Summer* is one of the most moving that Anni-Frid "Frida" Lyngstad recorded for ABBA.

Overleaf: The whole ABBA team during the sessions for *Our Last Summer*, June 1980.

OUR LAST SUMMER

(Benny Andersson, Björn Ulvaeus/4'18)

1980

Musicians
Anni-Frid "Frida" Lyngstad: lead vocals, backing vocals
Agnetha Fältskog: backing vocals
Benny Andersson: synthesizers, piano, glockenspiel, backing vocals
Björn Ulvaeus: acoustic guitar, backing vocals
Lasse Wellander: electric guitar
Rutger Gunnarsson: bass
Ola Brunkert: drums
Åke Sundqvist: percussion

Recording
Polar Music Studio, Stockholm: 4 to 6, 10 to 12 June 1980

Technical team
Producers: Björn Ulvaeus, Benny Andersson
Sound engineer: Michael B Tretow

HEADPHONES AT THE READY
The discreet piano line played by Benny Andersson at 2'47 on *Our Last Summer* is something he and Björn Ulvaeus liked so much they decided to keep it for the track *Anthem*, which would be performed as the conclusion of the first act of the musical *Chess* in 1984. "[…] We figured that no-one would have noticed that little part enough to say that we had 'stolen' anything from *Our Last Summer*," Benny joked several years later.[110]

Genesis

That our four Swedes were romantic at heart had been proven time and again, especially when it came to Björn Ulvaeus, who wrote the lyrics for the mostly autobiographical ballad *Our Last Summer*. In summer of 1959, Ulvaeus had visited Paris, where he met a Swedish friend who had recently moved there. "We had not been romantically involved in Sweden, but Paris tends to have that effect on people, and so it was with the two of us. She certainly took me to see the Quartier Latin, the Champs-Élysées and the Eiffel Tower, but to be honest I don't really remember much of Paris. I mostly remember her!"[110] Ulvaeus first alluded to this memory in *Monsieur, Monsieur*, the first version of *My Love, My Life,* recorded in August 1976. While Agnetha had performed lead vocals on that track, it was Frida's turn with *Our Last Summer*, which lists some of the features of the City of Love: the cafés, philosophical discussions, Mona Lisa's smile, the Seine, the Trocadero gardens, Notre-Dame, and of course the famous croissants for breakfast. While the lyrics are a rather caricatured collection of clichés of Parisian life, we can appreciate ABBA's attraction to the City of Light and the influence it had on Björn's lyrics, even though splendid Stockholm is just as much a dream destination for many non-Swedes.

Production

Lasse Wellander was invited to contribute a solo guitar line on *Our Last Summer*, a privilege that Benny and Björn rarely granted during recording sessions, ABBA's discography being almost entirely devoid of solo guitar. Lasse used his Fender Stratocaster 1962 for the occasion, plugged into one of his Music Man amps and using pedal effects stored in the pedalboard built by specialist Pete Cornish. The entire backline can now be seen at ABBA The Museum in Stockholm. "I always try to place the electric guitar amp in a different room," Michael B Tretow explained, "if the studio has access to a storage room or something like that. I believe that to get a really loud sound you must play loud and literally let the sound fill the room. I use one close-up mic in front of the amp and one omni, out in the room, to pick up rattling windows and the like."[109]

Stephen King, idol of Björn
and Benny, and world
superstar of fantasy fiction.

THE PIPER

(Benny Andersson, Björn Ulvaeus/3'25)

Musicians
Agnetha Fältskog: vocals, backing vocals
Anni-Frid "Frida" Lyngstad: vocals, backing vocals
Benny Andersson: synthesizers, piano, backing vocals
Björn Ulvaeus: acoustic guitar, backing vocals
Lasse Wellander: electric guitar, acoustic guitar
Rutger Gunnarsson: bass
Ola Brunkert: drums
Janne Kling: flute

Recording
Polar Music Studio, Stockholm: 6 to 7 February, 17, 20 April 1980

Technical team
Producers: Björn Ulvaeus, Benny Andersson
Sound engineer: Michael B Tretow

HEADPHONES AT THE READY
To accentuate what were already very dark lyrics, Björn asked Agnetha and Frida to sing a phrase in Latin after each chorus, "*sub luna saltamus.*" Echoing the chorus itself, it means "We dance beneath the moon."

Genesis

Hearing this strange song, recorded in February 1980, you'd swear you were listening to the soundtrack of the Midsommar festivities, the traditional Swedish festival in which Björn, Benny, and Stig Andersson participated every year, guitars and accordion slung over their shoulders. But if you listen carefully to the lyrics you'll notice it's not about a festival, but about people in thrall to a spiritual guide playing a flute to seduce his victims. "He gave them a dream/He seduced everybody in the land/The fire in his eyes/And the fear was a weapon in his hand," Frida and Agnetha sing to the rhythm of a hypothetical jig danced by the crowd in the song. Björn, who in 1978 had confided to readers of *ABBA Magazine,* "I'm a science-fiction freak,"[111] was inspired here by Stephen King's *The Stand* (1978), and in particular by the character Randall Flagg, the tyrant who used a global pandemic to win the people's trust. "The lyrics deal with the fear that there will come a time when people will want such a leader again."[108] The theme of fear was increasingly present in the music of ABBA, a band everyone once loved for their cheerfulness, and things would soon take an even darker turn with the album *The Visitors*.

Production

From *Super Trouper* onwards, ABBA decided not to specify in the album credits whether Agnetha or Frida supplied lead vocals on the songs. "We left the vocal credits off the sleeve on purpose," Björn explained at the time. "We think that the fans know the girls' voices so well now that they will be able to recognize who takes lead on every track. It is like a game that we have presented to the fans. If there are any doubts then I am sure that eventually they will all be cleared up in interviews."[102] No question as to who it is when you listen to *The Piper*, because Agnetha and Frida perform the track together to give it a group, if not exactly a party, feel.

Benny Andersson during
the Midsommar celebration,
Viggsö, 1980.

Single

LAY ALL YOUR LOVE ON ME

(Benny Andersson, Björn Ulvaeus/4'33)

1980

Musicians
Agnetha Fältskog: lead vocals, backing vocals
Anni-Frid "Frida" Lyngstad: backing vocals
Benny Andersson: synthesizers, backing vocals
Björn Ulvaeus: backing vocals
Lasse Wellander: electric guitar
Rutger Gunnarsson: bass
Ola Brunkert: drums

Recording
Polar Music Studio, Stockholm: 9 September 1980

Technical team
Producers: Björn Ulvaeus, Benny Andersson
Sound engineer: Michael B Tretow

Single
A-side: *Lay All Your Love on Me*/4'33
B-side: *On and On and On*/3'41
Released in the UK by CBS/Epic: July 1981
(maxi single ref.: A 13-1456)
Best chart ranking in the UK: 7

Genesis

If we didn't know that Benny Andersson and Björn Ulvaeus had a sense of adventure, we'd think that *Lay All Your Love on Me* was a choir singing on a Sunday morning in the little chapel in Lindingö, where Benny and Frida lived. Andersson's desire to write a song with such a mystical feel came to him when he was listening to Supertramp's albums, in particular 1979's *Breakfast in America*, which featured the hit singles *The Logical Song, Goodbye Stranger*, and *Take the Long Way Home*. The melody for this track is so effective that the two songwriters were even accused of taking it from an existing national anthem. "No, it is not the same tune," said Benny Andersson, "but it is meant to sound similar to the way hymns sound. That is the whole point. We wrote a hymn-like song on purpose because that is what we wanted."[112] They achieved their goal and it became one of ABBA's greatest tracks. The American label Sugarscoop, which had just launched its Disconet Program Service offering compilations of remixes of popular songs to nightclub DJs, included a version of *Lay All Your Love on Me* by remixer Raul A Rodriguez on volume four of the collection in May 1981. Following the success of the remix in clubs, Polar Music released a maxi single of the song in the UK: it would become the biggest-selling record in this format since star producer Tom Moulton launched it a few years earlier. In the USA, a promotional version of the record aimed at disc jockeys also found an audience in nightclubs.

Production

On 9 September 1980, *Lay All Your Love on Me* was recorded in one day from two segments that Björn and Benny had set aside some time before and that were never intended to go together: a very pop-sounding verse and a chorus that Agnetha Fältskog recited like a religious chant. Forerunner to a musical genre that was about to take the world by storm, ABBA's *Lay All Your Love on Me* introduces the synth-pop and new-wave sounds that would soon be developed by British bands such as New Order, Soft Cell, and Depeche Mode. The only feature these sounds have in common with disco is their fast, upbeat tempo.

Like Supertramp's songs, which inspired Björn and Benny when they wrote the melody for the verses, *Lay All Your Love on Me* is structured mainly around the synthesizer. Here, of

The Swedish singer Zara Larsson made a faithful but updated reinterpretation of *Lay All Your Love on Me* in 2021.

course, it's Benny's Dream Machine, his precious Yamaha GX-1, which is used extensively to add multiple layers of electronic sound to every bar of the song. Listening at 2'37 to the gimmick that bears an uncanny resemblance to the intro of *Africa Unite* by Bob Marley and The Wailers on the B-side of 1979's *Survival*, you can even hear the preset used by John Paul Jones for his legendary solo on *All My Love*. It was after he saw Led Zeppelin using the GX-1 when they came to Polar Music Studio in November 1978 that Benny Andersson decided to buy one for himself. Original, mysterious, intoxicating—there are many adjectives to describe this song, which is unique in ABBA's repertoire and whose boldness never ceases to amaze listeners.

Cover versions of *Lay All Your Love on Me* abound. While the hair-raising version by the German band Helloween on the 1999 compilation *Metal Jukebox* pleased metalheads, the one performed by Zara Larsson at her concert at Oslo Spektrum in Norway on 20 November 2021 delighted ABBA fans, with the young Swedish singer showing what audiences might have experienced had ABBA ever sung the song on stage.

THE WAY OLD FRIENDS DO

(Benny Andersson, Björn Ulvaeus/2'53)

1980

Musicians
Agnetha Fältskog: vocals
Anni-Frid "Frida" Lyngstad: vocals
Benny Andersson: synthesizers, accordion, vocals
Björn Ulvaeus: vocals
Anders Eljas: synthesizers
Åke Sundqvist: kettle drums
Tomas Ledin: backing vocals
Birgitta Wollgård: backing vocals
Liza Öhman: backing vocals

Recording
Wembley Arena, London: November 1979
Polar Music Studio, Stockholm: 6 to 8 October 1980

Technical team
Producers: Björn Ulvaeus, Benny Andersson
Sound engineers: Bernard Löhr (Wembley Arena), Michael B Tretow
Assistant sound engineer: Filip Lindholm (Wembley Arena)

Genesis

Without a doubt one of the most moving tracks in ABBA's repertoire, *The Way Old Friends Do* is one of those songs you link arms with the people next to you in a pub to sing, as you would with The Pogues' *Dirty Old Town*, U2's *Van Diemen's Land*, or Renaud's *La Ballade nord-irlandaise* ("The Northern Irish Ballad"), which are all built around the same harmonic development. ABBA used *The Way Old Friends Do* as the encore on their 1979 tour, with the four artists standing at the front of the stage, and Benny's accordion the only instrument. It is a song of peace and fraternity, melodious and melancholic like many of the band's compositions. It is also a song about separation, alluding to Agnetha and Björn's split, Benny and Frida's impending divorce, and ultimately the end of the band. "It came out so well, so we were thinking maybe we should have that as a live track on the next album," Agnetha said.[100] Listening to *The Way Old Friends Do* sends shivers down your spine: it is a song on which ABBA could have ended their career—or at least the first part of it—as they deliver a beautiful thank you and farewell message to their fans.

Production

"The live version has a very, very nice atmosphere to it," explained Benny. "We felt something would be lacking if we had done it here in the studio."[100] That said, as with most of the live albums released at the time, *The Way Old Friends Do* was recorded live (during the concerts at Wembley Arena, London, in November 1979), before being polished in the studio. A few accordion sections and some of the orchestration were added to the track at Polar Music Studio in October 1980, without diminishing it in any way. This is how the album ends, with ABBA waving at us as if to say goodbye, a friendly smile on their lips. It's a song that those who still insist ABBA are a disco band would do well to listen to.

ELAINE

(Benny Andersson, Björn Ulvaeus/3'44)

Musicians

Agnetha Fältskog: vocals, backing vocals
Anni-Frid "Frida" Lyngstad: vocals, backing vocals
Benny Andersson: synthesizers, backing vocals
Björn Ulvaeus: backing vocals
Lasse Wellander: acoustic guitar
Rutger Gunnarsson: bass
Ola Brunkert: drums

Recording

Polar Music Studio, Stockholm: 5 February, 21 April 1980

Technical team

Producers: Björn Ulvaeus, Benny Andersson
Sound engineer: Michael B Tretow

Single *The Winner Takes It All*

A-side: *The Winner Takes It All*/4'56
B-side: *Elaine*/3'39
Released in Sweden by Polar Music: 21 July 1980
(single ref.: POS 1272)
Released in the UK by CBS/Epic: 21 July 1980
(single ref.: S EPC 8835)
Released in the USA by Atlantic: 21 July 1980 (single ref.: 3776)
Best chart ranking in Sweden: 2
Best chart ranking in the UK: 1
Best chart ranking in the USA: 8

Genesis

The B-side of the single *The Winner Takes It All* is a pop track in the tradition of *Lovelight*, another ABBA song that didn't make it onto an album. In *Elaine*, Agnetha and Frida sing about a young woman caught in a trap; although they reveal no more about the situation, we imagine it is related to the character's home life. This theme had already been addressed in 1974's *Hey, Hey Helen*, when the women sang about someone who had had the courage to leave an unfaithful husband and a life she wanted to be free from. Interviewed on the subject in 1980, Agnetha talked openly about the role of women and her acceptance of motherhood, a status that is very much respected in Sweden. "Because I travel a lot, I have a nanny. But servants? No thanks! When I'm at home, I do everything myself. I hate to sit around and do nothing, and I prefer to cook and do the laundry myself. Of course, we don't have any worries financially, but that didn't go to our head. We are living an utterly plain life, we are living in simple houses and are driving ordinary cars."[113]

Production

Apart from a few overdubs added on 21 April, *Elaine* was recorded in one day, on 5 February 1980. The days at Polar Music Studio were long and busy, with no one leaving until the work in progress was finished. "Benny is an incurable worker who never wants to go home," said Michael B Tretow at the time. "Even if we've been working since early morning and it's past midnight, he wants to keep on."[114] Days spent in the studio all followed the same rigorous pattern at the time. After checking the equipment, the musicians took their places to record the backing tracks for that day's song, with Benny Andersson frequently handling the synthesizer parts from the control room. Björn or Benny then placed vocal cues to guide Agnetha and Frida when they sang the melody and, once the main vocal lines were committed to tape, it was time to add the final overdubs, backing vocals, and mixing, which was mostly done by Andersson, Ulvaeus, and Tretow.

Agnetha Fältskog has always put her family life before her career. Here she is with her daughter Linda in 1974.

Björn Ulvaeus and Benny Andersson in London, August 1980.

PUT ON YOUR WHITE SOMBRERO

(Benny Andersson, Björn Ulvaeus/4'32)

Musicians

Agnetha Fältskog: vocals, backing vocals
Anni-Frid "Frida" Lyngstad: vocals, backing vocals
Benny Andersson: synthesizers, backing vocals
Björn Ulvaeus: backing vocals
Lasse Wellander: acoustic guitar, mandolin?
Rutger Gunnarsson: bass
Ola Brunkert: drums, tambourine

Recording

Polar Music Studio Stockholm: 9 September 1980

Technical team

Producers: Björn Ulvaeus, Benny Andersson
Sound engineer: Michael B Tretow

Thank You for the Music box set

Released in Europe and the UK by Polar Music—Polydor: 31 October 1994 (CD box set ref.: 523 472-2)
Released in the USA by Polar Music—Polydor: 31 October 1994 (CD box set ref.: 314 523 472-2)
Best chart ranking in the UK: 17
Best chart ranking in the USA: did not make the charts

Genesis

Almost as if they wanted to prove that a leopard doesn't change its spots, just after they recorded *Lay All Your Love on Me*—a revolutionary song that would sow the seeds of the synth-pop sounds that would soon be used worldwide—Benny Andersson and Björn Ulvaeus put aside their desire to evolve artistically. Instead, on 9 September 1980, they took a huge step backwards when they recorded a track inspired by traditional Mexican music. Triplets, tambourines galore, and Frida's exaggerated vocal effects: everything here is totally overproduced. The band made a wise decision to exclude this pop-mariachi number from the album and put it at the back of a drawer at Polar Music until 1994, when it would be exhumed for the box set *Thank You for the Music*. It could then be appreciated for what it was: a song composed and recorded in record time, but not suitable for the ABBA of 1980.

Production

In 1980, the production of songs such as *Put on Your White Sombrero* was both ABBA's strength and their Achilles heel. Although fans have always loved the band's lighter tracks, as well as the more Spanish-sounding ones, such as *Hasta Mañana*, *Fernando*, and *Chiquitita*, the general public and the media soon grew weary of ABBA's musical experimentation, which made them seem outdated throughout the 1980s and overshadowed their many timeless compositions. "Some pedantic music critics have described ABBA's music as 'sugary and tedious,'" Benny Andersson commented at the time. "That doesn't bother us anymore, especially since millions of people all over the world keep on buying our music. We serve our customer, the only one who decides what's good or bad. I think it's less fun to hear, after having spent a whole year working very hard on a new album, that you didn't make an effort. But we even learned to live with remarks like these."[79]

THE VISITORS

The Visitors • Head Over Heels • When All Is Said And Done •
Soldiers • I Let The Music Speak • One Of Us •
Two For The Price Of One • Slipping Through My Fingers •
Like An Angel Passing Through My Room

Released in Sweden by Polar Music: 30 November 1981 (LP ref.: POLS 342)
Released in the UK by CBS/Epic: 30 November 1981 (LP Ref.: EPC 10032)
Released in the USA by Atlantic: 30 November 1981 (LP ref.: SD 19332)
Best chart ranking in Sweden: 1
Best chart ranking in the UK: 1
Best chart ranking in the USA: 29

1981

THE END OF A STORY

The changes that would upend the equilibrium that had lasted within ABBA for almost ten years began to take place from the beginning of 1981. On 5 January, Björn Ulvaeus and Lena Källersjö were married in the little church of Grythyttan. The event was followed by a small celebration at the Grythyttans Gästgivaregård restaurant, owned by the famous chef Carl Jan Granqvist. On 12 February the harmony that until recently had reigned within the group was once again disturbed, by the announcement of the divorce of Benny Andersson and Frida Lyngstad. Relations between the two had markedly worsened during the tour in 1979, and in the autumn of 1980 Benny had met Mona Nörklit, a 37-year-old journalist, at a dinner at the house of mutual friends. This brought the marriage to an end. "It took me a quarter of an hour to realize that I was sat next to a woman who would change my life," he said in 2010. "I don't know how it happened. Something hit me. It was as if I had no choice. We talked non-stop for about eight hours, but I have no idea about what! I was married to Frida then, and not interested in playing about, so it took three or four months before Mona and I were a proper couple."[11] The following 31 December, Benny married Mona, with whom he would have a child in 1982. At the time of writing, they are still a couple. "Actually, what has happened isn't sad at all," Frida explained. "We just grew apart due to different interests in life. We've always been honest to each other. We talked and talked and talked and eventually we both came to the conclusion that a divorce was the only way out."[5] "It was a very difficult and frustrating time," she added in a different interview. "Both of us wanted a different life, but as members of the group we had to keep on presenting ourselves to the audience as a happy couple. It even came to the point where we forced ourselves to go out in the evening, because we couldn't bear to be in each other's company at home any longer."[115]

A poisonous atmosphere at Polar Music Studios

Once they had moved on, in the spring of 1981 ABBA got down to work with their new album. In March, they recorded three new songs at their studio, recently renamed Polar Music Studios—the plural emphasizing more explicitly the size of the recording complex. The songs—*Two for the Price of One, Slipping through my Fingers*, and *When All Is Said and Done*—featured a pop flavor that was true to ABBA. But although melodies lay at the heart of these new compositions, their sound was older than formerly, as if it was a sign of the times—the early 1980s are notorious for the icy sound of the group's recordings. Polar Music Studios' acquisition of the brand-new 3M Digital Audio Mastering System 32-track digital tape recorder had a considerable impact on ABBA's sound; also, their production was ever more modern, thanks especially to the now extensive use of Yamaha GX-1 and Roland Jupiter JP-8 synthesizers. "Icy" also describes the atmosphere during those March sessions, for behind the professionalism of the group's members—who looked happy in public—relations in the studio worsened considerably. A journalist of the magazine *Privé*, who attended one of these recording sessions, described the experience: "There's a clear tension between [Benny and Anni-Frid]. There's nothing left of the fun and joyous atmosphere of the old days."[116] Although a few sessions were held in October and November, to complete the album by adding

Above: Michael B Tretow, Benny Andersson, and Björn Ulvaeus at the Harrison 40/32 console of Polar Music Studio.
Opposite: Rehearsals for the television special *Dick Cavett Meets ABBA*, filmed in April 1981.

certain overdubs, most of it was recorded from September 1981, and its release was set for 30 November.

A feeling that the end was nigh

The release of *The Visitors* confirmed in the eyes of the whole world the image of a group in the throes of disintegrating. Its favorite themes were no longer love and *joie de vivre*, but rather the social and political crises sweeping the world at the start of the 1980s, as well as the birth pangs of a new era. Björn's lyrics addressed—sometimes obliquely, sometimes explicitly—the geopolitical situation, such as the Cold War raging between the Soviet Union and the USA, threatening the world with imminent nuclear conflict. Moreover, his writing was tinged with a darkness that unsettled journalists who interviewed him. "The saddest thing in the industrial countries is that no one is looking at the future with confidence anymore," he told *Bravo* magazine. "Everyone is having a negative attitude. People are afraid of changes. The politicians are worse than ever. To me, they are worthless, because they have lost contact with the people. [...] These days, it seems to me that the brakes are put on young people. That's why so many of them are taking drugs. They don't have any reason to look at the future joyfully, because that's where unemployment, crises, and economic problems are waiting.

And they are escaping this hopelessness with alcohol and drugs."[105]

Rune Söderqvist, who was once more entrusted with creating the record's sleeve, had the measure of its anxiety-inducing character when he addressed the issue. Together with photographer Lasse Larsson, with whom he had created the festive sleeve of *Super Trouper* the previous year, Söderqvist decided to adopt the opposite approach from what he had used then, this time drawing inspiration from the album's enigmatic title: *The Visitors*. For him, the visitors in question were angels, who survey our world from a distance. Taking ideas from the work of the nineteenth-century Swedish artist Julius Kronberg, who produced numerous paintings of angels, Söderqvist decided to organize the photo shoot in his workshop, which had been converted to a museum, in Skansen Park, Stockholm. The members of ABBA posed, at a distance from each other, in front of Kronberg's canvases, as if impassive in the face of their group's unhappy fate. The cover of *The Visitors* was surprising, coming from a group recently criticized for the syrupy nature of their songs, and it disconcerted fans, who did not identify with ABBA portraying a dark world. "It really reflects what was happening," Benny Andersson declared years later. "Basically, we'd had enough."[3]

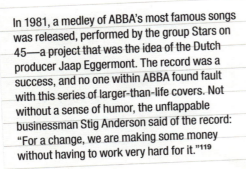

In 1981, a medley of ABBA's most famous songs was released, performed by the group Stars on 45—a project that was the idea of the Dutch producer Jaap Eggermont. The record was a success, and no one within ABBA found fault with this series of larger-than-life covers. Not without a sense of humor, the unflappable businessman Stig Anderson said of the record: "For a change, we are making some money without having to work very hard for it."[119]

1981

In order to quell increasingly persistent rumors in the press that the group might be breaking up, Görel Hanser, vice-president of Polar Music, decided to conclude the press release of 21 October 1981 for the launch of *The Visitors* with a formal denial: "There have been lots of rumors about ABBA splitting up, but we are very happy to tell you that there is no truth in these rumors. ABBA are working together as closely as before, and the recording sessions for the new LP have been very successful."[117] Built around the single *One of Us*, which once again tells the story, in a roundabout way, of Björn and Agnetha's separation, *The Visitors* made an impression in several European countries, reaching number 1 in the charts in Sweden, the UK, and West Germany. In other countries it had a more muted welcome. In France it languished at number 12, while in Italy it got no higher than 35. It made number 12 in Australia and Canada, and struggled to win over the American market, having to be content with number 29 in the *Billboard* chart. Despite positive reactions here and there, ABBA's success seemed to have been held back by an album that was unsettling, because it was very dark and anxiety-inducing. The band made no promotional tours linked to the record's release.

The failure of *Head over Heels*

The ABBA family was enlarged at the beginning of 1982: in January, Ludvig, the first child of Benny and his wife Mona, was born, while Björn and Lena's household grew with the arrival of little Emma. Aiming to devote themselves to fatherhood, the two men gave themselves some family time in the early part of the year, which inevitably emphasized the distance between the members of ABBA.

Agnetha Fältskog and her new layered hairstyle, 1982.

An unrecognizable Anni-Frid "Frida" Lyngstad, posing in front of the visuals for her solo album *Something's Going On*, 1982.

Agnetha took advantage of this to put the finishing touches to *Nu Tändas Tusen Juleljus* ("A Thousand Christmas Lights Are Now Lit"), the Christmas album she had recorded with her daughter Linda, while Frida embarked on the production of her new solo record, produced by the star of the moment, Phil Collins—whose 1981 album *Face Values* had been an international hit—and overseen by the latter's recording engineer, Hugh Padgham. March 1982 saw ABBA get back to business with the launch of their new single, *Head over Heels*, whose lyrics portrayed a modern young woman who loves fashion. With its clip showing Frida trying on various outfits, each more eccentric than the last, while grimacing like crazy, the song was faithful to ABBA's humorous spirit, but did not convince listeners, who were more interested in the nascent trends of the new romantics, cold wave, and new wave than in the plodding songs of a troupe of 40-somethings who represented in every way the lost insouciance of the 1970s. The single was a resounding flop—and, evidently, ABBA were in a bad way, seemingly struggling in a changing world.

A few songs before the end

The debacle of *Head over Heels* drove Benny and Björn to embark on the production of ABBA's new album in May 1982. In the same vein as the tracks on *The Visitors*, the group recorded three new songs: *Just Like That*, *I Am the City*, and *You Owe Me One*. But, with the team lacking both energy and desire, the project was quickly abandoned. In its place, ABBA decided to release a compilation celebrating their tenth

The Visitors was the first ABBA record to be released in compact disc format.

Overleaf: Photo shoot for the compilation *The Singles— The First Ten Years*.

anniversary, entitled *The Singles—The First Ten Years*. "There was something that wasn't like it used to be," Björn explained. "We didn't feel that same kind of strong spirit, and perhaps a feeling was starting to creep in that ABBA couldn't go on forever."[118] Two new songs were recorded to feature on the above compilation: *Under Attack* and *The Day Before You Came*. Unquestionably one of the darkest ABBA songs to date, *The Day Before You Came* was released as a single on 18 October 1982, accompanied by a brief promotion, by a group that looked happy in the media spotlight. On Saturday 11 December 1982, ABBA appeared on the television program *The Late, Late Breakfast Show*, recorded in Stockholm but broadcast live on BBC1 in the UK. After performing, in playback, their next single, *Under Attack*, the group paid tribute to their audience. It would be the very last time Agnetha, Frida, Benny, and Björn appeared together on television under the name ABBA. The clip of *Under Attack*, which was released as a single the following 21 February, also heralded the imminent end of the group, closing with a shot of the four artists seen from behind, leaving the stage side by side and heading towards a light outside, symbolizing a brighter future. The message was crystal clear: the ABBA adventure was coming to an end, and *Under Attack* would be the group's last single… until their great comeback, 40 years later.

Stig and Gudrun Anderson in Villa Ekarne, on the businessman's 50th birthday.

HOVAS VITTNE

(Agnetha Fältskog, Anni-Frid Lyngstad, Benny Andersson, Björn Ulvaeus, Michael B Tretow, Rune Söderqvist/2'56)

Musicians
Agnetha Fältskog: vocals, backing vocals
Anni-Frid "Frida" Lyngstad: vocals, backing vocals
Benny Andersson: synthesizers, vocals, backing vocals
Björn Ulvaeus: acoustic guitar, vocals, backing vocals
?: electric guitar
?: bass guitar
?: drums
?: flute

Recording
Polar Music Studios, Stockholm: 18, 20 January 1981

Technical team
Producers: Björn Ulvaeus, Benny Andersson
Sound engineer: Michael B Tretow

Side 1: *Hovas Vittne*/2'56
Side 2: *Tivedshambo*/2'10
Presented as a gift by Polar Music: 25 January 1981
(maxi single ref.: JUB 50)

Unheard-of celebrations for Stikkan's birthday

On Sunday 25 January 1981, at seven o'clock in the morning, Stig Anderson was woken in Villa Ekarne, his magnificent home in Djurgården—built by the architect Ragnar Östberg and formerly the property of Thorsten Laurin, a famous Swedish art collector. It was an important day for the businessman, for he was celebrating his 50th birthday. What he did not yet know was that his closest friends and associates had prepared for him a party that he would not forget in a hurry. The day began with breakfast in bed with his wife Gudrun, his daughter Marie, and his future son-in-law, the singer Tomas Ledin—all captured for posterity by the photographer Anders Hanser. There followed a performance by a troupe of cabaret artists formed for the occasion comprising, notably, Görel Hanser, Agnetha Fältskog, Frida Lyngstad, Lillebil Ankarcrona (wife of Rune Söderqvist), and Lena, Björn Ulvaeus' new wife. These women sang for him *Ljuva Sextital*, a hit he had made for Brita Borg in 1969, with music by Benny and Björn—who promptly appeared on the balcony singing *Happy Birthday*, Benny accompanying on the accordion. Stig then descended the staircase of his sumptuous home and discovered what his friends had prepared for him: domestic staff serving champagne, a buffet laid out for the occasion, and a choir that included Benny, Björn, Tomas Ledin, and Lasse Hallström, ready to sing in Stikkan's honor, as well as an orchestra awaiting the green light to entertain the 300 guests.

Return to Waterloo

Three videos were shown during the afternoon. The first showed the day's events, using footage hastily put together by a technician. The second was a photomontage made from pictures Stig Anderson had taken, while the third, shot the day before on the stage of the function room of the Berns Hotel in Stockholm, featured the members of ABBA sporting outfits similar to those they had worn the day they won the Eurovision Song Contest—6 April 1974. Guests watched ABBA performing a song written for the occasion by all four of them (with the help of Michael B Tretow and Rune Söderqvist), entitled *Hovas Vittne*. The piece, in *schlager* style, was sung in Swedish, and its title can be translated as "Hova's Witness"—a play on words referencing both Jehovah's Witnesses (*Jehovah Vittnens* in Swedish) and the town of Hova, Stig's birthplace.

Stikkan's closest female friends sing him one of his biggest hits, *Ljuva Sextital.*

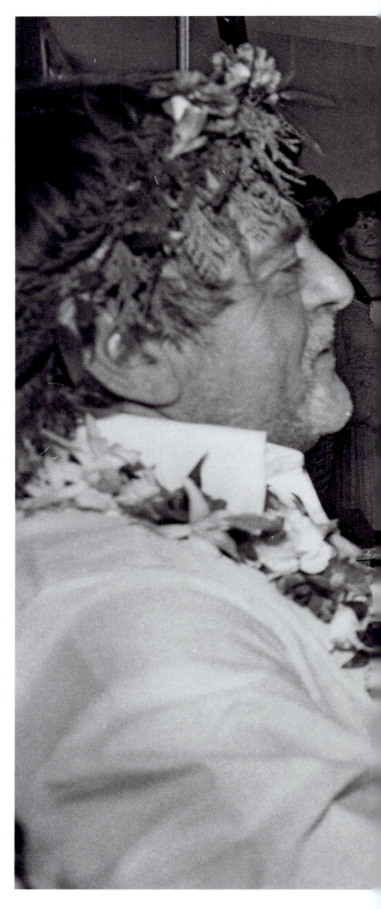

On 2 April 1981, ABBA also paid tribute to Gudrun, Stig Anderson's wife, as they had done to him and Görel Hanser before. For their friend's 50th birthday, the group's members recorded, in March, a medley of two birthday-party classics, *Ja Må Hon Leva* and *Happy Birthday to You,* simply accompanied by Benny's Yamaha GX-1 synthesizer. On the day in question, knowing that Gudrun was in England, ABBA managed to have *Ja Må Hon Leva* broadcast on the British radio station BBC Radio 2, with the connivance of the presenter Terry Wogan.

In it, ABBA made a list of certain character traits of their friend and manager, such as his passion for hot dogs, his affection for his dog, Lucas, and his annoying habit of vacuuming when he wanted to tell his guests that the party he had just thrown was over. The song had been recorded a few days earlier, and 200 copies were pressed in maxi single format by Hans "Berka" Bergkvist, one of Stikkan's close associates at Polar Music, so that it could be distributed to guests on 25 January. On the B-side of this record, now highly sought after by fans, was an instrumental version of *Tivedshambo,* one of Stig Anderson's biggest hits, re-recorded a few days earlier by Benny and Björn.

Single

THE VISITORS

(Benny Andersson, Björn Ulvaeus/5'49)

Musicians

Anni-Frid "Frida" Lyngstad: lead vocals, backing vocals
Agnetha Fältskog: backing vocals
Benny Andersson: synthesizers, backing vocals
Björn Ulvaeus: backing vocals
Lasse Wellander: electric guitar
Rutger Gunnarsson: bass guitar
Per Lindvall: drums

Recording

Polar Music Studios, Stockholm: 22 October 1981

Technical team

Producers: Björn Ulvaeus, Benny Andersson
Sound engineer: Michael B Tretow

Single

A-side: *The Visitors*/5'47
B-side: *Head over Heels*/3'47
Released in the USA by Atlantic: April 1982 (single ref.: 4031)
Best chart ranking in the USA: 63

Genesis

Sunday 13 December 1981 was a dark day for Poland. Aiming to crack down on the activities of Solidarność (Solidarity), the federation of trade unions led by Lech Wałęsa, General Wojciech Jaruzelski proclaimed a state of war, with the pretext that the country was about to be invaded by Soviet troops. The consequences were disastrous for the population: a reign of terror was imposed in Poland, with censorship and curfews enforced. More than 10,000 protesters were arrested in December 1981. Most of the world's democratic countries declared their opposition to this anti-democratic seizure of power. In the USA, on 31 January 1982, the government organized a special evening devoted to the crisis. The documentary *Let Poland Be Poland* by director Marty Pasetta was broadcast on NBC, followed by several appearances by personalities from the media. In order to show their support for Poland, which they had visited in 1976, Benny Andersson and Björn Ulvaeus recorded, at Polar Music Studios, a message on film, to be broadcast during the program. "Our thoughts are in Poland," Benny said at the beginning. "There are many rallies all over the world this weekend in support of the Polish people. But I think that this should also be a reminder that there are many countries around the world, for example, Chile, El Salvador, Afghanistan, and Iran, where people cannot express themselves openly and freely like we are doing now."[120] Björn added: "Human rights are things that we take for granted. And yet we are surrounded by so many examples how easily they can be crushed. I hope that this show will be something to keep us watchful and let us under-stand how delicate and vulnerable democracy is."[120] ABBA's sudden intrusion into the political debate did not seem to please the producers of *Let Poland Be Poland*, who decided arbitrarily not to include Benny and Björn's message in the program. It was not until an interview with the latter on the Swedish news program *Rapport* on 1 February that its contents became known.

A veiled political message

ABBA's speaking out at that time merely expressed their members' dread faced with an international geopolitical situation in which the Cold War, with tension between the USA and the USSR higher than ever, was a threat. It was precisely thinking about the plight of the people of the Soviet Union,

subject to permanent surveillance by the KGB intelligence service, that Björn wrote the lyrics of *The Visitors*, even though it was many years before he revealed their hidden meaning.

"I'm not saying what the song is about because it is full of double meanings," he announced to *International ABBA Magazine* in March 1982.[121] As lead vocalist, Frida sings of the terror of a Russian woman whose visitors—members of the KGB—knock on her door, conveying in an unsettling tone the climate of fear that existed in the USSR. When Björn revealed the content of the lyrics of *The Visitors*, fans finally came to know the hidden meaning of this atypical song. "I had a clear vision of that apartment, lots of bookcases on the walls…" he explained, "then suddenly the knock on the door, and that person realizes: 'Bloody hell—the time has come! They've found me out!' […] It was because I felt it would be more interesting if I didn't say exactly what it was about. I always thought it was so boring with the political music movement we had here in Sweden in the seventies, when everybody was so totally realistic and almost party-political. I wanted to retain a sense of mystery. Who were these 'visitors'?"[118]

Production

Its lyrics aside, *The Visitors* is characteristic of the new artistic direction ABBA were taking. Synthesizers were playing a bigger role in the group's production, influenced indirectly by the disturbing atmosphere of the albums of Joy Division, Depeche Mode, Peter Baumann, Spandau Ballet, Duran Duran, and Orchestral Manoeuvres in the Dark. Although Benny Andersson did not mention it, the music of the French pioneer of electronic music Jean-Michel Jarre, whose albums *Oxygène* (1976) and *Équinoxe* (1978) were huge successes worldwide, also seems to have left its mark in his mind, for he now made extensive use of synthesizers, both to provide ethereal synth pads in songs and for their Arpeggiator function, which adds a powerful rhythmic support. Although Andersson now used the Roland Jupiter 8 (JP-8) in many songs, he nevertheless remained faithful to his Yamaha GX-1, which is omnipresent on the album *The Visitors*. "It's a fantastic instrument," Andersson said at the time. "It is the first ever polyphonic synthesizer. That simply means you can add sounds and play chords but in reality it is so much more. There are three keyboards, two are for both hands to use and they each have the equivalent of 16 synthesizers operating on them. The top keyboard is for the right hand and for playing solos, which is just one synth. Add to that the three channels of the pedalboard and you have the equivalent of 36 synthesizers to play with!"[122]

The sleeve of the 1981 album *The Visitors* conveys the painful atmosphere within ABBA at the start of the decade.

In contrast to Björn, who had to turn into an actor for the clip of *Head over Heels*, Benny needed only to sit at his piano for the shoot.

Overleaf: Frida alternated between a sad face and a gallery of grimaces during filming of the clip of *Head over Heels*.

Single

HEAD OVER HEELS

(Benny Andersson, Björn Ulvaeus/3'45)

1981

Musicians
Agnetha Fältskog: lead vocals, backing vocals
Anni-Frid "Frida" Lyngstad: backing vocals
Benny Andersson: synthesizers, backing vocals
Björn Ulvaeus: acoustic guitar, backing vocals
Lasse Wellander: electric guitar
Rutger Gunnarsson: bass guitar
Ola Brunkert: drums

Recording
Polar Music Studios, Stockholm: September, 12 November 1981

Technical team
Producers: Björn Ulvaeus, Benny Andersson
Sound engineer: Michael B Tretow

Single
A-side: *Head over Heels*/3'45
B-side: *The Visitors*/5'49
Released in the UK by CBS/Epic: March 1982
(single ref.: EPC A 2037)
Best chart ranking in the UK: 25

HEADPHONES AT THE READY
The hand claps that double Ola Brunkert's snare drum in the choruses of *Head over Heels* (which can also be heard at 00'59 in *I Am the City*) were produced not by humans but by a revolutionary tool used in many disco hits of the time: the Clap Trap—a device marketed in 1979 by Simmons, which simulated all kinds of hand claps and applause.

Genesis

When the last single from *The Visitors* came out in March 1982, the reception it got was disastrous: number 10 in France, number 12 in Spain, and number 25 in the UK. With *Head over Heels*, ABBA suffered their worst chart ranking since the release of *I Do, I Do, I Do, I Do, I Do* in July 1975. It must be said that despite the quality of its production, the song—in which Agnetha lists the qualities of a working girl who is obsessed with fashion—has the dated character of a group who are apparently unable to adapt to the new musical trends in vogue. "I think it is a very happy song," Agnetha declared. "I can see this crazy girl in front of me. [...] It can be any girl [...]."[123] To illustrate the song, ABBA again called on Lasse Hallström (he can be glimpsed as an extra at 1'13 in the video), who in this made the very last ABBA clip of his career. As if to round off his oeuvre, on 21 January 1982 the film-maker created, at the Svensk Filmindustri Studios in Gröndal, a series of shots against a white background, as he had done for the videos of *I Do, I Do, I Do, I Do, I Do, Mamma Mia, SOS*, and *Bang-A-Boomerang*, in 1975. Other sequences were filmed in the streets of Stockholm and in the Nordiska Kompaniet shopping mall, with the budding actor Björn Ulvaeus playing the part of a husband who is despairing at having to follow his wife on an exhausting shopping expedition.

Production

The song's working title, *Tango*, matched the spirit of its composition fairly well, for it features the Spanish sounds from which ABBA seemed incapable of freeing themselves once and for all. The acoustic guitar rhythm, discreet but clearly audible, also recalls the Andalusian songs of which Benny and Björn were fond. Lasse Wellander plays all the guitar parts on the record, with the exception of a few overdubs added here and there by Björn. "Well, we have always used Lasse Wellander primarily in our recordings," Björn explained. "We always work well together and he was available. Janne is a fine guitarist and he has done some great things for us but he just wasn't [available] this time."[121] The year 1982 was definitely one of change for ABBA, for Janne Schaffer had played on all the group's albums since they formed, with the exception of *The Visitor*.

Single

WHEN ALL IS SAID AND DONE

(Benny Andersson, Björn Ulvaeus/3'20)

1981

Musicians
Anni-Frid "Frida" Lyngstad: lead vocals, backing vocals
Agnetha Fältskog: backing vocals
Benny Andersson: synthesizers, piano, backing vocals
Björn Ulvaeus: backing vocals
Lasse Wellander: electric guitar, acoustic guitar
Rutger Gunnarsson: bass guitar
Ola Brunkert: drums
Åke Sundqvist: percussion

Recording
Polar Music Studios, Stockholm: 17 to 18 March, 1 April, 13 November 1981

Technical team
Producers: Björn Ulvaeus, Benny Andersson
Sound engineer: Michael B Tretow

Single
A-side: *When All Is Said and Done*/3'20
B-side: *Should I Laugh or Cry*/4'30
Released in the USA by Atlantic: 9 January 1982 (single ref.: 3889)
Best chart ranking in the USA: 27

Genesis
A month and five days after the official announcement of his divorce from Frida, Benny Andersson went into the studio to record the group's new songs, accompanied by his faithful friend and lyricist, Björn Ulvaeus. Three songs were recorded in March 1981: *Slipping through my Fingers*, *Two for the Price of One*, and *When All Is Said and Done*. The last of these was reminiscent of *The Winner Takes It All*, built around a disco rhythm and a powerful melody. However, aside from its production, it was rather the theme developed by Björn Ulvaeus in the song's lyrics that echoed the July 1980 hit. Indeed, wanting to pay tribute to his two friends, whose relationship had just come to an end, Ulvaeus wrote lyrics that referred to their separation. "It was so sad," Ulvaeus told the biographer Carl Magnus Palm, "even sadder in a way than my own divorce not too long before, maybe because I was watching it from the outside. And when *When All Is Said and Done* was ready to be lyricized, I wanted to write something about them and what they went through. Something that gave my friends credit for courage and dignity."[39]

Production
It was Frida herself who performed the song, with unprecedented emotion and virtuosity. "All my sadness was captured in that song," she explained.[124] Then, in a separate interview, she added: "I know that we talked it over and Björn asked me if it was sometimes too emotional to sing those lyrics. But I mean, that was also in a way a challenge, to be able to put your emotions into the lyrics and the songs, and sing it."[125] On 24 November 1981, Frida (accompanied by Agnetha on backing vocals) recorded *No Hay a Quien Culpar* ("There Is No One to Blame"), a Spanish version of *When All Is Said and Done*, destined to feature on a special edition of *The Visitors* for the Spanish-speaking market. The promotional clip ABBA had filmed for the song in August 1981, when it was planned to release the song as a single, was re-used, this time including some shots of Frida and Agnetha singing in Spanish. It is amusing to watch the two videos one after the other, to see the two singers adopt the same pose, switching from English to Spanish with disconcerting ease, while maintaining a serious demeanor.

Per Lindvall's snare-drum rolls were Björn Ulvaeus's inspiration for the song's martial theme.

Overleaf: Despite the break-up of the two couples involved, ABBA remained a close-knit group.

SOLDIERS

(Benny Andersson, Björn Ulvaeus/4'38)

1981

Musicians
Agnetha Fältskog: lead vocals, backing vocals
Anni-Frid "Frida" Lyngstad: backing vocals
Benny Andersson: synthesizers, piano, backing vocals
Björn Ulvaeus: backing vocals
Lasse Wellander: electric guitar
Rutger Gunnarsson: bass guitar
Per Lindvall: drums

Recording
Polar Music Studios, Stockholm: 15 October, 14 November 1981

Technical team
Producers: Björn Ulvaeus, Benny Andersson
Sound engineer: Michael B Tretow

Genesis

A recurring theme in *The Visitors*, the fear of a nuclear world war once again lies at the heart of *Soldiers*, an outspoken song performed by Agnetha Fältskog. As he had done with *The Piper*, Björn Ulvaeus wrote the lyrics while thinking of the great dictators of the 20th century, and worrying about the future of the world. "I was talking about people that are Soldiers mentally," he explained, "those who actually cause wars and other atrocities—they are the people who 'sing the songs that you and I don't sing.' Dictators like Stalin: ice-cold, unimaginative, lacking in empathy, who just march forward and think they know what's important and are never interested in any other points of view."[118]

Production

Although the song's theme came to Ulvaeus quite quickly, its alarming martial quality, recalling the atmosphere of Hitler or Stalin's march pasts, was inspired by the drum rhythm Per Lindvall suggested during the recording session of 15 October 1981. Björn and Benny had not initially wanted to give the piece a drum part, but as Björn said later, "*Soldiers* has a serious style to it and I would like to say that [Per] added so much to that track. His contribution was invaluable because he came up with that odd beat."[121] It should be noted that only rarely before then had the sound of drums been so heightened in mixing as it was in the introduction of *Soldiers*. Michael B Tretow, the man behind "the ABBA sound," explained with amusement the difficulty of recording drums in 1982, and his relationship with the cymbals on this occasion when recording that instrument. "All drummers should get rid of their cymbals because they mess up the recording. I HATE cymbals! Do you know what they do? If you put a microphone above the drumkit, that mic captures the whole kit and you get better sound the further you put it. However, the cymbals are always higher up and therefore closer to the mic than the drums, but drummers always hit those cymbals harder than the drums and they come out too loud. It means that the drummer's tracks have to be brought right down in the mix and it ruins the sound. I always try to hide the cymbals in another room whenever I am producing."[126]

I LET THE MUSIC SPEAK

(Benny Andersson, Björn Ulvaeus/5'20)

1981

Musicians
Anni-Frid "Frida" Lyngstad: lead vocals, backing vocals
Agnetha Fältskog: backing vocals
Benny Andersson: synthesizers, piano, backing vocals
Björn Ulvaeus: backing vocals
Lasse Wellander: acoustic guitar
Rutger Gunnarsson: bass guitar
Ola Brunkert: drums
Jan Kling: flute

Recording
Polar Music Studios, Stockholm: 3 to 4, 8 to 9 September 1981

Technical team
Producers: Björn Ulvaeus, Benny Andersson
Sound engineer: Michael B Tretow

Genesis

In December 1981 the lyricist Tim Rice—who had written, among other things, the libretto for the hit musical *Jesus Christ Superstar* in 1970—traveled to Stockholm to meet Benny Andersson and Björn Ulvaeus. The pair had for many years wanted to embark on writing a musical of their own, and when Rice told them about a project he had in mind—the story of a love triangle at a world chess championship set during the Cold War, in which a Russian and an American go head to head—they were immediately convinced. While ABBA were recording their eighth studio album, the *Chess* project was launched. Certain very operatic songs written during this period were kept for the stage production (which saw the light of day in 1984), such as *Nationalsång* ("National Anthem"), which would become *Anthem*, while others were incorporated into ABBA's repertoire. One of these was *I Let the Music Speak*, whose structure and sequences seemed perfect for a musical. Indeed, Benny admitted as much: if ABBA had not recorded the song, he would have kept it for *Chess*.

Production

In the song's title and lyrics Björn referred to the way he wrote the words of ABBA's songs—letting the music speak to him and tell him a story that would inspire him. "A song or a piece of music has its own inherent language and story," Ulvaeus declared. "It's in there, you just have to listen."[118]

Frida sings lead vocals in the piece, her three associates providing the majestic backing vocals, recorded alongside her under specific circumstances, as Michael B Tretow explained: the sound engineer placed microphones a long way from Benny, Björn, Agnetha, and Frida, to simulate a recording made on stage. One need only listen to *I Let the Music Speak* to appreciate the creative genius of Benny Andersson and Björn Ulvaeus, whose talent would once again be celebrated with *Chess* a few years later.

Agnetha in the middle of
moving in—the clip of
One of Us.

Overleaf: Lasse Hallström
used mirrors to duplicate the
faces of the members of ABBA
in the clip of *One of Us*.

Single

ONE OF US

(Benny Andersson, Björn Ulvaeus/3'55)

1981

Musicians
Agnetha Fältskog: lead vocals, backing vocals
Anni-Frid "Frida" Lyngstad: backing vocals
Benny Andersson: synthesizers, accordion, backing vocals
Björn Ulvaeus: mandolin, backing vocals
Lasse Wellander: electric guitar, mandolin
Rutger Gunnarsson: bass guitar, mandolin
Ola Brunkert: drums

Recording
Polar Music Studios, Stockholm: 21 to 23 October,
12 to 13, 23 November 1981

Technical team
Producers: Björn Ulvaeus, Benny Andersson
Sound engineer: Michael B Tretow

Single
A-side: *One of Us*/3'55
B-side: *Should I Laugh or Cry*/4'29
Released in Sweden by Polar Music: 7 December 1981
(single ref.: POS 1291)
Released in the UK by CBS/Epic: 7 December 1981
(single ref.: EPC A 1740)
Released in the USA by Atlantic: 7 December 1981
(single ref.: 7-89881)
Best chart ranking in Sweden: 13
Best chart ranking in the UK: 3
Best chart ranking in the USA: 107

FOR ABBA ADDICTS
To give more credibility to Agnetha's moving-in
sequence in the clip of *One of Us*, Lasse Hallström's
team ordered in some boxes. On set, there was great
surprise when they all turned out to bear the name
"Björns Express AB" ("Björn Removals"). Although
the coincidence was amusing, it was decided to
hide the company's name for the video shoot.

Genesis
As was their wont, shortly before the release of *The Visitors*,
ABBA sent a cassette containing a selection of songs in the
running for being released as singles to certain partners around
the world, be they record labels or their records' distributors
abroad. Each was then invited to play along, ranking the songs
according to how much they liked them. When *One of Us*
came top of the list in 1981, Björn was ecstatic, because it was
one of his favorite songs at the time. In it, Agnetha plays the
role of a young woman who bitterly regrets having left her
sweetheart and hopes he will give her a second chance. Lasse
Hallström made a clip on 23 November 1981, a few hours
before ABBA went to record the song's backing vocals at Polar
Music Studios. It was shot in the film-maker's apartment—
Agnetha enacting moving in, unpacking her boxes, and even
putting up some strips of wallpaper. A few more images of
the group were filmed four days later at Filmstaden, the film
studios in Solna.

Production
The millions of fans of the Swedish group Ace of Base, who
were a lightning success in the mid-1990s and for whom the
press once forecast a career as prestigious as ABBA's, could
not (if they still dared to admit to their passion for the group)
deny the influence *One of Us* had on the singles *All That She
Wants*, *Happy Nation*, and especially *The Sign,* whose backing
vocals (at 0'55) bear an uncanny resemblance to those in the
ABBA song, audible between 1'27 and 1'31. Aside from this
small nod, the feature common to all four songs is the reggae
rhythm ABBA chose for *One of Us*, which Ace of Base would
re-use 15 years later. Benny Andersson plays the rhythm
essential to the reggae style on the accordion, while Lasse
Wellander plays, here and there, some well-chosen muted
guitar chords. The production is meticulous and the song very
pleasant, supported by the mandolins played by a group credited on the record sleeve as "The Three Boys." In fact they
are Björn Ulvaeus, Lasse Wellander, and Rutger Gunnarsson,
who had fun enhancing the song with this exotic sound.

TWO FOR THE PRICE OF ONE

(Benny Andersson, Björn Ulvaeus/3'36)

1981

Musicians

Björn Ulvaeus: lead vocals, backing vocals
Agnetha Fältskog: backing vocals
Anni-Frid "Frida" Lyngstad: backing vocals
Benny Andersson: synthesizers, piano, backing vocals
Lasse Wellander: electric guitar
Rutger Gunnarsson: bass guitar
Ola Brunkert: drums
Åke Sundqvist: percussion
Björn Borg: trumpet
Gunnar Gunrup: trumpet
Walter Brolund: trombone
Torbjörn Kvist: tuba
Bosse Persson: tuba

Recording

Polar Music Studios, Stockholm: 17 March, 8 April, 13 November 1981

Technical team

Producers: Björn Ulvaeus, Benny Andersson
Sound engineer: Michael B Tretow

FOR ABBA ADDICTS

In 1981 the Swedish city of Göteborg hosted the Ice Hockey World Championships. To support the national team, Benny Andersson recorded a musical theme on the Yamaha GX-1, to which he gave the obvious title *Fanfare for the Ice Hockey World Championships '81*. The piece, lasting 30 seconds, introduced each broadcast of the competition.

Genesis

What a strange story—that of a young man employed as a cleaner in the local train station who decides one day to reply to a lonely hearts advertisement offering a meeting with not one but two young women; the ad informs the reader that he will be thrilled to have "two for the price of one". The protagonist is astonished to discover that the two are a mother and a daughter! We can only wonder what was going through Björn Ulvaeus' head—unless he himself had had this strange experience. Indeed, Björn performs the song, supported by the voices of Agnetha and Frida in the choruses. "I was a bit reluctant to sing it myself," he explained, "because I thought it was a strong song, and it might have been a hit if one of the girls had sung it. To release a single with me as the lead singer really wasn't an option at this stage."[39]

Production

In the spring of 1981, having recorded four songs for ABBA's new album (*When All Is Said and Done*, *Slipping through my Fingers*, *Two for the Price of One*, and *Like an Angel Passing through my Room*), Björn and Benny felt more work was needed. "These songs aren't suitable to become a single A-side," Björn explained at the time. "That's why we've decided to postpone the release of the new single until September/October. That's the reason why we have to keep you in suspense for such a long time."[127] On 8 April of that year, ABBA decided to enhance the final part of the song with a fanfare sequence, which comes at the worst possible moment in the middle of this particularly dark pop album. In order to do this, five musicians recorded tubas, trumpets, and a trombone at Polar Music Studios, though their playing was partially replaced by the ultra-synthetic sounds of Andersson's Yamaha GX-1. If you listen carefully, you can still hear some of these parts deep within the mix, hidden behind the oompahs played on the synthesizer.

SLIPPING THROUGH MY FINGERS

(Benny Andersson, Björn Ulvaeus/3'51)

Musicians

Agnetha Fältskog: lead vocals, backing vocals
Anni-Frid "Frida" Lyngstad: backing vocals
Benny Andersson: synthesizers, piano
Björn Ulvaeus: backing vocals
Lasse Wellander: electric guitar
Rutger Gunnarsson: bass guitar
Ola Brunkert: drums
Åke Sundqvist: percussion

Recording

Polar Music Studios, Stockholm: 16, 18 March, 13 November 1981

Technical team

Producers: Björn Ulvaeus, Benny Andersson
Sound engineer: Michael B Tretow

Genesis

Recorded during the very first sessions for *The Visitors*, *Slipping through my Fingers* is one ABBA's favorite songs. It must be said that, in addition to its effective melody, the piece features lyrics that are wholly autobiographical. One morning Björn Ulvaeus had watched his daughter Linda setting off alone for school and, with an aching heart, was inspired to write the most beautiful song a father could write to his daughter. Although Agnetha would perform it, its words are definitely those of a dad. He said: "I thought, 'Now she's taken that step, she's going away—what have I missed out through all these years?'"[128] The song featured in a partnership with Coca-Cola, which in 1981 released in Japan a single bearing its brand name: *Coca-Cola Super Record—ABBA Slipping through my Fingers*. With its microgrooves colored bright red, bringing to mind the American brand, the record is an object every collector absolutely longs to own.

Production

In 1982, in the pages of *ABBA International Magazine*, published by Polar Music, Björn revealed some secrets of his way of working, which had contributed to the success of the group's songs for ten years. "I take the tape home for a couple of days and I play it over and over again and try different things. I sing together with the backing tracks, so when we go into the studio to put on the vocals we know that the lyric is absolutely perfect when it comes to syllables—sounding the way we want it […]. It's hard to say why it comes to me and how it comes to me, because when you work in the way that I do […] something just pops up very suddenly."[129] A Spanish version of *Slipping through my Fingers*—renamed *Se Me Está Escapando* and destined to feature on the South American edition of *The Visitors*—was recorded on 24 November 1981 by Agnetha and Frida.

Rarely with ABBA has melancholy been as powerful as in this song, the last track on *The Visitors*.

Overleaf: ABBA on the set of *Dick Cavett Meets ABBA* in April 1981.

LIKE AN ANGEL PASSING THROUGH MY ROOM

(Benny Andersson, Björn Ulvaeus/3'25)

1981

Musicians
Anni-Frid "Frida" Lyngstad: vocals
Benny Andersson: synthesizers

Recording
Polar Music Studios, Stockholm: June, October to November 1981

Technical team
Producers: Björn Ulvaeus, Benny Andersson
Sound engineer: Michael B Tretow

Genesis

In 2012 the deluxe edition of *The Visitors* was released. As well as a wealth of rare songs from the 1981 and 1982 sessions, and a DVD containing many videos of their idols, fans were treated to a medley concocted by Benny Andersson himself at the Riksmixningsverket, his recording studio on the island of Skeppsholmen, in the Stockholm archipelago.

From a Twinkling Star to a Passing Angel is built around the preliminary recordings made in May, June, October, and November 1981, which went into the making of the lullaby *Like an Angel Passing through my Room*, the last track on *The Visitors*. "It was fun to put this thing together," Andersson explained, "just to show what the process can be like. It's an interesting observation on how you labor over things before you reach the final result, although that doesn't necessarily mean that you make the right choice."[118] Indeed, Agnetha went back over the final choice of arrangements for the song. "You know we did two or three different backing tracks for that number and none of them came out that good," she said in 1982. "[...] Then they tried this very 'naked' approach and I think it sounds a bit exciting, but I have a feeling that it doesn't 'happen,' although I still like it. It is strong enough as a melody but I am not sure it has been given the right treatment."[130]

Production

The first version of the song, *Twinkle Twinkle Little Star*, is a lullaby sung by Björn over a Linn LM-1 drum machine. The second, *Another Morning without You*, features a majestic voice and piano duo by Benny and Frida. This gave way to the third preliminary recording of the song, which is as disco as can be—but a tad quirky. Two "ballad" versions were also tried, without success, before the basic framework for the song was chosen. With its effects covering Frida's voice and the ever-present "tick tock" of Benny's Minimoog synthesizer lasting throughout the song, *Like an Angel Passing through my Room* is one of the high points of the album—a lullaby for their children recorded by two parents shortly before they separated. Beyond the sadness peculiar to the group's most intimate songs, it shines because of its simple, effective treatment, as well as the performance of Frida, who seems to be saying goodbye to her fans with this delicate lullaby, before closing, for 40 years, the first chapter of ABBA's history.

Between 1981 and 1983, Benny Andersson used all kinds of synthesizers, such as this brand new Roland Jupiter 8 (JP 8).

JUST LIKE THAT

(Benny Andersson, Björn Ulvaeus/2'05)

Musicians

Agnetha Fältskog: lead vocals, backing vocals
Anni-Frid "Frida" Lyngstad: backing vocals
Benny Andersson: synthesizers, backing vocals
Björn Ulvaeus: backing vocals
Lasse Wellander: electric guitar
Rutger Gunnarsson: bass guitar
Per Lindvall: drums

Recording

Polar Music Studios, Stockholm: May 1982

Technical team

Producers: Björn Ulvaeus, Benny Andersson
Sound engineer: Michael B Tretow

Promotional maxi CD single Dream World

1. *Dream World*/3'38
2. *Put on your White Sombrero*/4'28
3. *Just Like That*/2'05
4. *Thank You for the Music (Doris Day Mix)*/4'02

Promotional distribution in Germany, Polar Music-Polydor: November 1994 (CD ref.: 853891-2)

Genesis

On 14 June 1982, Polar Music announced via a press release the start of recording for ABBA's ninth album, for which the songs *Just Like That* and *I Am the City* had just been recorded. Since the project was dropped during the summer, *Just Like That* was shelved until November 1994, when it appeared on the promotional EP *Dream World,* distributed in Germany. Although many ABBA watchers still regard the song as unreleased, its appearance on this CD justifies its presence in this book, as much for its quality as for its sacred status in the eyes of ABBA admirers. A bootleg version was in circulation during the 1980s, before being made available on the internet in the 2000s. Benny Andersson related the misadventure involving cassettes containing some preliminary recordings of songs for ABBA's new album, which were stolen from his car in 1983: "I left my car only a few minutes unguarded, but when I returned back, someone had managed to take the tapes away. At first, we thought that it wasn't such a big deal as the LP would be released only a few months later. We just ran the risk that songs would be played on the radio before their release date. That was not convenient, but surely not a disaster. It changed as we decided not to release that album. That meant that the stolen tapes with unreleased material would be floating around without our approval."[131]

Production

Fans regard the fact that this excellent song has never been officially released as an injustice, and ABBA must surely reconsider their decision one day. Björn Ulvaeus and Benny Andersson have explained in detail the reasons for banning it, justified above all by the lack of consistency between its verse and its chorus. Fans recognized in the introduction of *Just Like That* a guitar motif that was re-used for the melodic line of the verses of *Under Attack* during the summer of 1982, and consoled themselves in 1986 with the cover of the song made by the Swedish duo Gemini. True admirers of ABBA also had the opportunity, in 1994, to hear the saxophone part Raphael Ravenscroft recorded for the song in the medley *Abba Undeleted*, which brought together the group's demos and was available in the box set *Thank You for the Music*.

I AM THE CITY

(Benny Andersson, Björn Ulvaeus/4'00)

Determined to break free of her role within ABBA, Agnetha now appeared as an emancipated, dynamic woman.

Musicians
Agnetha Fältskog: vocals, backing vocals
Anni-Frid "Frida" Lyngstad: vocals, backing vocals
Benny Andersson: synthesizers, backing vocals
Björn Ulvaeus: backing vocals
Rutger Gunnarsson: bass guitar
Per Lindvall: drums

Recording
Polar Music Studios, Stockholm: May to June 1982

Technical team
Producers: Björn Ulvaeus, Benny Andersson
Sound engineer: Michael B Tretow

Compilation *More ABBA Gold: More ABBA Hits*
Released in the UK and Europe by Polar Music-Polydor: 24 May 1993 (LP ref.: 519 353-1, CD ref.: 519 353-2)
Released in the USA by Polar Music-Polydor: 9 June 1993 (CD ref.: 31451 9353 2)
Best chart ranking in Sweden: 7
Best chart ranking in the UK: 13
Best chart ranking in the USA: did not make the charts

Genesis
Like *You Owe Me One* and *Just Like That, I Am the City* was meant to feature on ABBA's ninth album, for which recording sessions began in May 1982. There is indeed a clear artistic coherence in these three songs, which feature modern production dominated by the almost exclusive use of electronic instruments, with the bass guitar, drums, and electric guitar (which is absent here) becoming ever more understated as recording sessions progressed. It was not until the release of the compilation *More ABBA Gold: More ABBA Hits* in 1993 that *I Am the City* was revealed to fans. Other tracks recorded during the same period resurfaced in the musical *Chess* in 1984, including *Opus 10* (also known to fans under the working title *Nationalsång*), which became *Anthem,* and *Every Good Man Needs a Helping Hand*, which was initially sung by Agnetha, and would be performed by Elaine Paige under the title *Heaven Help my Heart.*

Production
Production of ABBA's ninth album was abandoned after the sessions in the summer of 1982, and would have to wait almost 40 years to be completed. It must be said that *I Am the City* is far from being a potential hit such as ABBA had known how to make a few years earlier. The song aims to be ice cold, like many productions of the time, and it is even difficult to recognize Per Lindvall's acoustic drums in it. And yet the group used a drum machine on only one song throughout their entire career: *The Day Before You Came.* Doubtless weary of having to produce hits every time they set foot in Polar Music Studios, Benny and Björn tried here to record a more intimate song, even though the end result is hardly convincing. "You know," Benny said at the time, "a lot of people seem to think that our aim is to write only hits. But that's not the case. We write a song and we work on that until we feel that it's good ourselves. When the public thinks that that song is good as well, even so good that it becomes a hit, then that is so much to the good. We get an enormous kick out of the fact that our work is appreciated by millions of people. And that's also one of the reasons why we are planning to continue like this for years to come."[132] Less than a year after this declaration, ABBA went into standby mode, to the great dismay of their fans.

YOU OWE ME ONE

(Benny Andersson, Björn Ulvaeus/3'29)

Musicians

Agnetha Fältskog: vocals, backing vocals
Anni-Frid "Frida" Lyngstad: vocals, backing vocals
Benny Andersson: synthesizers, programming
Lasse Wellander: electric guitar
Rutger Gunnarsson: bass guitar
Per Lindvall: drums

Recording

Polar Music Studios, Stockholm: 3 May 1982

Technical team

Producers: Björn Ulvaeus, Benny Andersson
Sound engineer: Michael B Tretow

Single *Under Attack*

A-side: *Under Attack*/3'45
B-side: *You Owe Me One*/3'29
Released in Sweden by Polar Music: 21 February 1983
(single ref.: POS 1321)
Released in the UK by CBS/Epic: December 1982
(single ref.: EPC A2971)
Best chart ranking in Sweden: did not make the charts
Best chart ranking in the UK: 26

Genesis

What a joy to hear Agnetha and Frida once more, singing the verses of *You Owe Me One* together, as they had once sung on classics such as *Ring Ring*, *Waterloo*, and *Mamma Mia*. This return to the production values of former times marked a desire on ABBA's part to go back to basics, even though they certainly wanted to renew themselves. "There is something that happened between the *Voulez-Vous* and the *Super Trouper* album,"[133] Benny Andersson explained in October 1982, when plans for a new ABBA album were still on track. "I don't know if that shows. I hear it. I think that the next album will be even a little broader expression of what we're up to. We have in mind for the next album some sort of concept. That makes it a little different, because you can fit in things that normally wouldn't go with an album as separate tracks. If all the tracks are related to each other, it makes a whole of everything."[133] Benny and Björn certainly developed the project of a concept record, but outside ABBA: it was for the musical *Chess*, the soundtrack of which appeared on CD and vinyl in 1984.

Production

In March 1983, Michael B Tretow opened the doors of Polar Music Studios, now containing state-of-the-art equipment, to the editorial team of *ABBA International Magazine*. The facility's equipment held no more secrets for readers, who were able to see what Benny, Björn, and Tretow himself used to create the group's new sounds, which fans had encountered in songs such as *Under Attack* and its B-side, *You Owe Me One*. An exhaustive list of the peripheral audio equipment used was then drawn up; it featured several compressors, including two DBX 160 compressor/limiters, one Universal Audio LA-3A Audio Leveler, and a Universal Audio/UREI LA-4, as well an Eventide Omnipressor, chosen for its noise gate function. "Its function is to 'gate-out' unwanted sounds and noise," the sound engineer explained. "You can't really hear it working, it doesn't create a sound effect, it just tightens up the drums and cymbals, for instance."[134] A DBX 3BX 3-band dynamic range expander was also used, as was a White Instruments Model 142 sound analyzer.

Among all these now vintage racks, which today's recording engineers dream about, the Eventide Harmonizer H910 was without doubt the most legendary. Once used by Tony

Frida and Agnetha at the group's photo shoot on 11 December 1982, their last before they went into standby mode.

Visconti on songs by David Bowie (notably *Chant of the Ever Circling Skeletal Family* and *Speed of Life*), the H910 built the reputation of Brian May, who used it in Queen to simulate the sounds of synthesizers on the guitar. In ABBA's recordings it was used on Frida's voice in *The Visitors* and *When All Is Said and Done*.

CASSANDRA

(Benny Andersson, Björn Ulvaeus/4'50)

Musicians

Anni-Frid "Frida" Lyngstad: lead vocals, backing vocals
Agnetha Fältskog: vocals, backing vocals
Benny Andersson: synthesizers, accordion, backing vocals
Björn Ulvaeus: backing vocals
Janne Schaffer: acoustic guitar
Rutger Gunnarsson: bass guitar
Per Lindvall: drums
Åke Sundqvist: percussion

Recording

Polar Music Studios, Stockholm: 2 to 6 August 1982

Technical team

Producers: Björn Ulvaeus, Benny Andersson
Sound engineer: Michael B Tretow

Single *The Day Before You Came*

A-side: *The Day Before You Came*/5'50
B-side: *Cassandra*/4'50
Released in Sweden by Polar Music: 18 October 1982
(single ref.: POS 1318)
Released in the UK by CBS/Epic: 18 October 1982
(single ref.: EPC A2847)
Released in the USA by Atlantic: 18 October 1982
(single ref.: 7-89948)
Best chart ranking in Sweden: 3
Best chart ranking in the UK: 32
Best chart ranking in the USA: did not make the charts

Genesis

ABBA returned to their former musical loves with this folk ballad whose Spanish sounds recall *Hasta Mañana* (1973), *Fernando* (1975), and *Put on your White Sombrero* (1980). Despite its rather joyous feel, with triplets that invite the listener to dance, *Cassandra*'s lyrics are very dark. In them Björn Ulvaeus refers to a figure from Greek mythology, Cassandra, daughter of Priam and Hecuba, king and queen of Troy. Endowed with the gift of prophecy by the god Apollo in exchange for the promise of offering herself to him, Cassandra was punished with a curse when she refused: henceforth no one would believe her visions of the future. Frida, who sings the verses in the song, also refers to the consequences of the misfortunes of Cassandra, who saw the city of Troy destroyed after none of its citizens listened to her warnings.

Production

Recorded during the last sessions before ABBA went into standby mode, *Cassandra* features on the B-side of the excellent single *The Day Before You Came,* which, alas, did not enjoy the success it was expected to. This period followed a series of recordings that did not find favor with Benny, Björn, Agnetha, and Frida—nor with Stig Anderson who, since the summer of 1981, had been expressing his dissatisfaction with what the group were producing, and preferred to release the maxi single *Lay All Your Love on Me* rather than their new recordings. "We decided to pass on them," he explained at the time. "We listened to them for days but our unanimous decision remained the same, we don't think they are strong enough to release as a single. Oh, all of these songs would probably be able to occupy a position on the charts but our reputation has become more important to us than a hit that we're not completely satisfied with. We don't want to mislead the fans in any way."[135]

SHOULD I LAUGH OR CRY

(Benny Andersson, Björn Ulvaeus/4'30)

Musicians
Anni-Frid "Frida" Lyngstad: lead vocals, backing vocals
Agnetha Fältskog: backing vocals
Benny Andersson: synthesizers, backing vocals
Björn Ulvaeus: backing vocals
Lasse Wellander: electric guitar, acoustic guitar
Rutger Gunnarsson: bass guitar
Ola Brunkert: drums

Recording
Polar Music Studios, Stockholm: 4, 8, 9 September 1981

Technical team
Producers: Björn Ulvaeus, Benny Andersson
Sound engineer: Michael B Tretow

Single *One of Us*
A-side: *One of Us*/3'55
B-side: *Should I Laugh or Cry*/4'29
Released in Sweden by Polar Music: 7 December 1981
(single ref.: POS 1291)
Released in the UK by Epic: 7 December 1981
(single ref.: EPC A 1740)
Released in the UK by Atlantic: 7 December 1981
(single ref.: 7-89881)
Best chart ranking in Sweden: 13
Best chart ranking in the UK: 3
Best chart ranking in the USA: 107

Genesis

In this pared-down song, where all the space is occupied by Frida's voice, she tells the story of a woman who once looked on a man with wonder, but is now thrown into despair by the mere sight of him. Although it was not retained in *The Visitors'* tracklist, the song is of exceptionally high quality, both in the way it is put together and in the writing. Agnetha, Björn, and Benny's backing vocals are discreet but perfectly in keeping with the piece's delicate character, which is sustained by the effects of the voice of Frida, who perhaps saw something autobiographical in the lyrics. Yet Frida and Benny's divorce did not seem to have had any difficult consequences for the couple, who admitted at the time that the separation had been concluded peacefully. "I don't know how other people deal with things like this," Benny said. "Frida and I are still friends […]. We are still good friends, but are not married anymore."[136]

Production

Michael B Tretow subjected the vocals to the legendary MXR 113 Digital Delay rack unit, in order to give them this resonance and repetition of the sound signal. Launched in 1976, the device became an essential in recording studios, and was used notably by artists such as David Gilmour, Frank Zappa, Roger Waters, and Brian May. The MXR 113 Digital Delay could be used on all types of instrument, but also on vocals, and was an indispensable tool for wizards of sound who wished to fill their productions with the multiple effects the device offered, even though its chief feature was repetition of the signal (delay effect).

Benny Andersson records
The Day Before You Came alone,
in August 1982.

Overleaf: ABBA at the
Ch nateatern, Stockholm,
between two sequences of the
clip of *The Day Before You Came*.

THE DAY BEFORE YOU CAME

(Benny Andersson, Björn Ulvaeus/5'50)

Musicians
Agnetha Fältskog: lead vocals, backing vocals
Anni-Frid "Frida" Lyngstad: backing vocals
Benny Andersson: synthesizers, programming, acoustic guitar
Åke Sundqvist: snare drum

Recording
Polar Music Studios, Stockholm: 16 to 18, 20 August 1982

Technical team
Producers: Björn Ulvaeus, Benny Andersson
Sound engineer: Michael B Tretow

Single
A-side: *The Day Before You Came*/5'50
B-side: *Cassandra*/4'50
Released in Sweden by Polar Music: 18 October 1982
(single ref.: POS 1318)
Released in the UK by CBS/Epic: 18 October 1982
(single ref.: EPC A2847)
Released in the USA by Atlantic: 18 October 1982
(single ref.: 7-89948)
Best chart ranking in Sweden: 3
Best chart ranking in the UK: 32
Best chart ranking in the USA: did not make the charts

Genesis

It was summer 1982. Although Benny Andersson and Björn Ulvaeus had begun recording ABBA's ninth album in May, the desire had gone. The miserable atmosphere in Polar Music Studios when the four artists met did not, however, affect the composers' creativity, because the three songs recorded during this period are of a high quality. After *Just Like That*, *I Am the City, You Owe Me One, Cassandra,* and *Under Attack*, *The Day Before You Came* was recorded in mid-August. The song describes a young woman's monotonous day, and is sung by Agnetha. It would be the very last piece recorded by ABBA at Polar Music Studios in Stockholm, for a few months later, before the summer of 1983, the group decided collectively to pause, following the failure of their latest single, *Under Attack*. Yet *The Day Before You Came* is one of ABBA's greatest songs—but the way it was recorded and the sadness that fills it failed to convince fans, who had always been used to the jolly atmosphere inherent in the group's music. "We were again heading into something more mature, more mysterious and more exciting," Björn explained. "But this time it was one step too far from our audience. [...] It was beyond what our fans expected and consequently it was not a hit."[35] Like that of *Under Attack*, the clip of *The Day Before You Came* was shot not by the faithful Lasse Hallström but by two young film-makers, Kjell Sundvall and Kjell-Åke Andersson, whose first made-for-TV film, *Vi Hade I Alla Fall Tur Med Vädret* ("At Least We Were Lucky with the Weather"), had caught the eye of the members of the group. Filmed partly in a station in Tumba, in Stockholm's south-western suburbs, the video is like the song: infinitely sad and filled with despair. There was no possible doubt: the end of ABBA was nigh.

Production

For the first time in ABBA's history, Benny Andersson began the production of a song on his own, his sole companion being the sound engineer Michael B Tretow. The latter activated a metronome track, then a second track of a Linn LM-1 drum machine, which was retained in the mixing. Starting from an idea he had had in mind for some time, Benny began to record the song, adding the synthesizer tracks and—unheard of—recording some acoustic guitar chords he played himself. The only musician invited to work on the song was

the percussionist Åke Sundqvist, who left his mark on the piece with snare-drum beats in the break, starting at 4'30. The break also features ghostly vocal flights from Frida. When the time came to record the song's vocals, entrusted to Agnetha, Björn and Benny asked her not to display her characteristic technical skill but instead to interpret the lyrics in a more monotonous way, so that the artist and the protagonist of the song were one. Agnetha then asked Tretow to dim the lighting in the studio, and decided to record her voice drawing inspiration from the French singer Charles Aznavour, relating

her dull day in a thin tone. Although the song, which would feature on the compilation *The Singles—The First Ten Years*, is a marvel from all points of view, the group had a few regrets as regards this decision. "It's not the sound of a happy person," Björn explained, "and I think that if we'd done it like *Fernando* or whatever else, and let her sing her heart out instead of having her inhabit a role, it would have been a hit. But artistically we made the right decision. We wanted her to sound 'ordinary' and really be that person."[118]

Photo session with Lasse Larsson
for the sleeve of the single
Under Attack.

Overleaf: On the set of the clip of
Under Attack, directed by Kjell
Sundvall and Kjell-Åke Andersson.

UNDER ATTACK

(Benny Andersson, Björn Ulvaeus/3'45)

Musicians

Agnetha Fältskog: lead vocals, backing vocals
Anni-Frid "Frida" Lyngstad: backing vocals
Benny Andersson: synthesizers, backing vocals
Björn Ulvaeus: backing vocals
Janne Schaffer: electric guitar, acoustic guitar
Rutger Gunnarsson: bass guitar
Per Lindvall: drums, percussion

Recording

Polar Music Studios, Stockholm: 2 to 6 August 1982

Technical team

Producers: Björn Ulvaeus, Benny Andersson
Sound engineer: Michael B Tretow

Single

A-side: *Under Attack*/3'45
B-side: *You Owe Me One*/3'29
Released in Sweden by Polar Music: 21 February 1983
(single ref.: POS 1321)
Released in the UK by CBS/Epic: 11 December 1982
(single ref.: EPC A2971)
Best chart ranking in Sweden: did not make the charts
Best chart ranking in the UK: 26

Genesis

In February 1983, with a pang to the heart, ABBA fans learned of the clip of *Under Attack*, their favorite group's new single, shot on 16 November 1982 in a hangar in the Stockholm suburbs by the film-makers Kjell Sundvall and Kjell-Åke Andersson, who had already made the video of *The Day Before You Came*, unveiled the previous month. Agnetha and Frida are seen walking through the disused warehouse, before being joined at the end by Benny and Björn. The clip concludes with a shot of the four artists leaving the premises—symbolically emerging from the darkness to follow a blinding light coming from outside. The image is powerful and explicit: the end of ABBA has come. It was the group's last single before they went into standby mode.

Fans' frustration was all the greater because the song is exceptionally good. Inspired and inspiring, *Under Attack* is perfectly of its time, with its vocoder-drenched backing vocals, danceable rhythm, and catchy choruses. Although it was one of ABBA's best-produced songs since *Super Trouper*, the public did not agree. The song, which was released in December 1982, then the following February in Sweden, was a considerable flop worldwide and struggled in the charts, reaching number 26 in the UK, number 22 in West Germany, number 19 in Spain, and even number 96 in Australia, where the group had once been revered. Irreversibly, the failure of *Under Attack* would precipitate the end of ABBA.

Production

Here and there in *Under Attack* there are sections from songs that ABBA had never released. The end of the verses had already featured in *Rubber Ball Man* in 1979—a song that also went under the title *Under my Sun*, which fans would discover in 1994 on *Abba Undeleted*. The first part of the verses is borrowed from the guitar motif played by Lasse Wellander in *Just Like That* in May 1982. When the single *Under Attack* was released, Benny and Björn were already immersed in writing *Chess*, the musical they would create with the British lyricist Tim Rice. Listening to *The Day Before You Came* and its successor, we can hear ultra-modern sounds, which would be totally mastered in 1984 in *One Night in Bangkok*, a hit single from *Chess*, played by Murray Head and Anders Glenmark and recorded by Michael B Tretow.

Michael B Tretow turned into the group's archivist in order to make *ABBA Undeleted*.

ABBA UNDELETED

(Benny Andersson, Björn Ulvaeus, Stig Anderson/23'30)

Musicians

Agnetha Fältskog: vocals, spoken voice, backing vocals
Anni-Frid "Frida" Lyngstad: vocals, spoken voice, backing vocals
Björn Ulvaeus: vocals, electric guitar, acoustic guitar, spoken voice, backing vocals
Benny Andersson: synthesizers, Fender Rhodes, piano, spoken voice, backing vocals
Janne Schaffer: electric guitar
Lasse Wellander: electric guitar, acoustic guitar
Finn Sjöberg: electric guitar
Michael Areklew: guitar
Anders Glenmark: guitar
Mike Watson: bass guitar
Rutger Gunnarsson: bass guitar
Ola Brunkert: drums
Roger Palm: drums
Anders Eljas: synthesizers
Raphael Ravenscroft: saxophone
Malando Gassama: percussion
Åke Sundqvist: percussion

Recording

Studios Vogue, Villetaneuse: March 1974
Glen Studio, Stocksund: August, September, October 1974
Marcus Music, Solna: June, August 1977
Metronome, Stockholm: January 1974, March, May, July 1978
Polar Music Studios, Stockholm: June, August to October 1978, August 1979, May 1981, May 1982

Technical team

Producers: Björn Ulvaeus, Benny Andersson
Sound engineer: Michael B Tretow

Box set *Thank You for the Music*

Released in the UK and Europe by Polar Music-Polydor: 31 October 1994 (CD box set ref.: 523 472-2)
Released in the USA by Polar Music-Polydor: 31 October 1994 (CD box set ref.: 314 523 472-2)
Best chart ranking in Sweden: 17
Best chart ranking in the UK: did not make the charts
Best chart ranking in the USA: did not make the charts

Fifteen hitherto unseen songs for the fans

While he was working on the remastering of ABBA's songs for the compilation *ABBA Gold*, which would be released in 1992, Michael B Tretow made a very interesting discovery in the archives of Polygram, Polydor's parent company, which would distribute the record worldwide. Faced with the large number of tapes containing scraps of recordings, Tretow took them to listen to in his personal studio, and embarked on putting together a medley of 15 fragments of song. Entitled *Abba Undeleted* and lasting almost 24 minutes, the track was a treasure trove for fans, and was revealed in 1994 in the box set *Thank You for the Music*.

A few rare gems

Abba Undeleted contains preliminary recordings for songs that became famous, as well as some never heard before. On it, the musicians can be heard talking and laughing: it is a real plunge into the heart of a group's life in the studio. Among the songs that had never seen the light of day until then, fans could listen to *Scaramouche*, recorded in the studios of Marcus Music in Solna in June 1977, *Here Comes Rubie Jamie* and *Rikky Rock 'N' Roller*, recorded at Glen Studio, Stocksund, in September 1974 and September 1975, and *Hamlet III Parts 1&2* and *Free as a Bumble Bee,* recorded at Metronome in 1978—as well as others from Polar Music Studios, such as *Burning my Bridges*, *Rubber Ball Man*, *Crying over You*, and *Givin' a Little Bit More.* To the joy of discovering so many gems that had remained buried in the group's archives all these years was added the pleasure of discovering songs well known to the public in their embryonic stage. This was the case with *Summer Night City*, sung here with humor by Frida, exaggerating her English accent to make Agnetha laugh. There is *Baby*, the preliminary recording for *Rock Me*, sung by Björn in a register much too high for his vocal range. Also revealed are *Just a Notion*, a famous outtake from the time of *Voulez-Vous* which ABBA would bring back to life on *Voyage* in 2021, as well as an extract from *Just Like That* enhanced with Raphael Ravenscroft's saxophone part, recorded in 1982. Finally, this treasure also contains one of the first versions of *Fernando*, the group's flagship song. A beautiful gift that arrived right on cue to celebrate ABBA's return to grace, which began with the release of *ABBA Gold* in 1992.

ABBACADABRA: A FRANCO-SWEDISH COLLABORATION

In 1983, ABBA's French publisher, Alain Boublil, suggested to Benny and Björn that the group's songs could be adapted in French. His idea was not to revisit their existing classics, as Mireille Mathieu had done with *Bravo tu as gagné*, a Frenchified reinterpretation of *The Winner Takes It All*, but rather to create a musical based on the group's repertoire. The story was that of four children—John, Ellen, Peter, and Linda—who share the same punishment meted out by their headmistress: to tidy the school library. A book falls from a shelf, and sets free seven story characters whom the witch Carabosse had imprisoned in their respective books: Alice, Snow White, Cinderella, Aladdin, Bluebeard, the Little Prince, and Pinocchio. Various adventures follow, making up the musical *ABBAcadabra*, which was broadcast on French television in nine episodes, starting on 21 December 1983 with the program *Destination Noël* ("Destination: Christmas") presented by Plastic Bertrand, a Belgian singer who also plays Pinocchio in the piece.

ABBA in French

ABBA's songs were then translated into French, and the children included future celebrities, such as the politician Clémentine Autain and the actor Léa Drucker, who replaced her on the recording of the album *ABBAcadabra*, based on the musical. As regards the adults involved, they were also stars, for they included Frida in the role of Belle, whose marriage to the prince, played by the star of *Starmania*, Daniel Balavoine, occurs at the conclusion of the work. The ABBA songs used for *ABBAcadabra* include *When I Kissed the Teacher/Qu'est-ce que je vais faire plus tard?* ("What Will I Do Later?"), *Take a Chance on Me/Abbacadabra, Super Trouper/ Tête d'allumette* ("Matchstick Head"), and *Thank You for the Music/Envoyez le générique* ("Roll the Closing Credits"). The work, by Alain Boublil and his namesake Daniel Boublil, was adapted at the same time in the UK, and staged in its English-language version at the Lyric Hammersmith, London, on 8 December 1983, with lyrics by David Wood, Mike Batt, and Don Black. Peter James directed, and choreography was by Anthony Van Laast. For the occasion, Benny Andersson provided a composition that was once a preliminary recording for ABBA, *I Am a Seeker*, which became *I Am the Seeker* in the musical *ABBAcadabra—A Musical Adventure*.

Above: Produced by the star Phil Collins, Frida's album was a resounding success worldwide.
Right: Agnetha Fältskog reinvented herself too, with her album *Wrap Your Arms around Me*, produced by Mike Chapman.

ABBA AFTER ABBA

While the clip of *Under Attack* explicitly announced the end of ABBA, the song's worldwide failure would confirm it. Busy with other projects, the members of the group decided to put it on ice. "The boys have taken on the task to write three hours of music for the musical they are going to create together with Tim Rice," Agnetha explained in June 1983. "This means that they won't have any time to write songs for ABBA for the time being. I really don't know if they ever will be up for that. Where ABBA is concerned, the future is widely open. We are not saying that we will continue, but we are not saying that it's over either. I think that the development of our individual careers will be a deciding factor."[137] That year Agnetha was certainly riding the wave of the success of her first album in English, *Wrap Your Arms Around Me*, made by Mike Chapman, Blondie's legendary producer. The second single from the record, *The Heat Is On*, had a reggae quality identical to that of *Island of Lost Souls*, produced for Debbie Harry's group a year earlier. It was a resounding success, which promised a glorious future for Fältskog. "For me, my solo album is the first step on which many others will

follow," she said enthusiastically in September. "I want to compose more myself, I don't want to exist in the heads of the ABBA fans as just a singer."[138] For her part, Frida also benefited from the warm reception accorded to the album she released in 1982, *Something's Going On*, produced by Phil Collins.

In 1984, a year after *Wrap Your Arms Around Me* came out, the album of the musical *Chess*, by Benny Andersson, Björn Ulvaeus, and Tim Rice, was released. The first single from the record, *One Night in Bangkok*, performed by Murray Head (and sung by Anders Glenmark in the choruses), was a triumphant success in the USA and other countries, thanks especially to its irrepressible chorus. This was the moment Anni-Frid "Frida" Lyngstad chose to go and live abroad. "I have decided to leave Sweden because I can't be anonymous in my private life any longer," she explained in 1982. "In the near future, I would like to spend most of my time in London, which is better for me professionally and for my solo career as well."[139] The future now seemed radiant for the group's former members.

Benny Andersson and Björn
Ulvaeus at the premiere of
Chess in London, 14 May 1986.

Benny and Björn's first musical

Chess premiered at the Prince Edward Theatre, London, on
14 May 1986. Its three lead singers—Elaine Paige, Murray
Head, and Tommy Körberg—thus brought to life the wildest
dreams of Benny Andersson and Björn Ulvaeus: to create
their very first musical. The production ran for three years
before moving to Broadway where, alas, it was not a success.
This failure coincided with ABBA's image having deteriorated
considerably since the start of the decade. The group which,
ten years earlier, had been the most popular in the world was
now forgotten by everyone, and of no interest to record companies, which encouraged its members to disappear for good.
After several albums (Agnetha's *Eyes of a Woman* and *I Stand
Alone* in 1985 and 1987, and Frida's *Shine* in 1984), the two
former ABBA singers' hopes of successful solo careers had
evaporated. The latter even announced her retirement from
music in 1985. Despite their considerable musical legacy, the
group were then seen as old-fashioned, and the whole world
turned its back on them.

1992: the year of the return to grace

ABBA's fate would be decided during 1992, thanks to a series
of events that were as fortunate as they were unexpected. On
11 June, when they were playing at the Globen in Stockholm
as part of their *ZOO TV Tour*, U2 invited Benny Andersson
and Björn Ulvaeus on stage, and covered *Dancing Queen* with
them. This coup was a colossal surprise. On the following
30 August, at the Reading Festival in England, Nirvana
demanded the presence of the Australian group Björn Again,
who had specialized in covering ABBA hits since 1988, for
the first part of their set. "We were playing a show in Richmond
[Melbourne, Australia] and Nirvana were down the road [at
The Palace, 31 January to 2 February 1992]. They caught the
tail end of our set, bought all our T-shirts and buggered off.
The next thing, they're on MTV and Dave Grohl is wearing a
Björn Again T-shirt. Then we got the call: 'Nirvana wants you
to play with them at Reading. Moreover, Kurt [Cobain, Nirvana's

legendary lead singer] has said, Unless Björn Again are playing, they're not doing the gig.'"[140]

"It sounded like Abba!" said Dave Grohl, Nirvana's drummer at the time. "We immediately thought, we have to take these guys on tour—because who fucking doesn't like Abba?"[141] Also in 1992, the British duo Erasure, comprising Andy Bell and Vince Clarke (founder of Depeche Mode and later Yazoo), helped ABBA to regain popularity. Released on 1 June, their EP *Abba-esque* consisted of four reinterpretations of songs from the group's repertoire: *Lay All Your Love on Me, SOS, Take a Chance on Me*, and *Voulez-Vous*. Reworked with some new arrangements, and accompanied by clips in which the two artists good-naturedly caricatured those of ABBA, the songs thus came back to life thanks to the duo, who had already revisited *Gimme! Gimme! Gimme! (A Man after Midnight)* on the B-side of their maxi single *Oh L'Amour*, which had been a hit in 1986. "For me, the charts have lost much of their appeal after ABBA," Bell said in 1992. "I was too young for The Beach Boys, so for me ABBA was the first group that made those delicious, melodic pop-songs, with all those angelic choirs, that lifted you up. When they went disco with songs like *Voulez-Vous*, they seemed to fully understand that medium."[142] The critical success of *Abba-esque* naturally came to the notice of Polydor, now Polar Music's partner for the distribution of ABBA records, which decided to release a compilation of the group's greatest singles.

A cult compilation celebrating ABBA's legacy

The release of *ABBA Gold: Greatest Hits* on 21 September 1992 was accompanied by a return to grace for the group in the eyes of the public and the press, which once again emphasized the qualities of their repertoire. That year, ABBA's name was on everyone's lips. Also that year, Philip Lodge, a professor at Cambridge University in England, published a thesis entitled *Compositional Procedures in the Songs of ABBA*, which praised the work of Benny Andersson and Björn Ulvaeus, unhesitatingly comparing their talent to that of Mozart. When asked by the world's media what the reasons were for the group's return to center stage, Björn Ulvaeus replied: "I can only explain this renewed success with the possibility that people are getting tired of the fifties and the sixties. Lately, they have been milked dry to the last drop. Now it's time for the seventies. And since we were rather authoritative during that time, it's only natural that we're now present again as well."[143]

The year 1992 ended with the colossal success of the Swedish group Ace of Base, whose first album, *Happy Nation*, had just been released in Europe. Comprising two men and two women, the quartet were constantly compared with ABBA, both for their very pop-musical aesthetic and for the group's structure. Now, and for a long time to come, everyone was talking about ABBA. This state of grace was confirmed by the use of their songs in two major movies of the 1990s: *The Adventures of Priscilla, Queen of the Desert*, directed by Stephan Elliott, and especially *Muriel's Wedding*, directed by P J Hogan, whose screenplay was built entirely around the songs of ABBA, which punctuated the entire movie. The release of these two feature-length films in 1994 coincided with that of the longbox ABBA box set *Thank You for the Music*, which featured a delicious selection of the group's songs, together with a rich crop of rarities and unreleased material.

Björn Ulvaeus and Benny Andersson at the premiere of the film *Mamma Mia! Here We Go Again* at the Eventim Apollo, London, 16 July 2018.

Mamma Mia!: back to their peak

This happy situation drove Björn Ulvaeus and Benny Andersson to embark on writing the musical *Mamma Mia!* (whose title initially was *Summer Night City*), which premiered at the Prince Edward Theatre in London on 6 April 1999—25 years to the day after the group had won the Eurovision Song Contest. It was a huge success, and multiple adaptations of the work around the world over the years have attracted an audience totaling more than 50 million. When the film adaptation of *Mamma Mia!* appeared in 2008 it was also a success, leading the movie's producers, Judy Craymer and Gary Goetzman, to make a sequel ten years later entitled, logically enough, *Mamma Mia! Here We Go Again*. After their induction into the Rock & Roll Hall of Fame in 2010, and the opening of the ABBA Museum in Stockholm in May 2013, ABBA seemed in tune with the times more than ever before. This state of affairs led Benny and Björn to ask themselves a very simple question: was an ABBA comeback conceivable? Andy Bell of Erasure had already answered it in 1992, with a confidence that left no room for doubt: "They will never be able to completely get away from it, ABBA will always come back to haunt them. They will still see pictures of themselves everywhere."[142] It would take almost 40 years for Agnetha, Frida, Björn, and Benny to think about a comeback for their group—one of the most important in the history of modern popular music.

VOYAGE

I Still Have Faith In You • When You Danced With Me • Little Things •
Don't Shut Me Down • Just A Notion • I Can Be That Woman • Keep An Eye On Dan •
Bumblebee • No Doubt About It • Ode To Freedom

Released in Europe and the UK by Polar Music: 5 November 2021
(album ref.: 00602438614813, CD ref.: 00602438885800)
Released in the USA by Capitol Records: 5 November 2021
(album ref.: 00602438614813, CD ref.: B003460502)
Best chart ranking in Sweden: 1
Best chart ranking in the UK: 1
Best chart ranking in the USA: 2

Benny Andersson, Agnetha Fältskog, Anni-Frid "Frida" Lyngstad, and Björn Ulvaeus at the first performance of the show *Voyage*, ABBA Arena, London, 27 May 2022.

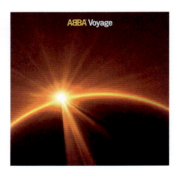

THE EMOTIONAL ENDING TO A SWEDISH STORY

In May 2013, while promoting the opening of ABBA The Museum, now a place of pilgrimage for ABBA fans from all over the world, Björn Ulvaeus granted an interview to *The Wall Street Journal* website. Inevitably questioned about a possible reunion, the musician and songwriter replied in no uncertain terms. "No […]—this is me talking, the other three will have to talk for themselves—I want people to remember us as we were. I think that's a fantastic legacy, that young people who get introduced to ABBA, maybe through *Mamma Mia* or something else, the videos that they look at are with a young and energetic group from the seventies and that's the way it should be. I don't think that four geriatrics wheeled on stage is what we should leave as a legacy."[144] A year later, Anni-Frid "Frida" Lyngstad confirmed this: "We have only one answer and that is no… No amount of money would change our minds."[145] Despite what they might say, the triumph of the first *Mamma Mia!* film, inspired by the musical of the same name, and the success of ABBA The Museum confirmed to the former band members that fans the world over were still hoping for something new from them. Those fans would have to wait until 2016 before ABBA fully emerged from their 34-year retirement.

No holograms for ABBA

In 2017, Benny Andersson and Björn Ulvaeus were approached by Simon Fuller, a British artist manager (of stars including The Spice Girls, S Club 7, and David Beckham) and creator of the UK TV series *Pop Idol*, known as *American Idol* in the USA. Fuller proposed a project to ABBA that would involve holograms of the four artists going on tour. Always on the lookout for new artistic projects, Benny and Björn agreed to a partnership with Fuller, who announced to fans in a press release that there would soon be "an extraordinary new virtual reality experience."[146] But the two Swedes' trip to Las Vegas in 2018 put a spanner in the works. They had gone to see the Cirque du Soleil show *Michael Jackson One*, in which the King of Pop appeared as a hologram for the track *Man in the Mirror*, and as a result they expressed reservations about this supposedly revolutionary technology. "We went to Vegas, saw that show, and went, 'No way,'"[147] Benny declared to *Life*. The collaboration between ABBA and Simon Fuller came to an abrupt end. "We had to abandon it because he was talking about doing a hologram show," Andersson explained in an interview with *The Guardian*. "Have you ever seen a hologram show? You have to sit smack in the middle, you can't have any lights, you can't have anything going on, so we said, 'No, we can't do that' … Simon Fuller wanted to do a TV show—a BBC and NBC special was also announced—and we thought, 'What do we want to do a TV show for?'"[146]

The partnership with ILM

Although the Las Vegas experience put paid to the partnership with Simon Fuller, it did give Andersson and Ulvaeus a new project, which they presented to Industrial Light & Magic (ILM), the special-effects company founded by George Lucas in 1975, now owned by the Walt Disney Company. The idea was to reproduce images of the band members as they were

Björn Ulvaeus at ABBA
The Museum, Stockholm.

in 1979, using the motion-capture techniques seen in movies such as Peter Jackson's *Lord of the Rings* trilogy and Rupert Wyatt's *Rise of the Planet of the Apes*, for which actor Andy Serkis's movements were recorded using multiple sensors to bring to life the characters of Gollum and Caesar the chimpanzee. The idea of resurrecting ABBA as avatars also appealed to Agnetha Fältskog and Frida Lyngstad, who gave the venture their go-ahead. The band would be reunited on the big screen with all four original members involved. "What interested us was the idea that we could send them out while we can be at home cooking or walking the dog,"[148] Benny Andersson joked.

Back in the studio

On 27 April 2018, while the show was being produced, a press release from Agnetha, Benny, Björn, and Anni-Frid took fans by surprise: "The decision to go ahead with the exciting ABBA avatar tour project had an unexpected consequence. We all four felt that, after some 35 years, it could be fun to join forces again and go into the recording studio. So we did."[149] The four met up again in June 2017 at Riksmixningsverket, aka RMV Studio, Benny's recording studio on Skeppsholmen island in the Stockholm archipelago. The name literally means "national mixing institute" (and had been invented by Michael B Tretow several decades earlier, but couldn't be used at the time because the term "institute" sounded so official). It was run by Ludvig Andersson, Benny's son, assisted by the talented sound engineer Linn Fijal. It was in this cozy hideaway in central Stockholm that ABBA, motivated by the idea of creating some new tracks for their fans for the upcoming tour and with the help of sound engineer Bernard Löhr, produced two new songs in 2017: *I Still Have Faith in You* and *Don't Shut Me*

Benny Andersson in his studio at Skeppsholmen, 20 October 2021.

Down. The fans' growing excitement at the prospect of seeing ABBA back on stage only increased when the recording of the new tracks was announced.

Some months later, the foursome, realizing how much they had enjoyed getting together again for creative purposes, decided to record more new tracks. While the initial project had been to come up with just two songs, they started talking about the possibility of taking their comeback a bit further. As Benny explained, "We said, 'Shouldn't we write a few other songs, just for fun?' And the girls said, 'Yeah, that will be fun.' So they came in and we had five songs. And we said, 'Shouldn't we do a few others? We can release an album.'"[148]

ABBA in motion capture

The sessions for the new album—called *Voyage*, the same name as the show that was currently under production—took place at Riksmixningsverket up to 2021, and were put on pause during the Covid pandemic in 2020 and 2021. In early 2020, before most of the world went into lockdown, ABBA just had time to do some motion-capture shots for the *Voyage* show (directed by Baillie Walsh and produced by Johan Renck, Svana Gisla, and Ludvig Andersson), over a five-week period at Stockholm's Svenska Filminstitutet. In the presence of 160 cameras and over 40 technicians, the four performed all the movements from Wayne McGregor's choreography before other motion-capture shots of young stand-ins were blended in to add youthful energy to the movements. "It was like going to the office in the morning," Björn recalled. "Then dressing in those funny costumes and going on stage and miming to the old songs exactly the way we had so many times in so many TV studios around the world in the '70s."[147] "They photographed us from all possible angles," he explained in another interview. "They made us grimace in front of cameras, they shaved our beards, painted dots on our faces, they measured our heads."[150] Choreographer Wayne McGregor described the atmosphere at the Svenska Filminstitutet in February 2020: "It was very emotional every day. It was like NASA in having so many people in the studio every day, but the whole studio were in tears most days. It was really extraordinary."[151]

The voyage begins

It was announced in a press release on 2 September 2020 that ABBA's ninth album, *Voyage,* would come out in November 2021. Mixed at Mono Music Studios, just along the street from Riksmixningsverket and also owned by Benny Andersson, the record was entirely produced by Andersson and has a modern sound and a modern cover, with an image of a sunrise above a planet we imagine to be Earth.

The album's tracklist consisted of nine new songs along with a rarity from the band's archives: *Just a Notion*, recorded in 1978 during the *Voulez-Vous* sessions. *Voyage* received a warm reception from the world's press and sold over a million copies within days of its release, topping the charts in almost 20 countries, including France, Australia, Germany, the UK, Sweden, and New Zealand. In the USA, ABBA scored a career best by reaching number 2 on the *Billboard* charts.

For the ABBA revival, the last living musicians who had helped to create the ABBA sound between 1973 and 1982 were called in, including guitarist Lasse Wellander and drummer Per Lindvall. Michael B Tretow was also invited to participate in the recordings, but sadly he was unable to join the emotional reunion for health reasons.

Opposite: Björn Ulvaeus gives a conference on the use of artificial intelligence at the Digital X exhibition in Cologne, 20 September 2023.

Below: The members of ABBA, forever young, on the poster for the *Voyage* show.

ABBA Voyage — ABBA Arena, London

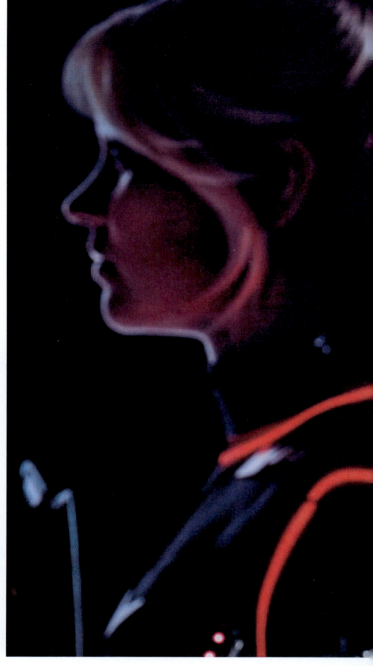

ABBA Voyage: the show

Alongside the international success of *Voyage* the album came the show of the same name, which premiered on 27 May 2022. Although it was initially planned as a touring show, the decision was taken to create ABBA Arena, a purpose-built venue that could easily be dismantled, near Queen Elizabeth Olympic Park in east London. "London is the best city in the world to be in when it comes to entertainment," Björn Ulvaeus explained. "Theaters, musicals, concerts, they've been here for years. And there's a big audience traveling here for that reason—so it was a no-brainer."[152] The show's setlist features 20 songs taken from ABBA's repertoire (*The Visitors, Hole in Your Soul, SOS, Knowing Me, Knowing You, Chiquitita, Fernando, Mamma Mia, Does Your Mother Know, Eagle, Lay All Your Love on Me, Summer Night City, Gimme! Gimme! Gimme! (A Man after Midnight), Voulez-Vous, When All Is Said and Done, Don't Shut Me Down, I Still Have Faith in You, Waterloo, Thank You for the Music, Dancing Queen,* and *The Winner Takes It All*), delighting fans who come to applaud the band's avatars, cleverly renamed ABBAtars by Ludvig Andersson, Benny's son and co-producer of the event. To the right of the stage, a group performs the songs live. James

Righton, former singer with Klaxons, had been asked to recruit musicians to form the group, which features Eoin Rooney and Dom John on guitar, Sarah Burrell and Victoria Hesketh on keyboards, Victoria Smith on drums, Joe Stoddart on bass, Anna Kirby on saxophone, Tuca Milan on percussion, and backing singers Rachel Clark, Amina Gichinga, and Grace Barrett. The show was an instant hit with sell-out performances, confirming Benny and Björn as visionary artists, supported by Agnetha and Frida on vocals.

Following the colossal success of the album *Voyage* and the show of the same name, the question is: what is ABBA's next career move? "I said 'that's it'," Benny said in 2021. "I don't wanna do another ABBA album. But I mean I'm not alone in this. There's four of us. If they twist my arm I might change my mind."[153] Björn Ulvaeus, sitting next to him, remarked: "Good to know."[153]

Let's hope Benny can be persuaded to change his mind (with no violence necessary) and that the greatest band of the 20th century will treat us to some more of their unparalleled and timeless songs.

Single

2021

I STILL HAVE FAITH IN YOU

(Benny Andersson, Björn Ulvaeus/5'08)

Musicians
Anni-Frid "Frida" Lyngstad: lead vocals, backing vocals
Agnetha Fältskog: backing vocals
Benny Andersson: piano, synthesizers, backing vocals
Björn Ulvaeus: backing vocals
Lasse Wellander: guitar
Lasse Jonsson: guitar
Per Lindvall: drums
Orchestra: Stockholm Concert Orchestra

Recording
Riksmixningsverket (RMV Studio), Stockholm: June 2017

Technical team
Producer: Benny Andersson
Sound engineer: Bernard Löhr
Assistant sound engineer: Linn Fijal
Conductor: Göran Arnberg
Orchestra arrangements: Göran Arnberg

45 rpm version
A-side: *I Still Have Faith in You*/5'08
B-side: blank

CD Single version
1. *I Still Have Faith in You*/5'08

Digital distribution by Polar Music: 2 September 2021
Released in Europe and the UK by Polar Music: 2 September 2021
(single ref.: 00602567807513, CD single ref.: 00602567899440)
Best chart ranking in Sweden: 2
Best chart ranking in the UK: 14

Genesis

I Still Have Faith in You was the first song to be recorded when ABBA got back together in June 2017 and is an homage to the friendship between the band members spanning almost 50 years. When Benny Andersson, who was the sole producer of *Voyage*, presented the melody to Björn Ulvaeus for him to write the lyrics, Björn instantly came up with a subject. "When Benny played the melody, I just knew it had to be about us. It's about realizing that it's inconceivable to be where we are. No imagination could dream up that, to release a new album after 40 years and still be the best of friends and still be enjoying each other's company and have a total loyalty. Who has experienced that? Nobody."[154] *I Still Have Faith in You* was released as a single on 2 September 2021, the same day the release date of the upcoming album was announced. It was accompanied by a second, more pop-sounding single called *Don't Shut Me Down*, reminding the public that Andersson's creative genius lent itself just as easily to pop-oriented tracks as it did to more operatic numbers.

Production

The main melody line for *I Still Have Faith in You* that Benny presented to Björn that day was not original. In 2015, he had composed the soundtrack for the fantasy film *Cirkeln* ("The Circle"), directed by Levan Akin. It included an instrumental piece called *Kyssen* ("The Kiss"), whose main theme from the opening bars was the one he reused for *I Still Have Faith in You*. "I felt it would be sort of a waste to have a melody line like that sort of disappear into thin air in a movie that people will not see again, I guess, so yeah, I completed it," Benny explained.[155] The song is an ode to friendship performed by Frida with backing vocals from Agnetha, Björn, and Benny—a perfect opening for ABBA's ninth album.

Benny Andersson and the team of the film *Cirkeln* ("The Circle"). *Chapter 1: The Chosen Ones* at the Berlin International Film Festival, 10 February 2015.

Single

WHEN YOU DANCED WITH ME

(Benny Andersson, Björn Ulvaeus/2'49)

Musicians
Agnetha Fältskog: vocals, backing vocals
Anni-Frid "Frida" Lyngstad: vocals, backing vocals
Benny Andersson: synthesizers, backing vocals
Björn Ulvaeus: backing vocals
Lasse Wellander: guitar
Lasse Jonsson: guitar
Per Lindvall: drums
Jan Bengtson: flute

Recording
Riksmixningsverket (RMV Studio), Stockholm: 2018 to 2021

Technical team
Producer: Benny Andersson
Sound engineer: Bernard Löhr
Assistant sound engineers: Linn Fijal, Vilma Colling

Single
1. *When You Danced with Me*/2'49
Digital distribution by Polar Music: November 2021
Best chart ranking in Sweden: 8
Best chart ranking in the UK: 67

Genesis

ABBA take us back to the folksiest songs in their repertoire with *When You Danced with Me*. Listening to this track with its Irish and Scottish sounds makes us think of *Hasta Mañana* (*Waterloo*, 1974), *Fernando* (1976), and *The Piper* (*Super Trouper*, 1980). In fact, Björn wrote the song—about two ex-lovers meeting up again in the small Irish town of Kilkenny years after one of them had left to explore the world—based on his memories of a trip there. "I drove around the coast from Limerick to Dublin with my family in the '90s and we stopped in Kilkenny," Björn explained in November 2021. "It was beautiful and very romantic, I thought. Castle, churches and the surroundings, County Kilkenny with its little charming villages. It has stayed with me. We drove through Cork as well and there's absolutely nothing wrong with that city, but try to replace Kilkenny with Cork in *When You Danced with Me!*"[156] he jokes.

Production

Although Jan Bengston's flute score is very much present in the mix of *When You Danced with Me* (it doubles the melody line of the verses at 0'23, for example), it's Benny Andersson's synth sounds that emulate the Irish bagpipes (also called uilleann pipes). Unlike the Scottish version, which is played by the piper blowing air from the mouth into the instrument, the Irish bagpipes deliver notes from the air in the pipes. This is irrelevant here, as Benny Andersson uses his synthesizers to produce the Celtic sounds on this track.

Aerial view of Kilkenny Castle, a landscape that inspired Björn to write the lyrics of *When You Danced with Me*.

Single

LITTLE THINGS

(Benny Andersson, Björn Ulvaeus/3'08)

Two young women dressed as Queens of Light at the important Swedish festival of St Lucia, December 1962.

Musicians
Agnetha Fältskog: vocals, backing vocals
Anni-Frid "Frida" Lyngstad: vocals, backing vocals
Benny Andersson: piano, accordion, backing vocals
Björn Ulvaeus: backing vocals
Lasse Wellander: acoustic guitar
Lasse Jonsson: acoustic guitar
Per Lindvall: percussion
Pär Grebacken: transverse flute, clarinet
Jan Bengtson: flute
Orchestra: Stockholm Concert Orchestra
Choir: Children's Choir of Stockholm International School

Recording
Riksmixningsverket (RMV Studio), Stockholm: 2018 to 2021

Technical team
Producer: Benny Andersson
Sound engineer: Bernard Löhr
Assistant sound engineers: Linn Fijal, Vilma Colling
Conductor: Göran Arnberg
Choir director: Kimberley Akester
Assistant choir director: Anneli Thompson

Single
1. *Little Things*/3'08
Digital distribution by Polar Music: 3 December 2021
Released in Europe and the UK by Polar Music: 3 December 2021
(CD single ref.: 602438971268)
Best chart ranking in Sweden: 20
Best chart ranking in the UK: 61

Genesis

The Swedes take Christmas and its traditions very seriously, especially Lussebruden, or the Queen of Lights, a celebration in homage to St Lucia, a young Christian woman who was persecuted and tortured for refusing to marry a Pagan man. Every year on 13 December, a ritual gets the winter season underway in Sweden: the oldest daughter in the family gets up in the morning, puts on a white robe with a red belt and a crown of nine candles on her head. She then wakes her family so everyone can enjoy some delicious saffron cakes called *lussekatters* by candlelight. "Here in Sweden, the Queen of Lights is something like Baby Jesus in Germany,"[157] Agnetha explained in an interview in 1976. As there was no Christmas song in ABBA's repertoire, our four friends decided to make up for this with *Little Things*, a tribute to the spirit of sharing and companionship that traditionally marks the festive season.

Production

As they had done before, with the recording of *I Have a Dream* in March 1979, ABBA decided to add a little extra touch to the production of their Christmas song by bringing in the children's choir from the Stockholm International School. In 2021, Kimberley Akester, the after-school activities coordinator, was invited to take part in a documentary on the genesis of *I Have a Dream*. So she and Anneli Thompson, the school's drama teacher, took the choir to Nalen, a famous entertainment venue in the city, where they sang with some of ABBA's session musicians.

A few weeks later, Akester received an email from Benny Andersson's assistant asking if she could get some children together to sing on a song ABBA were working on. She agreed to do so and, despite a few organizational issues caused by the Covid pandemic, the choir made it to Riksmixningsverket, Andersson's studio. "I picked eight students to sing," said Akester, "but even though we rehearsed a lot, Covid meant someone was always off sick or isolating. Even when the day of the recording came, we only had seven out of the eight students available to go."[158]

Single

DON'T SHUT ME DOWN

(Benny Andersson, Björn Ulvaeus/3'59)

Musicians
Agnetha Fältskog: lead vocals, backing vocals
Anni-Frid "Frida" Lyngstad: backing vocals
Benny Andersson: piano, synthesizers, backing vocals
Björn Ulvaeus: backing vocals
Lasse Wellander: guitar
Per Lindvall: drums, percussion
Margareta Bengtson: harp
Orchestra: Stockholm Concert Orchestra

Recording
Riksmixningsverket (RMV Studio), Stockholm: June 2017

Technical team
Producer: Benny Andersson
Sound engineer: Bernard Löhr
Assistant sound engineers: Linn Fijal, Vilma Colling
Conductor: Göran Arnberg

Single
1. *Don't Shut Me Down*/3'59
Digital distribution by Polar Music: 2 September 2021
Released in Europe and the UK by Polar Music: 2 September 2021
(CD single ref.: 00602438745692)
Best chart ranking in Sweden: 1
Best chart ranking in the UK: 9

Genesis
Without a doubt the most poppy number on *Voyage* and also the one that feels closest to the ABBA spirit, *Don't Shut Me Down* was a hit in the making, and on its release it shot to number 1 in the Swedish charts. Written to be performed on tour by the avatars, it would be one of the surprises for fans who attended the *Voyage* show when this was finally launched in London on 27 May 2022.

"At that time we were kind of getting the hang of what the ABBAtars would be," Björn explained to Apple Music in 2021. "This is about a woman who has broken up and regrets breaking up. And she is going to come back and see if the guy will take her back. So she sits on a bench in a park and it gets dark. And finally she gets the courage up to go and knock on the door. That's it at face value, but I see it as us, as ABBAtars, knocking on the doors of the fans: Please take us as we are now and don't shut us down."[159]

Production
Björn later stated that, musically speaking, *Don't Shut Me Down* is the only reference on *Voyage* to the kind of music ABBA were making in the 1970s. It certainly contains all the ingredients that made the band so successful: a disco drum pattern at 100 bpm, a funk guitar rhythm played by Lasse Wellander, accompanied to perfection by Benny Andersson's piano score, a totally irresistible melody, and impeccable vocal harmonies. "That was … perfect," Andersson commented. "It was exactly the same as it had always been. We came into the studio, the control room, I had made copies of the lyrics, we played the backing track, the girls sang along and asked questions, and then they took the sheets of paper into the studio and started singing. I have to tell you, when they came in the studio, I thought: maybe I should have asked them first, before we planned all this, if they can still sing. But after the first day, I didn't need to worry."[146]

On 2 September 2021, ABBA fans could see the first images of the show *ABBA Voyage* in front of the Hotel nhow in Berlin.

Back to 1978: Agnetha and
Frida recording vocals for
Just a Notion.

2021

Single

JUST A NOTION

(Benny Andersson, Björn Ulvaeus/3'29)

Musicians

Agnetha Fältskog: vocals, backing vocals
Anni-Frid "Frida" Lyngstad: vocals, backing vocals
Benny Andersson: piano, synthesizers, backing vocals
Björn Ulvaeus: backing vocals
Lasse Wellander: guitar
Per Lindvall: drums
Pär Grebacken: tenor saxophone
Jan Bengtson: baritone saxophone

Recording

Polar Music Studio, Stockholm: 7 September 1978
Riksmixningsverket (RMV Studio), Stockholm: 2018 to 2021

Technical team

Producer: Benny Andersson
Sound engineer: Bernard Löhr
Assistant sound engineers: Linn Fijal, Vilma Colling

Single

1. *Just a Notion*/3'29
Digital distribution by Polar Music: 22 October 2021
Released in Europe and the UK by Polar Music: 22 October 2021
(CD single ref.: 00602438921317)
Best chart ranking in Sweden: 22
Best chart ranking in the UK: 59

Genesis

In 1978, Charlie Bates, the new editor-in-chief of *ABBA
Magazine,* had been invited to meet the band members at
the recording sessions for their new album. "The girls go back
into the recording booth while the boys sit down at the
console with [Michael B Tretow]," he reported in the fanzine.
"The song is a newie called 'Just a Notion' from the new
album. The girls' voices are beautiful, they sound in top
form."[160] The piece was a 1950s-sounding rock track of the
kind Benny and Björn adore but, despite an effective melody,
it wasn't selected for inclusion on *Voulez-Vous*. Was it because
of this outdated feel, distancing the band from their disco
ambitions, that *Just a Notion* was shelved, with segments
reappearing in the 1994 *ABBA Undeleted* medley? "Why did
we decide against it?" Björn Ulvaeus wonders now. "In hindsight, I don't have a clue. It's a good song with great vocals.
I know that we played it to a publisher in France and a couple
of other people we trusted and as far as I can remember they
liked it very much. So it's a mystery and will remain a
mystery."[161]

Production

Whatever it was that led ABBA to put the *Just a Notion* tapes
back on the shelf at Polar Music Studios, the song stuck in
Benny Andersson's mind and in 2018 he decided to dust it off,
keeping only the vocal takes from the original recordings. He
then created a new instrumental track himself to make the
sound of *Just a Notion* coherent with the band's new songs.
The work done on this track is similar to the kind of alchemy
ABBA were trying to create with the *Voyage* show that was in
production at the time: a group of musicians on stage playing
the specially re-orchestrated songs alongside the original ABBA
vocal takes.

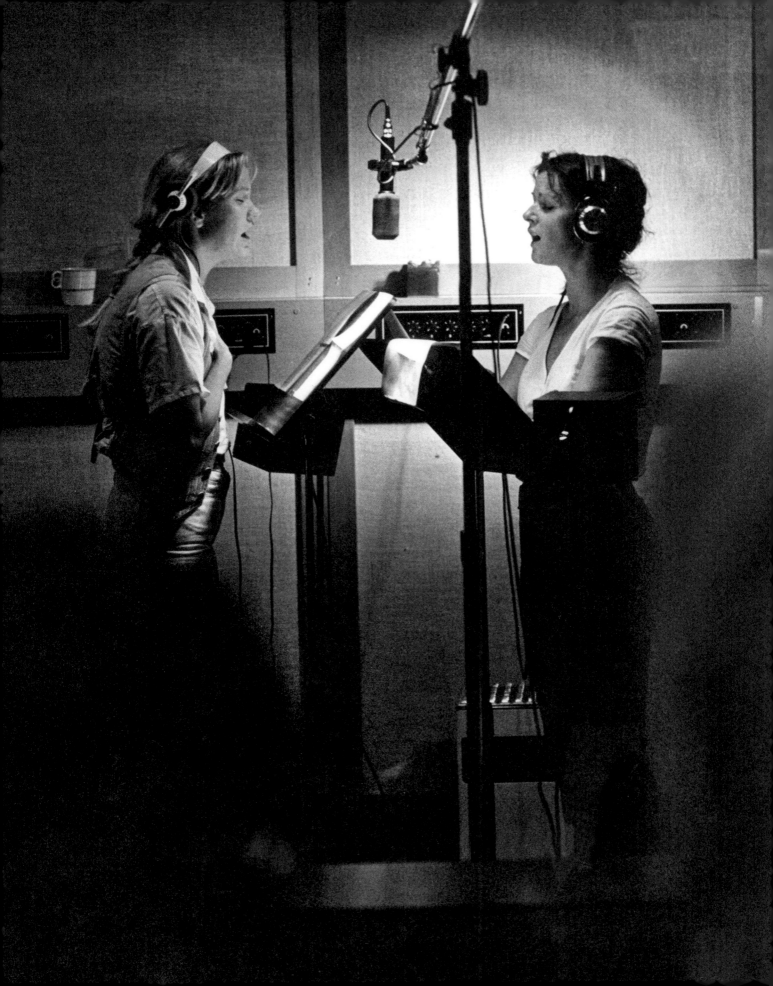

In homage to his love of country music, Björn Ulvaeus slipped a discreet reference to Tammy Wynette into the lyrics of *I Can Be That Woman*.

2021

I CAN BE THAT WOMAN

(Benny Andersson, Björn Ulvaeus/4'04)

Musicians
Agnetha Fältskog: lead vocals, backing vocals
Anni-Frid "Frida" Lyngstad: backing vocals
Benny Andersson: piano, synthesizers
Lasse Wellander: acoustic guitar
Mats Englund: bass
Per Lindvall: drums
Orchestra: Stockholm Concert Orchestra

Recording
Riksmixningsverket (RMV Studio), Stockholm: 2018 to 2021

Technical team
Producer: Benny Andersson
Sound engineer: Bernard Löhr
Assistant sound engineers: Linn Fijal, Vilma Colling
Conductor: Göran Arnberg

Genesis

Here, Benny and Björn pay homage to their fondness for country music, which is dotted here and there in ABBA's repertoire. As good as any of the greatest ballads of the genre, *I Can Be That Woman* also gives a nod to Tammy Wynette, a famous ambassadress of American country music, when Agnetha, the track's lead vocalist, sings about her dog Tammy lying on the couch. It's a song about regret, addiction, and relationship breakdowns. The lyrics have clearly been written by a mature songwriter, with the subject requiring a certain life experience that Björn wouldn't have had back in the 1970s, when he was in his twenties. He accepts that some lyrics are personal but uses his age as an excuse to claim he is allowed to keep secret which of the emotions are real and which invented. "We decided early on that we're not going to look at anything else," Björn said of the current charts. "We're just going to do the songs, the best songs we can right now. That meant writing lyrics I could get some of my thoughts of these past 40 years into, and add some kind of depth that, hopefully, comes with age and that makes it different from the lyrics I wrote 40 years ago."[146]

Production

Lasse Wellander, one of the last iconic musicians of the ABBA era who was still alive, was invited from the outset to participate in the band's 2017 recording sessions. He was sworn to silence and told to say nothing about the band's comeback. "I am good at keeping secrets," he revealed when *Voyage* was released. "And for many months no one knew. I mean, the studio is on an island, it's not like Abbey Road Studios in London where everyone sees who comes and goes."[162] His scores on the record are not as pre-eminent as the ones he had recorded in the past on tracks such as *Knowing Me, Knowing You*, *Take a Chance on Me*, *Does Your Mother Know*, and *The Winner Takes It All,* but what he brings to the album has inestimable value and adds to its heritage quality. "When I was doing my guitar tracks it felt like the old days. The only difference was that there was some preproduction this time around, which is very usual nowadays. It wasn't so in the late '70s when there was a bit more jamming in the studio and trying out new things."[162]

2021

KEEP AN EYE ON DAN

(Benny Andersson, Björn Ulvaeus/4'01)

Musicians
Agnetha Fältskog: lead vocals, backing vocals
Anni-Frid "Frida" Lyngstad: backing vocals
Benny Andersson: piano, synthesizers, backing vocals
Björn Ulvaeus: backing vocals
Lasse Wellander: guitar
Lasse Jonsson: guitar
Per Lindvall: drums, percussion
Orchestra: Stockholm Concert Orchestra

Recording
Riksmixningsverket (RMV Studio), Stockholm: 2018 to 2021

Technical team
Producer: Benny Andersson
Sound engineer: Bernard Löhr
Assistant sound engineers: Linn Fijal, Vilma Colling
Conductor: Göran Arnberg

HEADPHONES AT THE READY
A little nod to an old ABBA hit has been slipped in at 3'58 of *Keep an Eye on Dan*. When the song ends, Benny Andersson on piano plays the guitar melody intro to *SOS* originally recorded by Janne Schaffer in 1974.

Genesis

Keep an Eye on Dan is another song on the theme of divorce, a subject that appears numerous times in the older ABBA songs. Performed by Agnetha, who had previously sung about the upheaval of separation in *As Good as New, The Winner Takes It All*, and *One of Us*, this time the song describes a relationship breakdown through a mother's pain as she drops her child off at her ex-husband's. "All of us who have been divorced know what it's like to leave that little kid and seeing how absorbed that little kid is with the other parent," Björn confided. "And he waves, or she, and you stand there and you feel, 'Argh.'"[159]

Production

While ABBA's first eight albums were recorded by Michael B Tretow, the man at the controls for *Voyage* was Bernard Löhr, the sound engineer at Mono Music Studio, a specialist mixing business owned by Benny Andersson. The sound takes were done at Riksmixningsverket (generally shortened to RMV Studio), created in 2010 and managed by in-house sound engineer Linn Fijal, who was Löhr's assistant on *Voyage*. Löhr was one of Andersson's long-standing collaborators, having been in charge of the *Mamma Mia!* (2008) and *Mamma Mia! Here We Go Again* (2018) soundtracks, for which ABBA's songs had been totally re-recorded using the original arrangements. In an interview with the *Sound on Sound* website in October 2018, Löhr described his working environment at RMV, where ABBA's new songs had been recorded since the previous year. For the drums, the sound engineer placed a Neumann U 47 FET mic on the bass, a Shure SM57 on top of the snare, and an AKG C414 below it, next to the wire. Sennheiser MD 421s were used to capture the toms, and the hi-hat cymbals were recorded with an AKG 460 or a DPA 4011. The overhead takes were recorded using a pair of gold microphones that appeared on the photographs Ludvig Andersson had taken during the *Voyage* sessions, as they were also used for Agnetha and Frida's vocal takes. They were a pair of handcrafted Manibus Didrik De Geer static microphones worth around 15,000 euros each (over $17,000/almost £13,000). The bass guitar was recorded on a Direct Box (DI) and the guitar amps with Shure SM57 and Royer 121 microphones.

BUMBLEBEE

(Benny Andersson, Björn Ulvaeus/3'57)

Musicians
Anni-Frid "Frida" Lyngstad: lead vocals, backing vocals
Agnetha Fältskog: backing vocals
Benny Andersson: piano, synthesizers
Lasse Wellander: guitar
Lasse Jonsson: guitar
Per Lindvall: drums, percussion
Pär Grebacken: transverse flute
Jan Bengtson: flute
Orchestra: Stockholm Concert Orchestra
Recording
Riksmixningsverket (RMV Studio), Stockholm: 2018 to 2021
Technical team
Producer: Benny Andersson
Sound engineer: Bernard Löhr
Assistant sound engineers: Linn Fijal, Vilma Colling
Conductor: Göran Arnberg

Genesis

Björn Ulvaeus had already sung about bumblebees in *Free as a Bumble Bee* back in 1978. The song wasn't chosen for *Voulez-Vous* and the public was only able to hear segments of it in the *Abba Undeleted* medley in the 1994 box set *Thank You for the Music*. In that song, Björn sang about the life of a depressed man dreaming of being a bumblebee flitting from flower to flower. "I've always found bumblebees or squids as powerful symbols for what we might lose with climate change. It's a symbol of the loneliness we will feel when these creatures perhaps vanish because they cannot adapt," he explained.[159]

Production

Benny Andersson's Riksmixningsverket is packed with top-of-the-range instruments available for the use of artists who record there. Apart from the sumptuous guitars hanging on the corridor walls, including Rickenbackers, Fenders, and Gibsons, there are gems such as Andersson's Minimoog, repainted white for the band's 1970s tours (and the first to be imported into Sweden), a Fender Rhodes, a Mellotron M400, the Fazioli F212 grand piano on which Benny recorded his instrumental album *Piano* in 2017, as well as his legendary Yamaha GX-1 synthesizer used on the *Voulez-Vous*, *Super Trouper*, and *The Visitors* albums. But the owner's favorite instrument is the New England Digital Synclavier, acquired in 1985. Andersson used this synthesizer, which supplies myriad sounds, to write, make demos, and do the arrangements for most of his songs. In 2022, he even gave a solo recorded using this instrument to James Righton—who had previously created the band for the *ABBA Voyage* show—for the track *Empty Rooms* on Righton's album *Jim, I'm Still Here*. "He's never done anything like this before," the younger musician confided. "I nervously sent him the track and a couple of days later he sent back this keyboard line, which was perfect."[163]

Benny Andersson at the Synclavier in his studio Riksmixningsverket (RMV Studio), Stockholm, October 2021.

NO DOUBT ABOUT IT

(Benny Andersson, Björn Ulvaeus/2'52)

Musicians

Anni-Frid "Frida" Lyngstad: lead vocals, backing vocals
Agnetha Fältskog: backing vocals
Benny Andersson: piano, synthesizers, backing vocals
Björn Ulvaeus: backing vocals
Lasse Wellander: electric guitar, acoustic guitar, banjo
Lasse Jonsson: guitar
Per Lindvall: drums

Recording

Riksmixningsverket (RMV Studio), Stockholm: 2021

Technical team

Producer: Benny Andersson
Sound engineer: Bernard Löhr
Assistant sound engineers: Linn Fijal, Vilma Colling

Genesis

On 11 February 2022, Swedish radio stations broadcast a new song from *Voyage*. It was called *No Doubt About It*. Although it was not a single as such (the new rules for singles' distribution had long since transformed the old ways of promoting records), it was the 29th best-selling song on the streaming platforms. *No Doubt About It* has a very pop-rock sound, quite different from the two first tracks from the album, *I Still Have Faith in You,* a grandiose cinematic number, and *Don't Shut Me Down,* a highly effective disco pop song. Frida sings about a tumultuous relationship with a touch of humor, with the track's narrator to blame for causing the couple's issues due to a fiery temperament that she struggles to control. "*No Doubt About It* could be about me and my beloved one, but if you look upon any relationship with some sense of humor, you will certainly come out of it with a smile—until next time!!" Frida joked in 2022.[164] Björn added his own experience to the song when it came to relationship disputes that sometimes turn vicious. "I've known a few people who kind of flare up and can't help it, but then very quickly sort of get calm again and say, 'Sorry, sorry, I shouldn't have done that. I shouldn't have said that.' So it is this woman, in that situation she is incensed with her husband, who is very calm. He knows, he just waits for it. And in the end it comes."[159]

Production

While *Voyage* was mixed by Bernard Löhr and Benny Andersson on the SSL Duality 96 console at Mono Music Studios, it was recorded on the Rolls-Royce of analog consoles: a Neve 8068 that once belonged to star Swedish producer Max Martin. Linn Fijal, the manager of Riksmixningsverket, was in charge of installing the console when the complex opened in 2011, as well as acquiring the equipment that it now has. The story the sound engineer tells of how she met Benny Andersson sounds like something out of a fairy tale: "I happened to be at a mastering studio and bumped into Ludvig Andersson, Benny Andersson's son. We met in front of a coffee machine, and he said his father was opening a new studio and was looking for someone to manage it. He gave me an email address to contact if I was interested, but my first thought was that it had to be a joke. [...] I sent out the email and they responded, asking me to come in for an interview. Unfortunately, I couldn't find the address anywhere

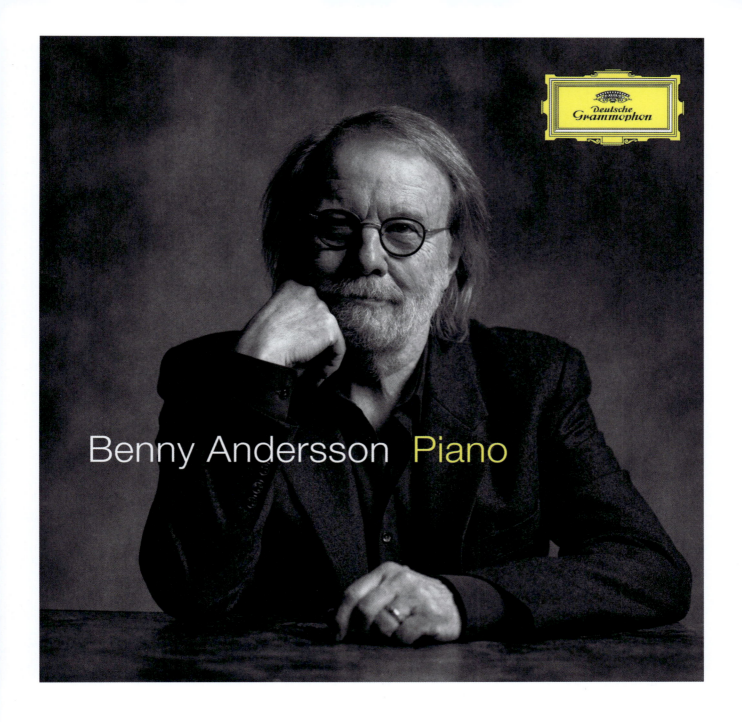

Benny Andersson Piano

even when I googled it, so I had trouble locating the building on the day of the interview. It all felt a bit sketchy, so I called my mom, gave her the address, and told her to call the police if she didn't hear from me in two hours (laughs). When finally I showed up at the address, the building was empty and had been falling apart, but Benny opened the door when I knocked and it was the shock of my life. I ended up getting hired soon after that, which was in 2010." [165]

Linn Fijal may have been only the assistant sound engineer on *Voyage,* but she was fully in charge of recording Benny Andersson's sublime album *Piano,* released by Deutsche Grammophon in 2017.

ODE TO FREEDOM

(Benny Andersson, Björn Ulvaeus/3'31)

Musicians
Agnetha Fältskog: vocals, backing vocals
Anni-Frid "Frida" Lyngstad: vocals, backing vocals
Benny Andersson: piano, backing vocals
Björn Ulvaeus: backing vocals
Lasse Wellander: acoustic guitar
Margareta Bengtson: harp
Orchestra: Stockholm Concert Orchestra

Recording
Riksmixningsverket (RMV Studio), Stockholm: 2018 to 2021

Technical team
Producer: Benny Andersson
Sound engineer: Bernard Löhr
Assistant sound engineers: Linn Fijal, Vilma Colling
Conductor: Göran Arnberg
Orchestra arrangements: Göran Arnberg

Genesis

No other track could have concluded ABBA's career with such elegance and emotion. When the record was released in 2021, Benny Andersson confided that producing a mix of diametrically opposed songs had always been the hallmark of ABBA's albums and he is rightly self-congratulatory about this. He also said that the instrumental part on *Ode to Freedom* had been lying dormant in his archives for 30 years and he'd never found the perfect way to bring it to the light of day. While Ludwig van Beethoven wrote his *Ode to Joy* (or *Symphony no. 9*) in 1824, here Ulvaeus and Andersson have written their *Ode to Freedom*, needed more than ever in today's world of geopolitical instability. On 27 March 2022, Benny walked on stage at the Stockholm Concert Hall with the harp player Margareta Bengtson, who plays on the album, the Swedish backing vocalists Eric Ericson Chamber Choir, and the Ukrainian Kyiv Soloists for an evening in honor of Ukraine, at war with the Russian invader. In front of the King and Queen of Sweden and the Ukrainian ambassador, the ensemble performed a majestic version of *Ode to Freedom*. There wasn't a dry eye in the house during this flawless rendition of one of ABBA's greatest works, once again testifying to the creative genius of Benny Andersson and Björn Ulvaeus.

Production

While *Ode to Freedom* is a masterpiece in Benny Andersson's discography, it owes much to the maestro Göran Arnberg, who provided the orchestral arrangements for *Voyage*. Arnberg shows his immense talent especially on the last track on the record (and the last ABBA song?), which does away with most of the musicians on the album and replaces them with an orchestra to perform this moving anthem. Arnberg was one of Andersson's long-standing collaborators, and was asked to transcribe the scores for the album *Piano* in 2017 with the aim of releasing a collection of scores alongside the record. "I try to keep my schedule clear during the periods I work with Benny," he observed, "as it always turns out to involve more work than it seemed to at the beginning. It's not a problem in the least though as we always have a good time when working."[166]

The inseparable Björn Ulvaeus and Benny Andersson, seen here in 2010.

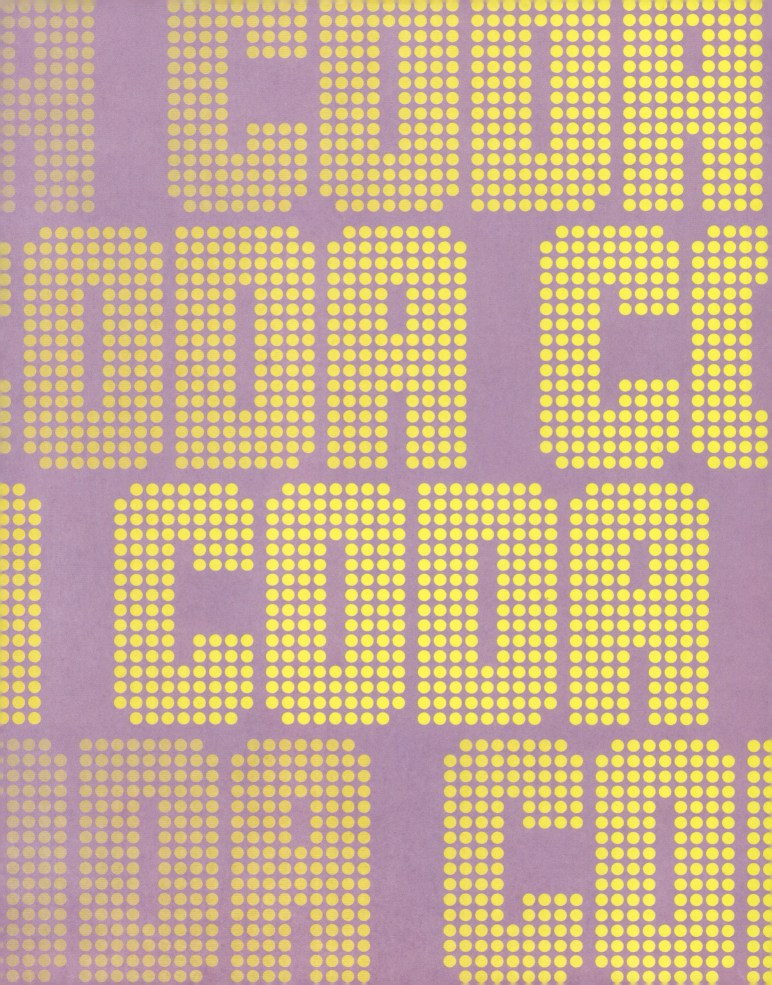

CODA

LIVES

ABBA Live
Live At Wembley Arena

COMPILATIONS

The Best Of ABBA
Greatest Hits
Greatest Hits Vol. 2
The Singles (The First Ten Years)
ABBA Gold – Greatest Hits
More ABBA Gold – More ABBA Hits
Thank You For The Music

ABBA LIVE

LP version / Dancing Queen (3'32) / Take a Chance on Me (4'12) / I Have a Dream (4'14) / Does Your Mother Know (3'54) / Chiquitita (5'10) / Thank You for the Music (3'28) / Two for the Price of One (3'18) / Fernando (5'11) / Gimme! Gimme! Gimme! (A Man after Midnight) (3'15) / Super Trouper (4'12) / Waterloo (3'18) / **CD version** / Dancing Queen (3'32) / Take a Chance on Me (4'12) / I Have a Dream (4'14) / Does Your Mother Know (3'54) / Chiquitita (5'10) / Thank You for the Music (3'28) / Two for the Price of One (3'18) / Fernando (5'11) / Gimme! Gimme! Gimme! (A Man after Midnight) (3'15) / Super Trouper (4'12) / Waterloo (3'18) / Money Money Money (3'11) / Name of the Game/Eagle (9'22) / On and On and On (3'42) / **Released in Sweden by Polar Music**: 18 August 1986 (LP ref.: POLS 412, CD ref.: POLCD 412) / **Released in the UK by Polydor**: 1986 (CD ref.: 829 951-2) / **Released in the USA by Atlantic**: 1986 (LP ref.: 81675-1) / **Best chart ranking in Sweden**: 49 / **Best chart ranking in the UK**: did not make the charts / **Best chart ranking in the USA**: did not make the charts

The 1980s were not a glorious time for ABBA. The band was forgotten—even despised—by everyone. In 1986 Polar Music (which was also experiencing a sharp downturn) suggested to the group that they release their very first live album. Despite the misgivings of Björn and Benny, who nevertheless gave their consent, the project was launched, overseen by sound engineer Michael B Tretow. The latter worked on remixing several songs taken from the group's archives and, with the Polar Music team, selected a handful that had been recorded on three occasions: at concerts performed at Wembley Arena, London, between 5 and 10 November 1979 (*Dancing Queen, Take a Chance on Me, I Have a Dream, Does Your Mother Know, Chiquitita, Thank You for the Music*, and *Waterloo*), during the 1977 Australian tour (*Fernando*), and on the set of the American television program *Dick Cavett Meets ABBA*, shot in April 1981 (*Two for the Price of One, Gimme! Gimme! Gimme! (A Man after Midnight),* and *Super Trouper*). Three additional songs were added to the CD version: *Money, Money, Money, On and On and On,* and a medley of *The Name of the Game* and *Eagle).*

But Tretow's enthusiasm and work on the songs were not enough to relaunch the ABBA machine, and the record was a resounding failure, even though it was an interesting testimony to what the group offered to fans when performing live. Disparaged by the group, even today *ABBA Live* does not feature on the webpage devoted to their official albums, and is relegated to the one for compilations, where it is stated that the record is no longer available to buy.

LIVE AT WEMBLEY ARENA

Gammal Fäbodpsalm (1'43) / Voulez-Vous (4'11) / If It Wasn't for the Nights (5'18) / As Good as New (3'26) / Knowing Me, Knowing You (4'30) / Rock Me (3'34) / Chiquitita (5'34) / Money, Money, Money (3'57) / I Have a Dream (6'51) / Gimme! Gimme! Gimme! (A Man after Midnight) (5'34) / SOS (3'30) / Fernando (4'13) / The Name of the Game (3'09) / Eagle (6'10) / Thank You for the Music (3'52) / Why Did It Have to Be Me? (4'32) / Intermezzo No. 1 (4'06) / I'm Still Alive (4'29) / Summer Night City (5'28) / Take a Chance on Me (4'25) / Does Your Mother Know (3'58) / Hole in Your Soul (4'39) / The Way Old Friends Do (3'05) / Dancing Queen (5'52) / Waterloo (3'51) / **Released in the UK and Europe by Polar Music**: 29 September 2014 (LP ref.: 00602537716074, CD ref.: 00602537928644) / **Released in the USA by Polar Music**: 29 September 2014 (CD ref.: B0021664-02) / **Best chart ranking in Sweden**: 15 / **Best chart ranking in the UK**: 30 / **Best chart ranking in the USA**: did not make the charts

Released on 29 September 2014 under the supervision of Ludvig Andersson, son of Benny and Mona, and head of RMV Film, RMV Publishing, RMV Grammofon, and RMV Studio—four subsidiaries of the label Mono Music, founded by his father in 1987—*Live at Wembley Arena* is the first live album that ABBA released officially. (They regarded *ABBA Live* (1986) only as a commercial project launched by Polar Music.) Having listened closely to recordings of the concerts performed at Wembley Arena between 5 and 10 November 1979, Ludvig decided to release only the last: "I listened to each night of the Wembley shows and devised an intricate scoring system, which I put onto a whiteboard. I was scoring things like vocals, sound quality, vibe, etcetera. In the end the feeling from the night I chose, 10 November 1979, was the winner. The songs were nearly all performed too fast but it still works."[167]

Bearing witness to a triumphal tour, the record, mixed by Bernard Löhr, in-house recording engineer at Mono Music Studio, is a real success, literally plunging the listener into the heart of the London venue. "My intention with that mix," Löhr explained, "was actually to have the feeling that you're sitting in maybe the tenth to twentieth row in the audience, listening to a real live concert. Instead of trying to do a studio type of mixing, I wanted to secure that, as a listener, you can sit here and visualize the band on stage."[62] As well as being a lasting testament to the magic that ABBA worked on stage, *Live at Wembley Arena* features a song by the group that was never recorded in the studio: *I'm Still Alive*. Composed by Agnetha with lyrics by Björn, she performed the piece every evening, accompanying herself alone at the piano in front of the Arena's 8,000-strong audience.

ABBA on stage at Wembley Arena, London, in 1979.

There are more than 100 ABBA compilations, each of the group's distributors abroad having released numerous "greatest hits" or "best of" selections. For this reason, only the group's major compilations are described here.

THE BEST OF ABBA

Waterloo (2'46) / Another Town, Another Train (3'13) / Watch Out (3'45) / I Am Just a Girl (3'04) / Me and Bobby and Bobby's Brother (2'52) / Hasta Mañana (3'10) / She's My Kind of Girl (2'45) / Ring Ring (3'04) / Gonna Sing You My Lovesong (3'39) / Honey, Honey (2'55) / King Kong Song (3'13) / Nina, Pretty Ballerina (2'54) / **Released in Japan by Philips:** 25 October 1974 (LP ref.: SFX-6008) / **Best chart ranking in Japan:** did not make the charts

By 1974 ABBA had recorded only two albums, yet in that year their Japanese distributor, Philips, released a "best of." Being the group's very first compilation, this Japanese CD, which brings together some songs from *Ring Ring* and *Waterloo*, thoroughly deserves its place in these pages. That said, there is nothing surprising on it, apart perhaps from *She's My Kind of Girl*, a song written by Benny Andersson and Björn Ulvaeus for the soundtrack of the erotic film *Någon Att Älska* ("The Seduction of Inga") by Joseph W Sarno, which also features on the B-side of the Swedish issue of the ABBA single *Ring Ring (English Version)*, released on 14 February 1973.

GREATEST HITS

SOS (3'22) / He Is Your Brother (3'15) / Ring Ring (3'00) / Hasta Mañana (3'05) / Nina Pretty Ballerina (2'50) / Honey Honey (2'55) / So Long (3'06) / I Do, I Do, I Do, I Do, I Do (3'15) / People Need Love (2'42) / Bang-A-Boomerang (2'50) / Another Town, Another Train (3'10) / Mamma Mia (3'32) / Dance (While the Music Still Goes On) (3'05) / Waterloo (2'46) / **Released in Sweden by Polar Music:** 17 November 1975 (LP ref.: POLS 266) / **Released in the UK by Epic:** 17 November 1975 (LP ref.: EPC 69218) / **Released in the USA by Atlantic:** 17 November 1975 (LP ref.: SD 18189) / **Best chart ranking in Sweden:** 1 / **Best chart ranking in the UK:** 1 / **Best chart ranking in the USA:** 48

The first official ABBA compilation released worldwide, in November 1975, *Greatest Hits* quickly became the group's biggest success, on its release exceeding the sales of their first three albums, *Ring Ring*, *Waterloo*, and *ABBA*. There are two sleeves, both equally legendary. The Scandinavian and Argentinian versions of the album feature a crazy drawing by the artist Hans Arnold, which shows the group wearing strange outfits (Benny even has the body of an imaginary animal). The other versions have a photograph that has become legendary, taken by Bengt H Malmqvist. It shows the two couples sitting side by side on a bench in Djurgården park in Stockholm; Frida and Benny are kissing lovingly, while Agnetha looks very alone next to Björn, who is engrossed in reading a medical booklet. Depending on the country where the record was sold, it featured a few distinctive characteristics, which are worth pointing out. In Brazil, for example, it was released with the sleeve and title of the album *ABBA*, the original version not having been released in that country. In Portugal the compilation was entitled *Fernando*, and bore the photo of the group around the fire which was used for the eponymous single. In other countries such as Singapore and Malaysia, the photograph of the group wearing white hats, made famous by the sleeve of the single *Dancing Queen*, was used. In Britain, ABBA's *Greatest Hits* became the best-selling record of 1976.

GREATEST HITS VOL. 2

Gimme! Gimme! Gimme! (A Man after Midnight) (4'45) / Knowing Me, Knowing You (4'02) / Take a Chance on Me (4'05) / Money, Money, Money (3'05) / Rock Me (3'03) / Eagle (5'51) / Angeleyes (4'20) / Dancing Queen (3'50) / Does Your Mother Know (3'13) / Chiquitita (5'26) / Summer Night City (3'34) / I Wonder (Departure) (4'38) / The Name of the Game (4'54) / Thank You for the Music (3'48) / **Released in Sweden by Polar Music:** 29 October 1979 (LP ref.: POLS 312) / **Released in the UK by Epic:** 29 October 1979 (LP ref.: EPC 10017) / **Released in the USA by Atlantic:** 29 October 1979 (LP ref.: SD16009) / **Best chart ranking in Sweden:** 20 / **Best chart ranking in the UK:** 1 / **Best chart ranking in the USA:** 46

Inevitably following on from the international success of *Greatest Hits*, released in 1976, *Greatest Hits Vol. 2* was also warmly received in the United Kingdom, where it easily climbed to the top of the charts, selling more than 1 million copies in 1979. That said, there is nothing very new on this CD which, apart from *I Wonder [Departure]*, brings together only more of the group's hits. But the presence of the exceptional and very disco *Summer Night City*, released as a single in September 1978 but absent from the album *Voulez-Vous*, is enough to make this Volume 2 a very appealing record.

THE SINGLES – THE FIRST TEN YEARS

Ring Ring (3'00) / Waterloo (2'46) / So Long (3'06) / I Do, I Do, I Do, I Do, I Do (3'15) / SOS (3'22) / Mamma Mia (3'32) / Fernando (4'15) / Dancing Queen (3'51) / Money, Money, Money (3'05) / Knowing Me, Knowing You (4'02) / The Name of the Game (4'53) / Take a Chance on Me (4'05) / Summer Night City (3'34) / Chiquitita (5'26) / Does Your Mother Know (3'13) / Voulez-Vous (5'11) / Gimme! Gimme! Gimme! (A Man after Midnight) (4'45) / I Have a Dream (4'44) / The Winner Takes It All (4'56) / Super Trouper (4'13) / One of Us (3'55) / The Day Before You Came (5'50) / Under Attack (3'45) / **Released in Sweden by Polar Music:** 8 November 1982 (LP ref.: POLMD 400-401) / **Released in the UK by Epic:** 8 November 1982 (LP ref.: ABBA 10) / **Released in the USA by Atlantic:** 8 November 1982 (LP ref.: 80036-1-G) / **Best chart ranking in Sweden:** 29 / **Best chart ranking in the UK:** 1 / **Best chart ranking in the USA:** 62

Although it is not as well known as *Abba Gold–Greatest Hits*, this compilation is undoubtedly the most interesting in ABBA's discography. Released when the plan for a ninth album was dropped, in the summer of 1982, *The Singles (The First Ten Years)* contains, as well as the group's essential hits, some of their very last singles, such as *The Winner Takes It All, Super Trouper,* and *One of Us.* Moreover, the presence of *The Day Before You Came* and *Under Attack,* which do not feature on any ABBA album, on their own justify buying this indispensable record. As well as being on LP and cassette, the compilation was also released as a CD in Sweden in 1983, to the great pleasure of fans who were lucky enough to own a player for this revolutionary format.

ABBA GOLD – GREATEST HITS

Dancing Queen (3'49) / Knowing Me, Knowing You (4'01) / Take a Chance on Me (4'01) / Mamma Mia (3'32) / Lay All Your Love on Me (4'32) / Super Trouper (4'10) / I Have a Dream (4'43) / The Winner Takes It All (4'54) / Money, Money, Money (3'05) / SOS (3'19) / Chiquitita (5'26) / Fernando (4'10) / Voulez-Vous (4'21) / Gimme! Gimme! Gimme! (A Man after Midnight) (4'46) / Does Your Mother Know (3'14) / One of Us (3'53) / The Name of the Game (3'56) / Thank You for the Music (3'51) / Waterloo (2'42) / **Released in the UK and Europe by Polar Music-Polydor:** 21 September 1992 (LP ref.: 517 007-1, CD ref.: 517 007-2) / **Released in the USA by Polar Music-Polydor:** 21 September 1992 (CD ref.: 314 517 007-2) / **Best chart ranking in Sweden:** 1 / **Best chart ranking in the UK:** 1 / **Best chart ranking in the USA:** 25

Who has not owned *Abba Gold–Greatest Hits*? The genesis of this compilation turns out to be as fascinating as its success was huge. By 1992, ABBA had fallen off the radar, but then British duo Erasure released an EP entitled *Abba-esque,* featuring four ABBA covers, which went to the top of the British charts. Polygram International, which had owned the ABBA catalog since 1989, when it bought Polar Music and Stig Anderson's publisher Sweden Music, decided, following insistent requests from fans, to release an ABBA compilation. Marketing director Chris Griffin was put in charge of the project. Once the songs had been selected (the group's American singles that had made the *Billboard* top 20 between 1974 and 1980), Griffin came up with the title: *ABBA Gold,* drawing inspiration from the 1983 Spandau Ballet hit *Gold.* Griffin travelled to Stockholm and obtained the consent of Benny, Björn, and Frida—Agnetha refused to come out of retirement at that time—even though he could perfectly well have produced the record without it. The songs were then entrusted to Michael B Tretow to be mastered anew so they could be released in CD format. British journalist John Tobler was asked to write the sleeve notes for the compilation. Following consumer testing, Polygram decided not to feature the group on the album cover, as their image was deemed too dated—unlike their songs, which were enjoying renewed popularity. The compilation, which has sold almost 30 million worldwide since its release in 1992, is one of the best-selling in the history of music, after The Eagles' *Their Greatest Hits (1971–1975)* (42 million), *1* by The Beatles (32 million), and *The Immaculate Collection* by Madonna (30 million). In short, it is essential to have *ABBA Gold–Greatest Hits* in your record collection.

MORE ABBA GOLD – MORE ABBA HITS

Summer Night City (3'28) / Angeleyes (4'16) / The Day Before You Came (5'47) / Eagle (4'23) / I Do, I Do, I Do, I Do, I Do (3'16) / So Long (3'06) / Honey, Honey (2'53) / The Visitors (4'27) / Our Last Summer (4'19) / On and On and On (3'38) / Ring Ring (3'00) / I Wonder (Departure) (4'34) / Lovelight (3'18) / Head over Heels (3'45) / When I Kissed the Teacher (3'00) / I Am the City (4'00) / Cassandra (4'50) / Under Attack (3'44) / When All Is Said and Done (3'16) / The Way Old Friends Do (2'52) / **Released in the UK and Europe by Polar Music-Polydor:** 24 May 1993 (LP ref.: 519 353-1, CD ref.: 519 353-2) / **Released in the USA by Polar Music-Polydor:** 9 June 1993 (CD ref.: 31451 9353 2) / **Best chart ranking in Sweden:** 7 / **Best chart ranking in the UK:** 13 / **Best chart ranking in the USA:** did not make the charts

It was inevitable that a sequel to *ABBA Gold–Greatest Hits* would be released. However, this second instalment was only modestly popular with the wider audience, for its track listing featured more intimate songs, as well as rarities such as *I Am the City*, unveiled for the first time on this record. A few B-sides also appear here, such as the splendid disco outpouring *Lovelight*, and the group's very last singles, *The Day Before You Came* and *Under Attack*. A second record that totally complements the first, but destined for a more inquisitive audience.

THANK YOU FOR THE MUSIC

Disc 1 / People Need Love (2'47) / Another Town, Another Train (3'14) / He Is Your Brother (3'19) / Love Isn't Easy (But It Sure Is Hard Enough) (2'56) / Ring Ring (3'02) / Waterloo (2'44) / Hasta Mañana (3'09) / Honey, Honey (2'57) / Dance (While the Music Still Goes On) (3'13) / So Long (3'06) / I've Been Waiting for You (3'39) / I Do, I Do, I Do, I Do, I Do (3'18) / SOS (3'22) / Mamma Mia (3'33) / Fernando (4'12) / Dancing Queen (3'51) / That's Me (3'16) / When I Kissed the Teacher (3'03) / Money, Money, Money (3'08) / Crazy World (3'49) / My Love, My Life (3'53) / **Disc 2** / Knowing Me, Knowing You (4'03) / Happy Hawaii (4'24) / The Name of the Game (3'58) / I Wonder (Departure) live version (4'31) / Eagle (5'49) / Take a Chance on Me (4'04) / Thank You for the Music (3'50) / Summer Night City (full-length version) (4'14) / Chiquitita (5'26) / Lovelight (3'20) / Does Your Mother Know (3'15) / Voulez-Vous (4'22) / Angeleyes (4'19) / Gimme! Gimme! Gimme! (A Man after Midnight) (4'48) / I Have a Dream (4'44) / **Disc 3** / The Winner Takes It All (4'55) / Elaine (3'46) / Super Trouper (4'14) / Lay All Your Love on Me (4'34) / On and On and On (3'40) / Our Last Summer (4'19) / The Way Old Friends Do (2'54) / The Visitors (5'48) / One of Us (3'57) / Should I Laugh or Cry (4'27) / Head over Heels (3'47) / When All Is Said and Done (3'16) / Like an Angel Passing through My Room (3'36) / The Day Before You Came (5'49) / Cassandra (4'50) / Under Attack (3'45) / **Disc 4** / Put on Your White Sombrero (4'28) / Dream World (3'36) / Thank You for the Music (Doris Day version) (4'04) / Hej Gamle Man! (3'21) / Merry-Go-Round (3'21) / Santa Rosa (3'02) / She's My Kind of Girl (2'45) / Medley (4'22) / You Owe Me One (3'26) / Slipping through My Fingers/Me and I (8'37) / Abba Undeleted (23'31) / Waterloo (French/Swedish) (2'40) / Ring Ring (Swedish/Spanish/German) (4'22) / Honey, Honey (Swedish) (2'57) / **Released in the UK and Europe by Polar Music-Polydor:** 31 October 1994 (numbered CD box set ref.: 523 472-2) / **Released in the USA by Polar Music-Polydor:** 31 October 1994 (CD box set ref.: 314 523 472-2) / **Best chart ranking in Sweden:** 17 / **Best chart ranking in the UK:** did not make the charts / **Best chart ranking in the USA:** did not make the charts /

The release of the longbox CD box set *Thank You for the Music* in October 1994 was undoubtedly the best gift to ABBA fans. It comprised the group's biggest hits, major songs that had never been released as singles (*That's Me, When I Kissed the Teacher, The Way Old Friends Do…*), and all their B-sides, most of which had never appeared on an album (*Crazy World, Happy Hawaii, Lovelight, Elaine, Should I Laugh or Cry…*). The box set was bursting with surprises that would satisfy both fans and new listeners. The collection, once again overseen by Chris Griffin, closely followed the international success of *Songs of Freedom*, a 1992 longbox by Bob Marley and The Wailers which presented the singer's discography in a similar way, as well as that of *Message in a Box: The Complete Recordings* (1993) by The Police, which sold 300,000

The Polar Music Studio, where magic was worked between 1978 and 1982.

worldwide. *Thank You for the Music,* of which 100,000 numbered copies were produced, was also popular because it featured unreleased songs such as *Put on Your White Sombrero* and *Dream World,* as well as the medley *Abba Undeleted,* consisting of the group's mostly unreleased preliminary recordings. The icing on the cake was the presence, in this comprehensive selection, of the full-length version of *Summer Night City,* complete with its splendid introduction, which had been cut during mixing because it was considered too long. Whether or not you are a fan of ABBA, this is a collector's item, to be obtained as a matter of urgency.

GLOSSARY

Arpeggiator: a function available on some synthesizers, which plays a chord as an arpeggio, with notes played one after another in sequence.

Backing band: a group of musicians accompanying an artist on stage or in the studio.

Backing tracks: instrumental or vocal tracks, sometimes purely rhythmic, recorded to accompany a singer or musical group.

Bootleg: a recording that has been made or sold illegally and without the authorization of the artist.

Bottleneck: a term used for the technique of playing slide guitar, when a glass or metal tube is placed over one of the guitarist's fingers (a slide), then slid over the strings to create a metallic sound. The expression comes from the method developed by blues guitarists that used the necks of bottles.

Bpm: beats per minute. A measure of the tempo of a song.

Delay: an audio effect that reproduces the acoustic phenomenon of an echo. Produced using an effects pedal or mixing console, and used for both vocals and instruments, it allows a sound to be repeated regularly by delaying the signal.

Direct Box (DI): a small box that allows musical instruments to be recorded, converting a high-impedance asymmetrical audio signal to a low-impedance symmetrical one that is suitable for direct connection to a microphone input on a mixing console. In a DI recording an instrument is plugged not into an amplifier but directly into the studio console.

Distortion: a sound effect produced by degrading the quality of an audio signal by means of the saturation of an amplifier channel, using the "distortion" effect contained in the latter or a distortion pedal.

Effects pedal: a small electronic device used to transform the sound of an instrument as it is being played.

EP: abbreviation for extended play. A record format that is often shorter than an album, containing only a few songs.

Harmonic: a guitar note produced by plucking a string while, with the other hand, touching it at a certain point without stopping it completely, to produce a soft sound an octave or a fifth higher.

Harmonization: the process of adding notes to a melody to produce a harmony—the blending of simultaneous notes.

Hi-hat: two cymbals set one above the other, facing each other, which are operated by the drummer's foot. The drummer also uses a drumstick to set the cadence of his/her rhythmic pattern.

Hook: a short series of notes, whose easily recognizable melody catches the listener's attention and is retained in their memory. Originally found in jazz, this was progressively adopted by other musical genres.

Humbucker: a double-coil pickup that gives a powerful sound, often fitted to guitars such as the Gibson Les Paul. By contrast, its great rival, the Fender Stratocaster, is fitted with a single-coil pickup, which produces softer, often crystal-clear sounds.

Lap/pedal steel guitar: a guitar that is played on the musician's lap (lap steel guitar) or on a special stand (pedal steel guitar), using a slide over the strings.

LP: abbreviation for "long play," a record format used for albums, usually around 25 minutes long on each side.

Metalhead: a fan of metal music.

Mid-tempo: a term applied to a song played at a moderate tempo.

Octaver: an effect used in a studio rack or pedal that doubles an audio signal an octave below or above.

Outtake: a piece of music recorded in the studio or live that has not been used in the official version of an album. It may be an unreleased piece or an alternative version of an existing song, and may be unearthed later for a compilation or a reissue.

Overdubs: new (vocal and/or instrumental) tracks recorded and added to an existing recording.

Power chord: a chord consisting of the root, fifth, and octave.

Reverb: a natural or artificial echo effect given to an instrument or voice during the recording or mixing of a piece.

Riff: a short fragment consisting of a few notes that recurs regularly during a piece and accompanies the melody.

Sampler: an electronic instrument that records and plays back samples (portions of sound recordings) to create new music.

Schlager: a musical style frequently associated with German pop music, but also present in the music of other countries, such as Italy and France. It features rhythmic melodies and lyrics that are easy to remember.

Slap: a technique of electric bass-guitar playing used chiefly in funk and disco music, in which strings are struck with the thumb and pulled using other fingers of the right hand.

Tracklist: the list of songs that feature on an album.

BIBLIOGRAPHY

1 – *ABBA Magazine*, no. 17, 1980.

2 – "ABBA intim: 'Wir Sind Sklaven unserer Karriere,'" *Joker*, April 1977.

3 – Paphides (Pete), "Supertroopers," *The Guardian*, 8 June 2002.

4 – "How They Met!", *Alphabeat Magazine*, 1977, p. 4.

5 – "Het nog nooit vertelde verdriet van ABBA," *Privé*, July 1977.

6 – "Intiem Portret, Agnetha (van ABBA)," *Popshop*, June 1977.

7 – Sleeve notes from box set *Thank You for the Music*, Polar Music International, 1994, p. 18.

8 – "Anna öffnet ihr Herz," *Bravo*, December 1976.

9 – "Benny ist mein Leben," *Das Freizeit Magazin*, 1976.

10 – "Benny verrät sein Geheimnis," *Bravo*, December 1976.

11 – Lindström (Kristina), "Kung Benny," *Vi*, 2010.

12 – "In Focus: Stig Anderson—Master of Words," abbasite.com.

13 – "Stig says," *ABBA Magazine*, no. 31, January 1981.

14 – *ABBA Annual*, 1981.

15 – "Benny Ger Mig Mod I Mina Mörka Stunder," *Min Värld*, no. 10, 1973.

16 – *ABBA Magazine*, no. 38, August 1981.

17 – "In Focus: Ring Ring—ABBA's Journey Towards Eurovision," abbasite.com.

18 – *ABBA Magazine*, no. 12, 1979.

19 – *ABBA Magazine*, no. 29, November 1980.

20 – "Benny hasn't said he's jealous but I bet he is!," icethesite.com, 2 September 2009.

21 – Jones (Peter), "ABBA. The History," *Billboard Magazine*, 8 September 1979.

22 – "Stig Andersongwriter," *International ABBA Magazine*, no. 9, August 1982.

23 – "Een kapotte geluidsinstallatie kostte ABBA bijna het songfestival," *Mix*, July 1977.

24 – "Facing Their Waterloo, ABBA. Their Songs. Their Story. Their Lives," *Life*, 2022.

25 – "ABBA, Liebe Auf Schwedissh," *Bravo*, October 1974.

26 – "ABBA liet de president van Amerika in de kou staan," *Mix*, 1977.

27 – "ABBA's Björn Ulvaeus, The Billboard Interview," *Billboard Magazine*, 3 April 1999.

28 – Hinson (Tamara), "Abba's Björn Ulvaeus on Stockholm," theguardian.com, 22 May 2015.

29 – Sharma (Amit), "Longtime ABBA guitarist Janne Schaffer picks his career-defining records," musicradar.com, 26 May 2017.

30 – "Guitarist Janne Schaffer (ABBA) Chats to Joe Matera," youtube.com, 20 August 2021.

31 – "The History Book on the Shelf", *Record Collector,* Christmas, no. 539, December 2022.

32 – Sky Magliola (Anna), "ABBA's Bjorn Ulvaeus reveals how The Beatles influenced their hit 'Waterloo,'" planetradio.co.uk, 31 January 2022.

33 – Van Leyde (Cees), "De ABBA Story, part 10," *Muziek Parade*, 1978.

34 – Fraser (Andrew), "The Winner Takes It All," *Attitude*, 23 April 2013.

35 – Andersson (Benny), Ulvaeus (Björn), and Craymer (Judy), *Mamma Mia! How Can I Resist You?, The Inside Story of Mamma Mia! and the songs of ABBA*, London, Phoenix Illustrated, 2006, revised edition 2008.

36 – Raab (Jared), *This Is Pop, "Stockholm Syndrome,"* Banger Films, 2021.

37 – "Ask Agnetha… Agnetha Answers—Question 5," youtube. com, 8 May 2013.

38 – "Diary 1973," rabbitwho.com.

39 – Palm (Carl Magnus), *ABBA. The Complete Recording Sessions, 1994/ABBA. The Complete Recording Sessions. Revised and Expanded Edition*, Croydon, CPI Group, 2017.

40 – Sharma (Amit), "ABBA guitarist Janne Schaffer: 'You can hear a lot of heavy rock guitars in the first and second albums. We'd been listening to Deep Purple,'" guitarworld.com, 8 December 2021.

41 – Mason (Neil), "Abba: Thank You for the Music," electronicsound. co.uk, 2017.

42 – Peplow (Gemma), "ABBA star Björn Ulvaeus: Waterloo took us from rat race—I wish that for other songwriters," news.sky.com, 5 May 2021.

43 – "ABBA People—Lasse Wellander", *ABBA Magazine*, no date, no. 15, p. 11.

44 – Marten (Neville), "Knowing Me. ABBA's Lasse Wellander," *Guitarist*, February 2022.

45 – "In Focus: Mamma Mia—The Song That Saved Abba," abbasite. com.

46 – Büchelmaier (Gerald), "Alles über die zur Zeit erfolgreichste Popgruppe der Welt: ABBA," *Bravo*, 1975.

47 – "Gaat Anna Abba Verlaten?," *Popshop*, 1976.

48 – Abba Acceptance speeches of Frida and Benny into Rock and Roll Hall of Fame, 15 March 2010, youtube.com, 17 March 2010.

49 – Pastel (Julius), "ABBA, Bedoel je de popgroep of de Zweedse haring?," *Veronica*, 12 July 1975.

50 – "Abba sind zu kess fürs Fernsehen," *Bravo*, July 1975.

51 – "ABBA bassist Mike Watson," thestrangebrew.com, 3 February 2020.

52 – Barr (Gordon), "Interview: Abba saxophonist Ulf Andersson," chroniclelive.co.uk, 18 November 2011.

53 – Paphides (Pete), "We Learned from The Beatles," *Record Collector*, Christmas, no. 539, December 2022.

54 – "Agnetha: ich glaube an eine höhere Macht," *Bravo*, 1981.

55 – Gradvall (Jan), Karlsson (Petter), Wanselius (Bengt), Wikström (Jeppe), *ABBA. L'album photo officiel*, Paris, Chêne et E/P/A, 2014.

56 – "In Focus: The Folk Medley—Abba's Rare Cover Versions," abbasite.com.

57 – Goddard (Simon), "The Agony of the Ecstasy," *Classic Pop*, "ABBA, A New Voyage," 2021.

58 – "Sieben daß sie ihr interessante Markenzeichen Fragen an ABBA BRAVO Wußtet Ihr, ABBA verdanken?," *Bravo*, June 1980.

59 – Fältskog (Agnetha) and Åhman (Brita), *As I Am. Abba Before & Beyond*, London, Virgin Publishing, 1997.

60 – "Abba People," *Abba Magazine*, no. 16, 1978.

61 – *Bass Player*, December 2000.

62 – Van Wymeersch (Stany), *The Legacy of ABBA Volume One (second edition)*, Gand, SVW Books, 2021.

63 – "ABBA The Hit Process", *ABBA Annual*, 1982.

64 – Eek (Leonard), documentary *ABBA-Dabba-Dooo!!*, October 1976.

65 – Hall (James), "ABBA's business brain: how Stig Anderson built—and almost broke—Sweden's greatest export," telegraph.co.uk, 5 July 2018.

66 – Meldrum (Ian "Molly"), interview with ABBA, *Network 7 Production*, July 1976.

67 – "ABBA: The Making of Dancing Queen," youtube.com.

68 – "Arrival, ABBA Their Songs. Their Story. Their Lives," *Life*, 2022

69 – "In Focus: Money, Money, Money—Some Kind of Tension," abbasite.com.

70 – "ABBA's Views," *ABBA Annual*, 1982.

71 – "A Day in the Life of Stig Anderson," *Billboard Magazine*, 14 January 1978.

72 – "ABBA Verovert Polen," *Joepie*, October 1976.

73 – Sleeve notes from *ABBA—The Album* Deluxe Edition, 2007.

74 – *ABBA—The Movie: Looking Back (BENNY & BJÖRN)*, bonuses from *ABBA: The Movie* DVD, 2005.

75 – "Dear ABBA," *ABBA Magazine*, no. 24, May 1980.

76 – Documentary *ABBA in Concert*, 1980.

77 – *ABBA Magazine*, no. 3, 1978.

78 – "Olivia's TV special with guests Andy Gibb and Abba," onlyolivia. com.

79 – "ABBA bereidt zich voor op nieuwe hitaanval!," *Joepie*, November 1980.

80 – "ABBA versprechen: 'Im Herbst kommen wir nach Deutschland!,'" *Pop*, 1979.

81 – "Die Wahrheit über uns," *Bravo*, 1979.

82 – "ABBA's toont nieuwe Liefde," *De Telegraaf*, 1979.

83 – "ABBA-Extra," *Fan Magazin*, no. 12, 1979.

84 – "How the Hits Are Made—Abba in the Studio," *ABBA Magazine*, no. 2, 1978.

85 – "ABBA The Meeting," *ABBA Magazine*, no. 9, 1978.

86 – Sleeve notes from *Voulez-Vous* Deluxe Edition, 2010.

87 – "ABBA The Meeting," *ABBA Magazine*, no. 10, 1978.

88 – "Single Van De Week," *Hitkrant*, April 1979.

89 – "ABBA in Switzerland," *ABBA Magazine*, no. 14, 1979.

90 – "ABBA People—A Voulez-Vous Virtuoso," *ABBA Magazine*, no. 14, 1979.

91 – *For Us, The Studio Is an Instrument That You Play*, ABBA Record Collector, 2021.

92 – Simper (Paul), "Abba legend Benny Andersson doesn't find Eurovision fun anymore—but was impressed by the UK's Sam Ryder," metro.co.uk, 26 May 2022.

93 – Documentary *Thank You ABBA*, Polygram Video, 1994.

94 – Sleeve notes from *Super Trouper* Deluxe Edition, 2011.

95 – "Detwee Abba-vrouwen: We Willen Best Stoppen, Maar We Kůnnen Niet," *Viva*, March 1980.

96 – "Agnetha Fältskog in da Livet," *VeckoRevyn*, 29 May 1979.

97 – *ABBA Magazine*, no. 20, 1980, p. 2.

98 – "The Winner Takes It All," *ABBA Magazine*, no. 27, August 1980, p. 14.

99 – "The Greatest Show on Earth," *ABBA Magazine*, no. 30, December 1980.

100 – Wilkinson (Anthony), *ABBA Words & Music*, documentary, Shooting Lodge, 1980.

101 – Oscar Alejo Smirnov, "The Spanish Lyrics," *Official International ABBA Fan Club*, no. 100, September 2009.

102 – "Circus Games," *ABBA Magazine*, no. 31, January 1981.

103 – "Björn Ulvaeus Discusses Songwriting at Way Out West Music Conference," icethesite.com, 11 August 2014.

104 – Eames (Tom), "How ABBA's Two Marriages and Divorces Split the Group Apart for Nearly 40 Years," smoothradio.com, 7 January 2022.

105 – "Björn: Ich Würde Gern Zum Mind Fliegen," *Bravo*, 1981.

106 – "ABBA," *ABBA Magazine*, no. 41, November 1981.

107 – "ABBA Bjorn and Benny Writing Their Songs on an Island," youtube.com, 17 June 2017.

108 – "In Focus: The Making of Super Trouper," abbasite.com.

109 – "Abba in the Studio," *Sound International Magazine*, February 1980.

110 – "In Focus: Our Last Summer," abbasite.com.

111 – "Off the Cuff," *ABBA Magazine* no. 4, 1978, p. 19.

112 – "Blow by Blow with Benny," *ABBA Magazine*, no. 40, October 1981.

113 – "Agnetha und Annafrid, (K)Ein Leben Wie Im Märchen," *Rocky Das Freizeit-Magazin*, April 1980.

114 – "ABBA, The Story Goes On," *ABBA Annual*, 1980.

115 – "Ik Geniet Van Mijn Nieuwe Leven," *De Telegraaf*, September 1982.

116 – Powers (Ed), "The Ultimate Break-Up Album: Why Making *The Visitors* Destroyed ABBA*," telegraph.co.uk, 30 April 2018.

117 – Hanser (Görel), Polar Music press release, 21 October 1981.

118 – Sleeve notes from *The Visitors* Deluxe Edition, 2012.

119 – "Om Artistieke en privé-Problemente Overwinnen, Grote Baas Verplichtte ABBA Vakantie Te Nemen," *Joepie*, August 1981.

120 – Interview with Benny Andersson and Björn Ulvaeus for "Let Poland Be Poland," report, STV2, 1 February 1982.

121 – "A Bell from Björn," *International ABBA Magazine*, no. 4, March 1982.

122 – "We are the Music Men," *International ABBA Magazine*, no. 12, November 1982.

123 – *International ABBA Magazine*, no. 7, June 1982.

124 – Burke (David), "Album Insight—*The Visitors*," *Classic Pop*, *ABBA, A New Voyage*, 2021.

125 – Cole (Steve) and Hunt (Chris), documentary *The Winner Takes It All: The ABBA Story*, Iambic Productions, 1999.

126 – "Blow by Blow with Micke Tretow," *ABBA Magazine*, no. 38, August 1981.

127 – "In diesen Häusern verstecken sich Abba," *Bravo*, 1981.

128 – "In Focus: The Making of *The Visitors*," abbasite.com.

129 – "That Golden Touch (Part One)," *International ABBA Magazine*, no. 10, September 1982.

130 – "A Bell From Agnetha," *International ABBA Magazine*, no. 5, April 1982.

131 – "ABBA Bestolen," *Hitkrant*, 1985.

132 – "In De Studio Hebben Wij De Grootste Lol," *Pop Foto*, April 1982.

133 – "That Golden Touch (Part Two)," *International ABBA Magazine*, no. 11, October 1982.

134 – "We Are the Music Men," *International ABBA Magazine*, no. 17, March 1983.

135 – "Grote Baas Verplichtte ABBA Vakantie Tenemen," *Joepie*, August 1981.

136 – Yates (Henry), "Slipping Through My Fingers," *The Story of ABBA*, Future, 2023.

137 – "Agnetha: Geen Tijd Meer Voor ABBA," *Panorama*, June 1983.

138 – "Starke Töne Von Agnetha," *Popcorn*, September 1983.

139 – "ABBA Privat," *Bravo*, 1982.

140 – Allen (Matt), "Inside Nirvana's Last Ever UK Show: 'The band was fractured in more than a few ways… it was touch and go,'" Mojo4music.com, 30 August 2023.

141 – Buchanan (Brett), "Grunge Legend Reveals How Courtney Love 'Didn't Help' Kurt Cobain," alternativenation.net, 23 October 2017.

142 – "Björn Again, Het Tweede Leven Van ABBA," *OOR*, August 1992.

143 – "Björn, tretet ihr noch mal gemeinsam auf?," *Bravo*, October 1992.

144 – "Interview: Bjorn Ulvaeus of ABBA, *The Wall Street Journal*." youtube.com, 10 September 2013.

145 – Beaumont-Thomas (Ben) and Brown (Mark), "Abba reunite for *Voyage*, first new album in 40 years," theguardian.com, 2 September 2021.

146 – Petridis (Alexis), "Super troupers! Abba on fame, divorce, ageing backwards—and why they've returned to rescue 2021," theguardian.com, 27 October 2021.

147 – "Here We Go Again, ABBA. Their Songs. Their Story. Their Lives," *Life*, 2022.

148 – Vincentelli (Elisabeth), "After 40 Years, Abba Takes a Chance with its Legacy," nytimes.com, 27 October 2021.

149 – ABBA press release, 27 April 2018.

150 – "The ABBA Voyage journey," icethesite.com, 5 November 2021.

151 – Trendell (Andrew),—"ABBA Voyage's creators tell us how they made the show, and what's next," nme.com, 28 May 2022.

152 – Welsh (Daniel), "ABBA Voyage: 15 Things We Learned From The Music Icons' Long-Awaited Reunion Announcement," huffingtonpost.com, 3 September 2021.

153 – "Abba on new album *Voyage*: 'We don't need to prove anything', BBC News, youtube.com, 5 November 2021.

154 – "ABBA Voyage: The Journey Is About To Begin," youtube.com, 2 September 2021.

155 – "Q&A with Björn And Benny," youtube.com, 31 October 2022.

156 – Henderson (Chelsea), "ABBA's Björn Ulvaeus shares Kilkenny inspiration behind 'When You Danced With Me,'" hotpress.com, 8 November 2021.

157 – "ABBA wünschen Euch fröhliche Weihnachten", *Das Freizeit-Magazin*, December 1976.

158 – "ABBA Say 'Thank You for the Music' to SIS choir," stockholmis.se.

159 – Interview with Björn Ulvaeus for Apple Music, 2021.

160 – "ABBA the Meeting," *ABBA Magazine*, no. 8, 1978.

161 – Pearis (Bill), "ABBA share new single 'Just A Notion' that dates from 1978," brooklynvegan.com, 22 October 2021.

162 – Dyke (Peter), "ABBA guitarist Lasse Wellander and the secret story behind their great comeback," express.co.uk, 10 October 2021.

163 – Richards (Will), "James Righton shares new song 'Empty Rooms' with ABBA's Benny Andersson," nme.com, 27 April 2022.

164 – ABBA Instagram account, November 2022.

165 – "Riksmixningsverket—Linn Fijal [Engineer]," speakhertz.com, 28 September 2015.

166 – "Göran Arnberg talks to icethesite," icethesite.com, 27 March 2013.

167 – "Interview with Ludvig Andersson," icethesite.com, 11 January 2019.

Web Sources

abbaannual1972.blogspot.com

abbacharts.com

abbafanclub.nl

abba-intermezzo.de

abbaomnibus.net

abbaoncd.wordpress.com

abbaontv.com

abbasite.com

abba-theconcerts.de

abbathemuseum.com

agnethaarchives.com

carlmagnuspalm.com

discogs.com

equipboard.com

facebook.com/TheABBAmagazinearchive

icethesite.com

instagram.com/abba

officialcharts.com

raffem.com

sverigetopplistan.se

thesecondhandabbastore.nl

thorsven.net

vinylcollector.store

worldradiohistory.com

INDEX

The songs, albums, and singles analyzed in the text are indicated in **bold**.

ACKNOWLEDGMENTS

This book is the result of collaboration with the irreplaceable Marie Laure Miranda and Katia de Azevedo, who are capable of switching from Metallica to ABBA with surprising ease.
I would like to thank Boris Guilbert and Charlotte Couture of Les Éditions E/P/A, as well as Sara Quémener and Zarko Telebak of ZS studio.
Finally, I would like to thank the authors cited in the bibliography for their passion and for the time they devoted to writing books that have often been invaluable in my research.

And thank you to two new ABBA fans: Rose and Vera.

PICTURE CREDITS

First published in Great Britain in 2024 by Cassell,
an imprint of Octopus Publishing Group Ltd
Carmelite House
50 Victoria Embankment
London EC4Y 0DZ
www.octopusbooks.co.uk

An Hachette UK Company
www.hachette.co.uk

Original title: *ABBA, La Totale*
Texts: Benoît Clerc
Published by Les Éditions E/P/A–Hachette Livre 2024

Distributed in the US by
Hachette Book Group
1290 Avenue of the Americas
4th and 5th Floors
New York, NY 10104

Distributed in Canada by
Canadian Manda Group
664 Annette St.
Toronto, Ontario, Canada M6S 2C8

ISBN 9781788404822

A CIP catalogue record for this book is available from the
British Library.

Printed and bound in China

10 9 8 7 6 5 4 3 2 1

For this edition:
Publisher: Trevor Davis
Project Editor: Sarah Reece
Art Director: Yasia Williams
Senior Production Manager: Peter Hunt
Translators: Simon Jones and Andrea Reece
Copy Editor: Caroline Taggart
Proofreader: Helena Caldon
Typesetter: Jeremy Tilston

Disclaimers:
All information correct at time of printing.
Details that are unknown are marked by "?"; for example, the name
of the flute musician for *Me and Bobby and Bobby's Brother* on page 62.